Quality ESL Programs
An Administrator's Guide

Judith Simons and Mark Connelly

The Scarecrow Press, Inc.
Technomic Books
Lanham, Maryland, and London
2000

SCARECROW PRESS, INC.
Technomic Books

Published in the United States of America
by Scarecrow Press, Inc.
4720 Boston Way, Lanham, Maryland 20706
http://www.scarecrowpress.com

4 Pleydell Gardens, Folkestone
Kent CT20 2DN, England

British Library Cataloguing in Publication Information Available

Library of Congress Cataloging-in-Publication Data
Simons, Judith, 1947–
    Quality ESL programs : an administrator's guide / Judith Simons, Mark
Connelly.
        p. cm.
    Includes bibliographical references (p.).
    ISBN 0-8108-3757-9 (alk. paper)
    1. English language—Study and teaching—Foreign speakers—Management.
I. Connelly, Mark, 1951 Oct. 17–
PE1128.A2 S57 2000
428'.0071—dc21

                                                            00-027687

∞™ The paper used in this publication meets the minimum requirements of
American National Standard for Information Sciences—Permanence of
Paper for Printed Library Materials, ANSI/NISO Z39.48–1992.
Manufactured in the United States of America.

Contents

Preface

The purpose of this book is to provide basic education (K–12) administrators with a framework for understanding issues and programming for students who are speakers of English as a second language (ESOL) and to conceptualize the role of educational administrators in promoting equal educational opportunity for culturally and linguistically diverse (CLD) students. Once primarily the concern of large urban school districts, quality programming for ESOL students is now the responsibility of suburban and even rural districts throughout the nation. Demographic predictions from a wide variety of sources indicate that the number of students in our nation's schools who come from backgrounds where English is not spoken at home, and who therefore may experience difficulty learning in mainstream classrooms because of limited English proficiency (LEP) or cultural differences, is going to continue to increase at a rapid rate well into the twenty-first century. Children and adolescents who are acquiring English are frequently at risk for academic failure or underachievement owing to a multitude of variables other than language that affect their lives, including poverty, transience, and parental disempowerment. While several books have been published that specifically focus on teaching ESOL students in the regular classroom setting (Faltis, 1993; Peregoy & Boyle, 1993, Snow & Brinton, 1997), there is currently no resource guide for educational administrators; yet, the central office administrator or building principal is the person most likely to be responsible for the development, administration, and evaluation of programs for ESOL students. Likewise, a review of professional educational journals uncovered few articles on the administration of K–12 basic education programs that provide equal educational opportunities for ESOL students.

School boards facing legal and fiscal decisions associated with the provision of federally mandated programs for ESOL students often have limited access to valid research and detailed accounts of effective programs and practices. The information that is readily available is often skewed, inaccurate, and limited in scope as the result of sensationalism by the media or poorly designed research on the part of so-called experts. Scholars who are not well versed in the multidisciplinary nature of the issues surrounding the provision of equal educational opportunity for CLD students provide heavily biased or isolated analyses of research and theory, which can result in confusion and frustration on the part of the administrators and staff attempting to interpret the data to make program decisions. Additionally, development and implementation of successful programs involves much more than understanding theory, methods, and materials. Administrators endeavoring to meet the needs of CLD students in a district, school, or even a single classroom must take into consideration an incredibly wide scope of complicated variables to develop programs that are valid in relation to the knowledge currently available in a variety of fields, such as cognitive linguistics, child development, and education, and the varied and practical experiences of districts that have pioneered program development. The tendency to become sidetracked by sociopolitical issues, combined with a trend toward emphasizing political correctness over research, experience, and even common sense, continues to have an extremely negative effect on the lives of one of our nation's most valuable resources: the children and adolescents who are most capable of becoming the bilingual and bicultural adults necessary for the United States to remain a leader in the twenty-first century. Even worse, many of our nation's ESOL children may never achieve their potential academically or professionally.

This book attempts to provide educational administrators with an ecological (Bronfenbrenner, 1979) understanding of educating ESOL students that will facilitate policy decisions and the creation of an infrastructure for quality programming. Bronfenbrenner's theory emphasizes the interdependent nature of children's development, involving not only the family and the school but also the current context of the community, the state, the nation and even the world situation. The education of CLD students is particularly affected by these broad variables. If administrators and school directors are to become successful leaders in positively influencing the improvement of ESOL students' academic performance, English language development, and acculturation and social integration into the larger community, these leaders must begin with a realistic perspective of ESOL students' native languages and cultures, home lives, motivations, needs, and the broader national and international social, political, and economic variables. Most critical, educational leaders must acknowledge ESOL students' potential contributions to society. Until now, no single source for the background information administrators need to provide the best services for ESOL students has been available. Therefore, this book was written for central office administrators, building principals, school board members, parents, and interested community members. It contains integrated perspectives on and insights into theory, research, and practice that permit leaders to make valid, grounded decisions about educating the increasing numbers of CLD students in our nation's schools.

The education of CLD students is currently an issue of considerable contention among various constituencies, not only among U.S. educators, but among the general public, as well. Until recently, the primary focus of this contention was a heated debate over "language of instruction," an issue that has been a political minefield throughout U.S. history. Americans cannot seem to reach agreement on whether bilingualism is an asset to the individual and the United States, or a condition that demonstrates a lack of loyalty to our nation's democratic ideals. While few Americans deny the economic and social benefits of a multilingual population, and while we institute laws against discrimination rooted in language or ethnic origin, we have only belatedly provided resources for foreign language learning by native English speakers, or for maintaining the first language of our newest citizens. It is both ironic and sad that we tend to equate fluency in one or more foreign languages as evidence of being well-educated, intellectually gifted, and sophisticated, yet continue to elect many state legislators who attempt to enact "English-only" legislation, or who refuse to enact budget legislation to help promote or maintain bilingualism.

It is evident that both the general public and educational leaders are divided and confused about how to best meet the needs of ESOL students, and that they are even more sharply divided over what the needs of this population are. Additionally, while we tend to readily admit that we have a long way to go in providing quality services to ESOL students, especially those who are dealing with a multitude of other problems that make them increasingly at risk for educational failure such as poverty, family dysfunction, and homelessness, we fail to plan programs for this population based on what research and common sense dictate. In the midst of this confusion, we are largely failing in our endeavors to facilitate the academic achievement, English language development, acculturation, and social integration of our ESOL students, as evidenced by the poor level of academic achievement, high level of school dropouts, and low proportion of ESOL students who attend college because they enter our schools (and frequently exit them) with limited English proficiency and are largely unprepared for employment in our economy. Administrators need a source that integrates information on the issues, legal mandates, and findings on what constitutes the special educational needs of ESOL students. It is this inclusive type of resource that the authors strive to provide for educational leaders, especially those from districts that are involved in the initial development of programs for their ESOL students, and for districts that are implementing program models and seeking strategies to refine and improve these programs.

The authors' experience with a coalition of ESL (English as a second language) program coordinators in Pennsylvania, our participant-observations in classrooms and schools, and our conversations with parents and students, support staff, teachers, and administrators who work with ESOL students across the nation have convinced us that district administrators frequently are at a loss when it comes to strategic planning to serve the needs of ESOL students. These administrators are at even a greater loss when they attempt to understand the needs and frustrations of both ESOL students and staff at the building level. This book tries to provide educational leaders with an integrated perspective based on interdisciplinary insights of a linguist and an educator. We hope that after reading this volume, educational leaders will be better able to balance intervention and advocacy, preservation of first languages and cultural heritage and acculturation, social integration, academic content learning, and English language development, and the opinions and demands of various interest groups in the community with the needs of ESOL children as they learn with the same scope and rigor of native-English-speaking students. First and foremost, we hope this work will help improve the educational experiences of the many ESOL students we have come to know and respect.

The Format of the Book

We have divided this book into three parts. Part I promotes a general understanding of ESOL students' special needs by discussing historical, sociopolitical, and legal context within which decisions about the education of ESOL students take place, by presenting in chapter one the characteristics of these students as the heterogeneous group they are, and by helping educational leaders gain an up-to-date understanding of second language learning from a linguistic perspective in a straightforward and readily understandable manner in chapter two. Chapter three explains the legal mandates and controversy related to equal educational opportunity for ESOL students and offers resources for staying abreast of the legal debates that will continue to occur.

Part Two focuses on program development issues and procedures, including important policy issues that form the infrastructure for program development. Special attention to the controversial issue of language of instruction provides the reader with insights from history and from the sociopolitical perspectives of various parties to the debate. Within this context, program evaluation research is the focus of chapter four. Information on specific program models to provide equal education opportunities for ESOL students and important ecological considerations connected to the implementation of various models are discussed in detail in chapter five. Descriptions of specific experiences of the Bethlehem Area School District, currently implementing an exemplary program model, provides an example of a positive experience that may be replicated with appropriate contextual variation. The authors also investigate the rationale for collaboration with ESOL students' families and the larger community and strategies for doing so in chapter six.

Part Three presents specific information to allow the educational leadership of a district to design a plan for administering and evaluating programming for ESOL students. In chapter seven, the authors provide a step-by-step format for designing a context-sensitive paradigm for the development of a high-quality structured-immersion program and introduce general guidelines for accommodating CLD special education students. Chapter eight considers the specific task of administering ESL programming by including a detailed view of the program director's responsibilities and staff development. In addition, chapter eight considers the important issue of formative and summative program evaluation. Chapter nine presents sources and directions for resourcing ongoing program refinement and for obtaining information on legal issues, grants, and research.

Our Perspective

Self-esteem and preservation of native languages and cultural heritage should be supported in every school system by every staff member, but educators are not meeting their professional responsibility to our newest citizens and their children if they allow preservation of native language and culture to be the overriding focus of ESOL children's K–12 education. We believe that while all students in our basic education systems should learn to respect and appreciate diversity, ESOL students must also learn the skills and knowledge they need to succeed and to negotiate differences successfully.

We have found that if schools truly work in partnership with parents, and by doing so, provide ESOL students with the tools they need to navigate both the U.S. mainstream culture and their native culture and language, we will be ensuring ESOL students' long-range success as individuals, employees, and citizens of a world where bilingualism and multilingualism are viewed as advantages rather than deficits. We firmly believe that ESOL students have the right to the same high-quality core curriculum as native speakers, and that the expectations for the performance of ESOL students should be aligned with the content standards established by professional organizations such as NCTE, NSTA, NCTM, and by federal and state agencies. Researchers and practitioners must continue to integrate knowledge and experience until we develop a better understanding of organizational structures and pedagogical strategies that foster the development of every child.

A Few Words About Terminology and Acronyms

Few fields have the enormous number of terms and acronyms associated with them that the field of educating English as a second language learners does. We feel the need to comment on some of the terms and acronyms used in the book, and explain our choices of acronyms when more than one term or acronym is available. The Glossary at the end of the book serves as an extended resource with easy access to terms used.

Because of the inherent danger of selecting terms that become negative labels, we use the term, "ESOL students," because this term has been used for many years by a majority of educators, so it is more immediately understandable to the reader who is not familiar with the field. Since the recently published ESL Standards for Pre-K–12 Students (TESOL, 1997) uses the term ESL to refer to the field of English as a second language and to the standards themselves, and uses ESOL to refer to the learners who are still in the process of acquiring English as an additional language, we have used these acronyms with the same denotations. Although we prefer the term culturally and linguistically diverse (CLD) student, and have used this term throughout the text to contribute to the style and readability of the manuscript, we realize that the term is not as widely recognized and used by education professionals who do not work with this population. Therefore, we opted against exclusive use of this acronym. Although ESOL students may speak one or more languages other than English, and in many cases may speak

English to some extent, we caution readers that oral fluency in English does not necessarily equate with the degree or type of language proficiency necessary for academic learning and success (Cummins, 1989). Many students who complete special programming for ESOL students may continue to have special learning needs since verbal fluency and even a high level of literacy in a language does not automatically mean a level of acculturation that precludes learning difficulties based on a mismatch between home and school cultures.

We avoid the term language minority (LM) students because this term is already inaccurate in some districts, and is rapidly becoming inaccurate in many additional districts in which children who are not native speakers of English may in fact be the majority at a particular school or at several schools. We also believe that the term "minority" has a negative connotation and that in the not-so-distant past, has been incorrectly equated with some kind of deficit on the part of ESOL students. We also avoid the labels Non-English Proficient (NEP), Limited English Proficient (LEP), and Fully English Proficient (FEP) because they are frequently associated with the level of English proficiency classification criteria employed by countless numbers of school districts, each of which is likely to have different criteria for assigning these labels in terms of students' competencies in listening, speaking, reading, and writing in a second language (L2). Therefore we believe these terms might be confusing to readers who might have difficulty putting aside their own working definitions to adopt ours.

We use the acronym, TESOL (Teachers of English to Speakers of Other Languages) to refer to the national professional organization of teachers and other professionals who have the specific training and/or responsibility for planning and implementing lessons for ESOL students toward the goal of oral fluency and literacy in English. Administrators should recognize from the start that these acronyms are used with many different meanings in different contexts, and that this reality is just one of the many hindrances to understanding the concerns, issues, research, and processes of providing ESOL students with equal educational opportunity.

Because the term, bilingual education has been defined in a variety of ways, we are careful to delineate the specific characteristics of programs where instruction in content areas takes place in the primary language or in some combination of the native language and English. We feel that the confusion over the term bilingual education has to do with comparing and contrasting program successes or failures and we intend the term to refer to programs in which students are educated in both their native language and English.

If we have offended anyone in our use of terminology, we apologize; however we feel that it is important to recognize that stereotyping ESOL student is inappropriate, because ESOL population in our schools is heterogeneous. While we would purport that ESOL students are all advantaged because they have all been exposed to two languages and cultures, their individual experiences vary greatly. It is important therefore, that educational leaders remember that ESOL students are children first, and second, culturally and linguistically different.

Finally, this book is among the first to incorporate TESOL's ESL Standards for Pre-K–12 (TESOL, 1997). As members of TESOL, we agree with the standard developers that integration of these standards into the general curriculum of elementary, middle, and high schools may help bring about the necessary adaptations to our educational system if we are to provide CLD children with the best opportunities for success in school and in their adult lives.

Acknowledgments

We extend special thanks and appreciation to the experts in our field who have guided us in developing our own knowledge of linguistics and education: Dr. Herbert Stahlke (Ball State University), Dr. Joseph Kender (Lehigh University), Dr. Herbert Rubenstein (Lehigh University), Dr. JoAnn Nurss (Georgia State University), Dr. Barbara Frankel (Lehigh University), and Dr. Andrea Calabrese (University of Connecticut). To Myrna Delgado, director of minority education for the Pennsylvania Department of Education, we extend thanks for her encouragement and motivating presentations, chats and reality checks. We thank Ana Sainz de la Peña for her insights on the needs of CLD students and encouraging us to write this book. Finally, we thank the students, faculty, parents, and administration of the Bethlehem Area School District (BASD), and in particular Mr. Thomas Dolusio, superintendent; Mrs. Ann Goldberg, coordinator of the English Acquisition and Literacy Program; Dr. William Nelson, director of Elementary Education; Sandra Figuoroa; and all the faculty and students at Donegan and Freemansburg elementary schools, a true community of lifelong learners in every sense. Among the faculty from BASD who have helped us along the way are Iris Cintron, Camie Modjadidi, Sue Lucrezi, Martha Nieves, Olga Ramirez, Rita Hatten, and others too numerous to name here. These friends spent countless hours with us over the past four years sharing their ideas, concerns, dreams, teaching strategies, and needs. We are fortunate to have had the opportunity to work with these professionals who are the true experts in our field.

Part One

❧

The Background Issues
and Questions

Part One provides necessary background information for the administrator. Chapter one considers the history of structural responses to the presence of ESOL students in U.S. schools. Chapter two outlines the pedagogical responses to the task of learning a new language and the kinds of issues and topics that teachers have been wrestling with for some time. This information is provided so that the administrator be able to assess what teachers are doing in the classroom and why. Chapter three sketches legal developments in response to the needs of ESOL students over the past decades. Many of these developments directly shape the choices and responses of administrators as they structure programs to meet the needs of ESOL students.

Chapter One

Providing Equal
Educational Opportunities
for ESOL Students

Goldenberg's (1996) assertion that "our schools' response to the challenge of non-English-speaking students has been uneven, fitful, and laced with political, ideological, and methodological controversies such as those swirling around bilingual education" (p. 353) accurately describes the confusion and discomfort experienced by many educational leaders when faced with the challenge of planning, implementing, administering, and evaluating programs for English as a second language (ESOL) students. The overall status of ESOL student success in U.S. schools is far from satisfactory, although some programs have demonstrated success with this population (Krashen & Biber, 1988). The challenge faced by educational administrators in making decisions about the special needs of ESOL students is not easily met. Children who are not native speakers of English must at the same time learn a new language and the accompanying culture, strive to achieve academic competencies at their grade or age level, adjust to new cultural norms and mores, and seek social integration within a classroom, school, and community that may often be hostile and rejecting.

This chapter provides educational administrators with the history of the education of ESOL students in Grades K–12 in the United States, the demographic variables that make our ESOL students a highly heterogeneous group, and other variables that must be considered in a context-specific and ecological manner by any district attempting to design and implement a quality program for this population. Such programs for ESOL students must, at the same time, foster the academic achievement, English language development, acculturation, and social integration of these students if they are to provide equal educational opportunities to these students.

Education of Non-English-Speaking Immigrant Children in the United States

Educational administrators planning programs for an ESOL student population must understand the historical and sociopolitical issues surrounding programming. The history of the education of ESOL children in the United States since early colonial times provides insights into the origins of the emotionally charged and frequently illogical reactions of many Americans to language and culture in our nation and schools that may deeply affect a school district, as its leaders attempt to provide ESOL students with federally mandated but ill-defined services. The education of immigrant students using their native language as the language of instruction was acceptable in many communities throughout the country during our early history. The schools in a community frequently used the immigrant settlers' native language as the language of instruction, because either parents wanted to maintain their children's original cultural heritage, or the only teachers in the communities were monolingual speakers of the native language of the community's immigrants. The Continental Congress published official documents in German, French, and English, and newspapers in many languages were available for the literate colonist (Crawford, 1992a) because bilingualism or even multilingualism was a fairly common phenomena and was not viewed negatively.

In the midwest, Pennsylvania, and Ohio, German immigrants set up numerous German language schools for their children; by 1900, more than 4% of the elementary school population in the United States was taught partially or totally in German. In California and New Mexico, students were permitted to attend classes in both English and Spanish, or Spanish only. In 1839, Ohio was the first of a dozen states and territories to pass laws authorizing bilingual education. Other states and territories unofficially supported native language or bilingual education in their schools. The New Mexico Territory authorized bilingual education in Spanish and English in 1850 (Crawford, 1991). During the same period, French language public schools existed in areas of Louisiana and northern New England (August & Garcia, 1988). Instruction in English, French, or both was authorized in Louisiana in 1847, and parents had the right to choose the language of instruction of their children (Crawford, 1991). Several other states permitted the use of other languages for instruction, including Czech, Dutch, Lithuanian, and Norwegian (Anderson & Boyer, 1970).

"Language of instruction," currently a topic of much dispute and debate among researchers, education practitioners, politicians, and general U.S. citizenry, did not become an issue in educational policy until the latter part of the nineteenth century, when the Common School movement and compulsory education were widely instituted to "Americanize" or assimilate the country's newest immigrants. With the arrival of an increasing number of immigrants of lower socioeconomic status (SES) from southern and eastern Europe who were often illiterate and largely Catholic, the "old immigrants" (mostly Anglo-Saxon Protestants from northern Europe) reacted with what was almost xenophobia, apparently fearing changes in their community from the impact of "the children of the foreign born" (Esterlin, Ward, Bernard, & Rueda, 1982). Descendants of the English settlers resented the large numbers of Italian, Slav, and Jewish immigrants who were settling in the eastern United States. In the west, additional immigration by Asians and Mexicans was viewed as an increasing an unwelcome influence on societal mores and values. American citizens began to view the United States as the "great melting pot" and giving up one's native language and culture was an expected step toward becoming an American citizen. Refusal to give up one's native language and culture in the interest of being American was often viewed as unpatriotic.

English literacy and instruction in American values were deemed critical to ensuring that the newcomers assimilated and acquired the common value system of a democracy. A single common language of instruction became an educational issue that continues to be hotly debated today. The ability to quickly "shed" one's native language and learn English was viewed as an important measure of assimilation and came to be associated with upward social and economic ability. State legislatures soon began passing laws regulating the language-of-instruction in public and private schools. California and New Mexico both adopted "English-only" instruction laws. By 1898, the use of Spanish for instruction was banned in the U.S. territory of Puerto Rico, even though the entire population there spoke Spanish (Diaz-Rico & Weed, 1995). In 1906, the requirements for U.S. citizenship were changed, and, for the first time, all immigrants seeking naturalization had to demonstrate English-language skills. This change provided support for opposition to public school instruction in any language other than English.

During World War I, the anti-German and anti-foreign reaction of the American populace made the idea of bilingual education unthinkable (Cartagena, 1991). The few remaining foreign-language schools in existence (mostly German) were eliminated, either by withholding public funding or by enacting laws that mandated "English-only" instruction. Several states even banned the teaching of foreign languages in public and private schools with criminal penalties for teachers who broke these laws. Linguistic unity actually became the focus of the civil defense effort of Franklin K. Lane, Secretary of the Interior during World War I (Crawford, 1991). When the Japanese attacked Pearl Harbor during World War II, the Japanese-language schools were closed. It was not until late in the 1960s that schools in Rio Grande, Texas, discontinued "Spanish detention," being kept after school for using Spanish during the school day or on school grounds.

Bilingualism: Asset or Liability?

Well before the national isolationist policy, ESOL children were viewed as disadvantaged and so-called culturally deprived. Cultural deprivation theory included factors such as lack of English-language skills, lower SES values, and lack of parental support for the importance of education, and related particular cultures rather than genetic differences as the cause of lower academic achievement of minority children. Early research views bilinguals as handicapped and purports that they have less intelligence than monolingual learners. While much of this research demonstrates evidence of flawed designs and biased results, Jensen's (1962) review of more than 200 studies found correlations between bilingualism and handicaps in language development and reading problems, handicaps in academic and intellectual achievement, emotional development problems, lack of creative thought, shyness or aggressiveness, contempt and hatred toward parents, and even schizophrenia.

Darcy (1953) and Weinreich (1953) conducted separate reviews of research done between 1920 and 1950, and concluded that bilingualism affected children negatively. For example, Goodenough (1926) asserted that ethnic groups with inferior intellectual ability did not learn English readily. Until the 1970s, only Leopold's (1939) case study documented the advantages of bilingualism until additional positive effects of bilingualism were documented in studies by Liedtke & Nelson (1968), Torrance, Wu, Gowan, & Alliotti (1970), Ianco-Worrall (1972), Bain (1974), Ben-Zeev (1977), De Avila (1987), Bain & Yu (1980), and Hakuta & Diaz (1984). Although the cognitive benefits of early bilingualism are not in question, one must consider the effect of the earlier research on current debates. Some teachers today continue to accept the cultural deficit standpoint, which may lead to second-class status for some CLD students, and lowered teacher expectations. The deficit research resulted in negative stereotypical beliefs, which contributed to the stereotypic attitudes about student expectations of many classroom teachers today in regard to working with ESOL students, in spite of clear research evidence to the contrary (Constantino, 1994; Penfield, 1987; Simons & Connelly, 1997). This view of a deficit on the part of ESOL students may be part of the reason that a disproportionate number of ESOL students are assigned to special education classes, a condition that has only begun to be rectified by recent mandates for inclusion. From the 1920s until the 1960s, little was done to provide special support for ESOL students; they were usually placed in regular classrooms where they sank or swam. This approach, generally termed "submersion" is illegal, although throughout the United States, in many districts with few ESOL students scattered one or two to a class among many schools, "submersion" is the norm for children whose English fluency and literacy is limited.

It was not until 1968 that bilingual education programs were actually legislated. The Civil Rights Movement and increasing demands for cultural pluralism produced Title VII of the 1964 Civil Rights Act, the enforcement legislation by which courts came to order services for ESOL students. Title VII prohibited discrimination on the basis of race, color, or national origin. The Bilingual Education Act (BEA) (1968) established the federal government's role in providing bilingual education and allotted funding for innovative projects and support programs. The melting pot ideology that had been so widely adopted by citizens of the United States slowly began to be replaced by respect or at least tolerance for diversity. Some have come to refer to the acceptance and appreciation of diversity as the "salad bowl" approach. Concomitantly, a successful experimental bilingual education program in Dade County, Florida, and research on successful bilingual programs in Europe and Canada, contributed to congressional passage of the first Bilingual Education Act in 1968. However, Laosa (1984) notes that in 1971, 35 states still maintained some type of English-only instruction laws.

English Only, First, or Also

A movement to make English the official language of the United States resulted in major opposition to bilingual education. The most active English-only group in the United States is "U.S. English," which operates a political action committee that continues to strive for adoption of an English-only amendment to the Constitution. In 1981, Senator S. I. Hayakawa of California introduced the first English-only bill in Congress, proposing the designation of English as the official language of the United States. Like many other members of U.S. English, he supported limits on the use of languages other than English. In spite of Congress's failure to pass Hayakawa's bill, English-only advocates continue to support English-as-the-official-language legislation at the federal and state levels. These advocates seek a repeal of laws that mandate multilingual voting ballets and more controlled enforcement of the English-language requirements for citizenship. With more than 200,000 members, U.S. English has been moderately successful by financing statewide efforts to have English become the official language of individual states. In California, U.S. English spent more than $700,000 on Proposition 63, which passed by a three-to-one margin in 1986. Today, 21 states have official English language laws (Porter, 1996).

In recent years, the overemphasis on the question of language-of-instruction appears to be a reaction by some to the increasing numbers of documented and undocumented immigrants who have entered the United States since the 1960s. Most of the new immigrants come from Third World nations that are largely undeveloped. Since the middle 1980s, the trend of loyalty to the English language seems to be a subtle disguise of racial politics, and bilingual education has become an integral part of the issue. The English-only lobby labels any effort to provide language support to ESOL speakers as "un-American" (Diaz-Rico & Weed, 1995, p. 149). The English-only movement also attempts to alarm monolingual English-speaking teachers by claiming a potential loss of status and jobs as the result of bilingual programs being implemented in public schools. Most important, the focus on the language-of-instruction debate has resulted in the neglect of research that examines the usefulness of specific teaching strategies for ESL strategies to better meet the learning needs of ESOL students who are in mainstream classrooms.

Government-sponsored research repeatedly focused on comparing a variety of program models classified as either primary-language (native language) or English only (immersion). In most cases, this criterion grossly oversimplifies program design variations. In addition, few qualitative studies have been designed to discover the specific characteristics of highly effective programs for

ESOL students. Essentially, valuable time, effort, and fiscal resources have been wasted over a period of more than 30 years to produce research that is essentially invalid and unreliable because of methodological flaws and poor program evaluation design.

Perspectives of U.S. citizens today are widely divided with regard to bilingualism and multilingualism. Depending on the individual queried, language differences are seen as a problem, a right, or a resource (Ruiz, 1984). Students who do not speak English as their native language are still viewed by many as intellectually less capable. Even the 1968 Bilingual Education Act and many states' statutes on the education of ESOL students were initiated based on the premise that native speakers of a language other than English face learning problems caused by their native language. As a result, many programs for ESOL students have a primary goal of developing English, often at the cost of ESOL students' lack of exposure to the core curriculum and lack of opportunities for social integration. Since the original BEA instituted poverty as an eligibility requirement, many people adopted the perspective that bilingual education is only for the impoverished.

Some U.S. citizens view language as an individual's right, equating language to civil and minority rights. American citizens and immigrants should have the freedom to communicate with one another in whatever language they choose. In relation to educational programming, this stance often results in support for primary-language instruction—that is, educational programs in which all or a large part of the students' academic content learning takes place in the students' native language (theoretically, until the students gain sufficient proficiency in the English language to attend mainstream classes conducted in English). The primary-language instructional model also tends to result in segregation of ESOL students who are unable to attend class with native-English-speaking peers when matriculating in a primary-language program. Students who attend primary-language programs frequently find it difficult to integrate socially into situations with native-English-speaking peers when they are mainstreamed at a later time, thus the primary-language model may inadvertently contribute to marginalization of ESOL students. Problems related to recruiting qualified bilingual teachers also contribute to the difficulties associated with implementation of a primary-language model.

Unfortunately, the language-of-instruction controversy tends to result in a competition in which different groups (i.e., teachers, parents, businesspersons, the community) attempt to exert their own rights over each other, and a multitude of sociopolitical issues emerge, none of which directly relates to providing ESOL students with equal educational opportunities. The language-of-instruction controversy may divide faculty in a school or district, parents and administration, district administration, and even entire communities in disputes that cannot be settled to the satisfaction of everyone, since they are largely emotional and/or political, and since research that might provide evidence of greater effectiveness of one model or another has been limited in scope and weak in both internal and external validity.

Nationally, the reality is that compliance with federal regulations and state mandates in regard to ESOL students is frequently ignored in states with few of ESOL students, and ESOL children are not receiving equitable educational opportunities despite federal legislation ensuring them of special services. Only through increased awareness on the part of school administrators will the injustice of districts failing to provide appropriate services end. Few educational administrators will develop or supervise programming for ESOL students without coming face to face with language-of-instruction issues.

Another perspective that is currently accepted as politically correct, but is probably less realized in terms of program design and implementation, views language diversity as a personal and national resource that school districts should facilitate for all students. Supporters of this perspective are critical of both the lack of resources for foreign-language education and the failure of the majority of school districts to develop programs that help students maintain their native languages. Numerous reasons are documented by research and economic projections that support the development of multilingualism among U.S. students, including diplomatic needs, the trend toward economic interdependence of nations, international communication, and enhancement of students' cognitive flexibility and earning power. However, even in affluent school districts with substantial advanced placement curriculum offerings, few schools have implemented dual-immersion or foreign-language elementary school (FLES) programs consistently. It is paradoxical that the very Americans who agree that fluency in a foreign language is indicative of a better education, greater social sophistication, and more cognitive ability, view bilingualism of recent immigrants as a trait that needs to be eliminated to prove patriotism and to achieve success in learning English and academic content. In effect, politics being what they are, we have lost sight of, or at least minimized, larger issues such as determining effectiveness of various models of instruction in second-language development for all students, and on academic achievement of ESOL students, with the goal of general educational improvement and, specifically, reducing the staggering dropout rate of many ESOL students.

These varying perspectives on language, its role in education, and in more global contexts result in communities that frequently disagree over how to best meet the needs of ESOL students. The language-of-instruction issue remains a major source of contention, and school district leaders need to understand the foundations of the many perspectives related to this controversy and at the same time understand what the available research does and does not support. More than 30 years of research largely provide us with literature reviews of poorly conceptualized and invalid designs of evaluation studies that attempt to determine which models are more effective, and with position papers that focus on the language-of-instruction debate, which are often based on biased interpretations of linguistic theory and research. Most education scholars lack a background in applied linguistics and know very little about the variety of ecological problems faced by school administrators, yet they often take a militant stand supporting one model or another. Many administrators of ESOL programs view their program models as "emerging" even after 5 or 10 years of implementation, a position that the authors view as appropriate in light of the lack of definitive longitudinal support for any particular model. The typical administrator is left with minimal and often conflicting resources when attempting to examine program effectiveness to help select a program model appropriate for his or her context.

While many Americans acknowledge the advantages of instruction in a foreign language by native speakers of English at an early age, only a small number of elementary programs offer FLES, and even fewer provide dual-language immersion models, integrating native and non-native speakers in the same classroom where they receive daily academic content in two languages. Unfortunately, even if district administrators are convinced that dual-immersion programs are the best approach for all students, dual-immersion models or FLES programs (in the case of schools with all native-English-speaking students) are seldom implemented because of a lack of staff who are qualified to teach in two languages or a lack of economic resources. The United States simply lacks sufficient numbers of qualified bilingual teachers to implement such programs.

Ultimately, school administrators are faced with the fact that researchers and practitioners have yet to define what constitutes the community's or nation's responsibility to immigrant children in terms of language and content instruction. Since education is the vehicle for upward social and economic mobility, most scholars and practitioners agree that we must provide ESOL students with the education they need to become productive members of society. Yet, it is evident that we are not succeeding in fostering this level of education when the dropout rate of minority students is in excess of 50% a year. At the same time, we have evidence that some ESOL students do succeed. An encouraging number of Asian students graduate from our high schools and are well represented in our nation's colleges and universities. However, the data on most immigrant students, and on Hispanic students in particular, remains disappointing (Suarez-Orozco, 1987).

The Need for Sensitivity to Community Concerns

The history of the relationship between language and education in the United States demonstrates that educational leaders need to be very sensitive to the current attitudes and beliefs of the members of their community about the language of instruction when planning programming for ESOL students. Community members and parents of ESOL students and monolingual English-speaking students need to understand the rationale for program decisions that are made about the language of instruction since many of these parents and community members only have access to what is printed in the local newspaper and, thus, lack a complete picture when forming opinions and voting. While there has been little in our experience or research that has built an airtight case for English-only instruction, transitional bilingual education, or primary-language maintenance programs, administrators should at the very least recognize that the question of language of instruction is an issue of considerable division and great emotional response. Administrators must be prepared to deal in a professional and forthright manner with constituents who will disagree with program design decisions. (See chapter four for an extended discussion of language-of-instruction controversy and appendix A for a summary of relevant research.)

ESOL Students in Our Nation's Schools

Increasing numbers of school districts throughout the United States are facing the challenge of providing federally mandated services to ensure equal educational opportunity for substantial numbers of students who speak little or no English and are therefore eligible for special services to ensure equity in learning opportunities. The federal government's description of students eligible for special services because of lack of fluency in English is broad and imprecise, and results in yet another difficulty faced by a district's educational administrators in decision making in regard to ESOL students: Which students need special services and for how long? The operational definition of "limited English proficiency," "English second-language student," and "language minority student" varies from state to state and even from district to district within a given state. Current federal mandates (BEA, 1994) indicate that all students who meet the following criteria are eligible for services:

1. Students who were not born in the United States or whose native language is not English.
2. Students who come from environments where the dominant language is not English.
3. Students who are American Indian or native Alaskan and have come from an environment where a language other than English has significant impact on their level of English proficiency.
4. Students who, by reason thereof, have sufficient difficulty speaking, reading, writing, or understanding English to deny them the opportunity to learn successfully in a classroom where the language of instruction is English or to participate fully in our society.

Thus, the federal government's description of students eligible for services provides little guidance for a school district in developing specific guidelines about which students are mandated to receive services. The very general student characteristics outlined by the federal government indicate that all students who speak another language prior to learning English are eligible for special services. However, Porter (1996) reports, "In a private conversation with one of the regional GAO managers, I was told that the agency has not found an agreed upon definition of what a 'limited English' person is and that they have included in this category children who speak English well, but may not read and write it well enough for school work" (p. 8). Administrators must depend on state legislation or state department of education policy guidelines, or develop their own criteria for assessing students' English proficiency, and deciding on criteria for including ESOL students in special programs as the result of their linguistic and cultural backgrounds. In addition, even theoretical research on delineating English-language skills necessary for successful learning of *content* presented in the English language is still not clearly identified because researchers are still shaping practical, proficiency-, and communication-based definitions of successful acquisition, particularly as they relate to the degree and type of proficiency necessary to ensure academic content learning success.

Heterogeneity of ESOL Speakers in the United States

Demographic predictions indicate that by the year 2000, there will be 260 million people in the United States. One out of every three will be African American, Hispanic American, or Asian American, representing a dramatic change from the Anglo-Saxon, Protestant, northern or western European heritage of our earliest settlers. Changes in immigration patterns and birthrates among various ethnic groups are responsible for this unprecedented demographic change. Gonzalez (1990) reports that in 2000, European Americans will constitute 64% of the U.S. population (a 10% decrease since 1980); Hispanics will make up 17% of the population (a 9% increase since 1980); African Americans will constitute 16% of the population (a 2.5% increase since 1980); and all others (Asians, Pacific Islanders, native Americans, etc.) will constitute 3% of the projected ethnic composition of the United States. Predictions of the U.S. population's ethnic makeup in the year 2040 are: 59% European Americans, 12.4% African Americans, 18% Hispanic Americans, and 10.3% all others.

Compared with the previous decade, between 1980 and 1990 alone, there was a 63% increase in immigration to the United States, for a total of 7.3 million immigrants (Waggoner, 1993). The greatest rates of growth in immigration were from Mexico (300% increase), El Salvador (600% increase), Ireland (178% increase), Iran (200% increase), Haiti (200% increase), Poland (200% increase), Romania (200% increase), and Vietnam (62% increase). Demographic predictions indicate a continued increase in immigrants from Third World countries well into the twenty-first century. Waggoner (1993) compared data from the 1980 and 1990 U.S. censuses, and discovered that there was a significant increase in the number of U.S. residents who speak a language other than English in their homes and neighborhoods. Approximately one in seven individuals ages 5 and older spoke a language other than English at home in 1990, as compared with one in nine in 1980. Waggoner also discovered that the majority of persons who speak a language other than English in the United States are native-born Americans rather than immigrants. In addition, Spanish speakers constitute almost half of the people speaking a language other than English, but over 1 million people speak one of the following languages: Chinese, German, Greek, and Italian. Waggoner's analysis also indicates that the largest increases in immigrant languages were from Asian countries such as China, Korea, Laos, Thailand, and Vietnam. Waggoner reported that 6.3 million American students spoke a language other than English in their homes in 1990. The reader is invited to consult the Web site for the National Clearinghouse for Bilingual Education (http://www.ncbe.gwu.edu) for comprehensive statistics on LEP enrollments in the United States and its territories.

These changing demographics are having a major effect on U.S. society and, consequently, on the demands on our educational system. Immigrant parents expect schools to help their children adjust to a new cultural identity and a technological society where educational success is vital to financial security. These immigrant parents want their children to study the same curriculum as native English speakers and to become thoroughly proficient in the English language. The demographic predictions indicate that in the twenty-first century, the future of the U.S. economy will rest more on the Asian and Hispanic worker than it does now. Therefore, the K–12 education of the members of these groups will have an important effect on U.S. economic welfare and global competitiveness. Unfortunately, our track record in providing for the needs of these students is poor. We must provide educational leadership with the information they need to improve decision making about programming for ESOL students in our nation's schools.

The Hispanic population is experiencing a particularly high growth rate, and Hispanics may make up 30% of the U.S. population within the next two generations. More than two-thirds of the Hispanic population in the United States is under age 35, compared with just a little more than half of the non-Hispanic population. In addition, the mean size of a Hispanic-American family is 3.75, compared with 3.11 for the non-Hispanics (National Educational Association, 1991). Hispanic children constitute the greatest ethnic group growth in our current school population, and the majority of these students come to school speaking little or no English. Some also lack fluency in a standard variety of English, and speak what is referred to in a derogatory fashion as "Spanglish." Still another subgroup of non-native English speakers shows some fluency in basic communication skills and the foundation for literacy. For a variety of reasons, including proximity of other native speakers of the language, opportunities to visit the native home frequently, and a growing professional and blue collar population actively involved in community action, Hispanic Americans tend to actively promote pride in and maintenance of their native language.

During 1990–1991, 33 states had some criteria to identify students who were limited in their English language proficiency; by 1994–1995, there was a 75% increase in the number of states that had identified criteria (42). Fleischman & Hipstock (1993) contend that nearly 90% of students who are classified as LEP receive some service to meet their needs for approximately 3.5 years. They further report that nearly 34% receive services in a regular classroom environment, and the remaining 66% receive at least some instruction in their native language. However, we must recognize that the quality and scope of services reflects a broad continuum of quality from intensive, longitudinal services of the highest quality grounded in interdisciplinary research to "lip service," consisting solely of tutoring by a native-language speaker that has little or no impact on the education of ESOL students because such services are designed solely to meet legal mandates, rather than truly provide equal educational opportunity. This also means that some ESOL students receive services from highly qualified professionals with specific training in meeting their needs while others receive services from someone who may take on the challenge only reluctantly for a variety of reasons that may be unrelated to an interest in working with ESOL students.

The results of Fleishman and Hipstock's (1993) survey further indicate that ESOL high school students are less likely to receive services than elementary students, and that students in districts with high concentrations of ESOL students are more likely to receive services than those who attend school in districts with minimal ESOL student populations. Finally, Fleishman and Hipstock found that less than 30% of the teachers who serve ESOL students have certification in either ESOL education or bilingual education. These data reflect major differences in the quality of services ESOL students receive. Federal Chapter I, Migrant Education, and Emergency Immigrant Assistance reportedly served higher numbers of ESOL students than Title VII. While only 298,787 students received instruction funded by Title VII in 1994–1995, 1,482,943 students were served through Chapter I. Migrant Education funded 1,333,142 students, and 757,918 students were served through emergency Immigrant Assistance funds. Title VII-funded programs identify the number of students receiving services in transitional and developmental bilingual education, family literacy programs, special alternative instruction (content-based ESL and sheltered content programs), and programs for special populations. Slightly more than 30% of the programs are considered to be ESL only.

Heterogeneity of ESL Programs in the United States

Nationwide, ESOL students receive a mixture of several types of instruction and services in the course of a single day, week, or school year, but no studies have been conducted to examine the effect of these sorts of mixtures on students *longitudinally*. Little effort has been made to provide educational leadership with objective analyses of data on effective programming, so many administrators are at a total loss when it comes to deciding what services are most cost effective and likely to produce desired outcomes.

According to the U.S. Government Accounting Office (GAO) (1987), greater heterogeneity among ESOL students is predicted to continue, especially in suburban and rural communities, for the next 40 to 50 years. Administrators' decision-making process is often made more difficult by major variations in ESOL population from one school to another or even within a single building. For example, the Bethlehem School District in northeastern Pennsylvania has three elementary schools and one middle school that have been designated as "high-impact schools" in terms of numbers of students attending with limited English-language proficiency. In high-impact schools, ESOL students make up 40–50% or more of the total school student population. Students attending these schools are predominantly, but not exclusively, Hispanic and are largely from lower-SES families who are on public assistance and are first- and second-generation U.S. residents. Another three schools within the district are designated "medium-impact schools," and percentages of ESOL students in these schools range from 12–30%. Many of these ESOL students are also from lower-SES families who are on public assistance, others are from middle-SES families. In contrast, "low-impact schools" with less than 6% ESOL students matriculating serve mostly children of middle-SES or professional immigrant families, and the range of language backgrounds in these schools is often more heterogeneous than in low- and medium-impact schools. A significant number of parents whose children attend schools in the Bethlehem Area School District (BASD) express their belief that their children should not be educated in their native tongue. Many of these parents say they are perfectly capable of de-

---

The Allentown School District in Allentown, Pennsylvania, has addressed the needs of ESOL students for 28 years. Currently, 18 different languages are represented among the 1,000+ students receiving ESL services out of a total student population of 14,831. Students in this district receive ESL services using a variety of different models; however, a bilingual model was implemented recently in one middle school to accommodate the needs of students who are trying to grasp more complex concepts typical of the middle-school level. The Allentown School District is using two models of structured-immersion: one is a push-in ESL program in the early elementary grades in which the ESL teacher goes into the elementary classroom during academic content instruction for some time each day, working with ESOL students as they participate in the regular classroom learning experiences; the other is a pull-out ESL program in which ESOL students are assigned various periods of time, depending upon their level of English language development, to attend an ESL class in which an ESL teacher plans and implements a lesson specifically designed to facilitate English-language development and support academic-content learning. During the 1999–2000 school year, the district will implement a dual-immersion program in one middle school. In this context students in Grades 6–8 will have the option of attending a middle school with both native speakers of English and native speakers of Spanish in a true bilingual program in which half of their content area instruction takes place in Spanish and half in English. Additionally, the native English speakers take classes in Spanish while the native Spanish speakers attend ESL classes for a period each day. This middle school is located in a bilingual (English and Spanish) community. Thus, the program for ESOL students meets the needs of the sudents and communities in which the schools are located.

veloping their own children's facility in their native language, and of fostering their children's pride in their native culture. They assert that schools should teach their children English and content (Simons, 1992, unpublished data).

This trend toward language heterogeneity combined with a shortage of bilingual teachers makes the question of whether to implement a primary-language instruction model a moot point in many communities such as Bethlehem. Thus, the density of ESOL student population in a particular school and the specific language backgrounds of the students are context variables that should affect decisions regarding the language of instruction. This type of variation makes it difficult if not impossible to select one program model that is effective across all schools in a district. On the other hand, placing all ESOL students in a single school at each level (elementary, middle, secondary) usually results in a watered-down curriculum, fewer opportunities for meaningful social integration with peers who are native speakers of English, and, in many cases, segregation or at least marginalization of a particular ethnic group (frequently Hispanics) from mainstream students at neighborhood schools.

The two districts just described are typical of districts throughout the country that serve small to moderate numbers of ESOL students, and the insights into decision making and solutions they have developed will be valuable to the readers of this book.

Many ESOL students are native-born American citizens who have had minimal exposure to English until they enter public school

---

Serita was born in Bethlehem, Pennsylvania, and has lived in the Marvine Housing Projects since her birth 7 years ago. At home, only Spanish is spoken. Her mother does speak some English, but her father is monolingual in Spanish, so English is not used. Her playmates during her preschool years were all Hispanic, and only a few of the neighbors speak English in their homes. Thus, Serita arrives at Marvine Elementary School with no proficiency in English at the age of 7. Meanwhile, Carmen, age 8, is the only child of Sr. and Sra. Gonzalez and has heard both English and Spanish from birth, with her mother speaking only English to her and her father speaking only Spanish to her.

in kindergarten or first grade, because they live in communities most of whose members speak the native language. Many of these students arrive at school lacking fluency in a standard dialect of the native language and English, a situation that produces additional instructional and learning problems. Other ESOL students learn their native language and English at the same time in home environments where their parents speak different native languages and only use English to communicate with each other.

ESOL students also vary significantly in the age at which their family immigrates to the United States, and in the age at which they begin to learn English. These two variables also affect appropriate curriculum adaptation, teaching strategies, and potential for the development of native-like English pronunciation. Circumstance of immigration to the United States also influences students' socioemotional adjustment, particularly during their first years here. Parents of ESOL students may have left their country of origin because of a desire for economic or social mobility and a better life in the United States, or they may have fled their homeland to save their lives. Children who experience severe trauma either before or during the immigration need different services from children who arrive in the United States to the welcoming arms and homes of relatives who are established members of a community with an understanding of the culture and the school system and experience in making the adjustments that the newcomers now face. Some ESOL students immigrate directly into the United States while others spend time in refugee camps or even in several different countries before gaining permission to come here. Therefore, it is not unusual for ESOL students to arrive at their U.S. school already speaking two or more languages, or to have already experienced difficulties and frustration attending school in an unknown language other than English. Still other students may be children of illegal immigrants. Many times students of illegal or undocumented aliens attend school with the constant fear of being identified as illegal aliens by government officials through tips from school officials. These ESOL students may view teachers and administrators as potential enemies, and this perspective may affect students' sense of acceptance and belonging and their motivation to learn English. While all immigrant students tend to follow a pattern of cultural adjustment that includes a period of culture shock, it is not surprising that students who have experienced serious trauma in the emigration process will need additional services from the guidance department and possibly long-term therapy.

ESOL students also arrive in classrooms with very different types of past educational experiences. ESOL students may come from war-torn countries where schools operated only intermittently because of widely spread chaos and destruction, or they may come from countries where they received a quality education until the day the family emigrated. A small percentage of ESOL students arrive in the United States without their parents, and may face long stays with relatives or even previously unknown friends of their family before their parents arrive. Some may even be uncertain about whether their parents will ever make it to the United States. If the student attended a school in another country, the culture of a U.S. classroom itself may require adjustment on the part of the child. ESOL students may have expectations of teachers, appropriate classroom behaviors, and learning and achievement that are significantly different from what they experience in educational settings here. There is a valid argument that language differences are not as difficult for ESOL students as the mismatch between the home and school culture (Heath, 1983). Still other students may arrive in the United States as capable readers and writers of English, but still lack functional English communication skills. That is, some ESOL students at the secondary level may be able to read and write English but lack oral proficiency. The BASD developed specific services for students whom it characterizes as "low schooled," recognizing that students who are far behind their age cohorts in academic experiences and literacy cannot be placed in classrooms with children many years younger than they are. Instead, these children need additional services to enable them to catch up and avoid embarrassment that may cause them to drop out of school because of the humiliation of "being with the babies."

Why Are ESOL Students at Risk?

The socioeconomic status of the families of ESOL students differs widely, but many ESOL students are doubly at risk because of the high incidence of poverty among immigrant families that makes focusing on learning difficult. Some ESOL students have educational difficulties due not of any lack of cognitive capabilities, but to familial transience caused by poverty issues, temporary economic problems such as parental unemployment, or parent or parents' employment as an underpaid migrant worker.

Although many ESOL students share a lack of sufficient English fluency to succeed in academic endeavors, and their lack of comfort with the English language may negatively affect their social integration, they exhibit the same range of individual differences in ability, motivation, and personality characteristics as students who are native-English speakers. Educational leaders must keep in mind that ESOL students are, first of all, children or adolescents, and that their cultural and linguistic differences are compounded by the same variety of individual differences that are found in monolingual English-speaking students. Educational administrators should also recognize that the ESOL population is far from heterogeneous, and that the number of variables affecting the English-language development, academic achievement, acculturation, and social integration of ESOL students are complex and intermeshed. A single ESOL program in a mid-sized district may serve students who are the children of government officials or corporate senior management, students who are children of professionals who immigrated to the United States because of political adversity in their native land, students who are living with their grandparents and seldom see their blue collar working parents during the week, children of poverty and abuse, and children experiencing every possible permutation of the variables mentioned.

Concerns Common to the Education of ESOL Students

In a GAO study (1994), *Limited English proficiency: A growing and costly educational challenge facing many school districts,* a careful analysis of ESOL students in five representative districts found several problems common to ESOL students and administration of programs for these students in public schools nationwide. These problems are important considerations in program planning and administration:

1. Immigrant students are almost 100% non-English proficient (NEP) when they arrive in the United States.
2. The arrival of limited-English-proficiency students in the district is unpredictable, occurring at various times throughout the year with little warning, which generates frustration on the part of many regular classroom teachers.
3. Some middle and high school ESOL students lack schooling in their native countries and are preliterate in any language.
4. A high level of family transience and poverty exists among families of ESOL students, increasing their academic jeopardy.

5. Some parents of ESOL students lack an understanding of their children's new schools and American schooling and tend not to be involved in school activities.
6. There is a critical shortage of bilingual teachers and texts in native languages, the texts that do exist in Spanish are of poor quality, and materials and texts that are available in other languages are frequently so out of date that they include misinformation.
7. There is a lack of valid instruments for assessing ESOL students' English development and academic achievement.
8. There are inadequate funds for teacher training and program development.

The administrator who considers each of these variables in program development will immediately have an advantage in meeting the complex needs of ESOL students. However, only if school administrators insist on internal and external formative and summative assessment of these programs will the educational community be able to move beyond its current tentative position in recommending services for meeting the needs of ESOL students in a holistic manner.

ESOL Students and Learning Academic Content

Educational researchers and practitioners continually note difficulty in developing and implementing comprehensive language-and-content programs that meet the educational needs of the diverse ESOL population (e.g., Fuchs & Reklish, 1992; Gottlieb, Alter, & Gottlieb, 1991; Pallas, Natriello, & McDill, 1989; Stevens & Grimes, 1993). ESOL students have less opportunity to learn (Arreaga-Mayer & Greenwood, 1986; Oakes, 1985; Ortiz & Yates, 1987; Ortiz, Yates, & Garcia, 1990; Willig, Swedo, & Ortiz, 1987), and lower academic success rates, which potentially delay their academic and linguistic development (Benavides, 1989; Miramontes, 1993). ESOL students tend to be confined to a passive learning role (Arreaga-Mayer, Carta & Tapia, 1994; Grossman, 1991; Sugai, 1989; Swedo, 1987), and experience difficulties with receptive and expressive communication within the classroom (Mattes & Omark, 1984; Moll & Diaz, 1987; Sugai, 1989). They also experience learning difficulties and delays because of inadequate instruction (Baca & Cervantes, 1989; Campos & Keatinge, 1988; Chamot & O'Malley, 1994; Fradd & Correa, 1989; Garcia, 1994; Gay, 1993).

When ESOL students experience problems with academic content learning, teachers typically refer them to special education, resulting in a disproportionate number of ESOL students who are so referred (Gersten & Woodward, 1994). An ESOL student with a disability is especially at risk because the majority of teachers and psychologists are not prepared to deal with the interaction of language, culture, behavior differences, and learning problems (Gonzalez, Brusca-Vega, & Yawkey, 1997). If teachers reduce standards and expectations of ESOL students, the well-documented impact of teacher expectations on student achievement may, in this case, substantially increase ESOL students' risk of academic and social integration problems.

The disproportionate numbers of culturally and linguistically different students referred to and placed in special education has been attributed to lack of acculturation, inappropriate assessment, language problems, academic/cognitive problems, and poor school achievement, which has resulted in negative expectations for these students in terms of their academic performance (Malave, 1991; Payan, 1984; Rodriguez, Prieto, & Rueda, 1984). Many school districts lack measures or personnel capable of fairly testing ESOL students referred by regular classroom teachers or ESL teachers. Although commonly used by school districts, retention of ESOL students is not a suitable way of dealing with these students' inability to handle grade-appropriate content. From a social, emotional, and academic development perspective, it is easier to be a 12-year-old in a sixth-grade classroom than a 12-year-old in a fourth-grade classroom, although the fourth-grade curriculum may seem more appropriate for ESOL students. Twenty-eight percent of Hispanic students are in grade levels below those expected, given their chronological age.

The effect of this retention on motivation and self-esteem has yet to be documented, but one can logically predict a strong correlation between retention and dropout rates. In addition, many ESOL students are placed in programs that result in underpreparation for college (Page, 1991). This placement can be seen as a form of tracking or segregation. If students with inadequate English-language abilities are segregated, then ESOL students (and in particular, Hispanic students) are more likely to be in a segregated school setting than Black students. This type of segregated grouping makes it difficult for ESOL students to interact with native speakers of English, which would help them achieve the fullest potential for English language development and social integration.

Many of the programs developed and implemented to meet the needs of ESOL students in the United States have resulted in only marginal improvements in the education and acculturation of these students. There is abundant documentation that many U.S. educational systems have been weak or even negligent in meeting the needs of the very same school populations that are experiencing the most rapid and substantial growth. Education is the vehicle for upward social and economic mobility, so we readily admit that schools must provide ESOL students with the education they need to become productive members of society. Yet, we are not succeeding in fostering this end as evidenced by dropout rate among minority students in excess of 50%.

Mexican-American youth are more likely to be enrolled two or more years below grade level than other Hispanic youth or other minorities, and only 53.3% of Mexican Americans graduate from high school. In fact, 17% of Mexican Americans have less than a fifth grade education. Among African-American and Hispanic students in California, there is a 43% dropout rate from high school (Highsmith, 1990). Dropout rates by ethnicity for 8th and 10th grade students continue to indicate that Hispanic students have the highest dropout rates of any group. About 40% of Hispanic students ages 19 and older drop out of school and do not have high school diplomas. Almost 1 in 5 leaves school without a diploma, compared with 1 in 16 Black students, and 1 in 15 White students. Only 50% of young Mexican-American adults ages 25–34 have completed four or more years of high school (National Council of La Raza, 1986). These alarming statistics are a challenge to administrators who have Mexican immigrant students in their districts.

At the same time, there is evidence that some ESOL students do succeed. Asian American students are well represented among college students, while college enrollment statistics for Hispanic American students are dismal (Suarez-Orozco, 1987). While Asian immigrant children are often viewed as academic superstars (Suzuki, 1989), this image is in reality a negative stereotype that is not true of students from all Asian ethnic groups. Many youths do not learn English well enough to enter mainstream classrooms, and the U.S. labor force contains substantial numbers of undereducated Asian males. Unemployment statistics for Asians are higher than those of Whites and Hispanics, and are rapidly approaching the average for Blacks (32%). Subethnic Asian groups experience differing educational success rates. Khmer and Laotian students have lower grade point averages than White students, while Vietnamese,

Chinese-Vietnamese, and Hmong students are well above the average. Japanese, Korean, and Chinese students also have higher averages than their White cohorts. Interestingly, Asian students attending graduate study enter engineering, physical sciences, mathematics, and computer sciences at both the undergraduate and graduate levels and aspire to careers in dentistry, medicine, and pharmacy, majors and occupations that require fewer communicative language skills (Trueba, Cheng, & Ima, 1993). Although these students may experience academic success in school, our educational system may not be meeting their need to develop their functional English proficiency.

The Effect of ESOL Students on Teachers

In a survey of public school teachers conducted by Waggoner and O'Malley (1985), only 6% of the respondents had taken one or more credit or noncredit courses to learn how to teach ESOL learners effectively, while more than half of these teachers had some experience teaching ESOL students. Research suggests that learning problems and delays experienced by ESOL students are often because of inadequate instruction (Campos & Keatinge, 1988; Fradd & Correa, 1989; Ortiz & Ramirez, 1989). While districts provide a variety of programs for ESOL students, the majority of these students spend only a small part of their day in ESL or bilingual classrooms; the rest of the day is spent in mainstream classrooms with teachers who are generally ill-prepared to integrate ESOL students into their classes (Clair, 1993; Simons & Connelly, 1997; Penfield, 1987; Wong-Fillmore & Meyer, 1990).

Anglo faculty comprise 95% of the teaching staff in public schools, and there is a nationwide shortage of minority and bilingual teachers (Farrell, 1990). The majority of elementary grade teachers are White women who are monolingual speakers of English and exhibit values and behaviors of the mainstream population. Olsen (1988) noted that fewer minority group members are majoring in education in college, increasing the likelihood that teachers will become more homogeneous in language and cultural backgrounds, while their students are at the same time becoming increasingly culturally and linguistically diverse.

Even with the adoption of multicultural norms in the accreditation standards of the National Council for Accreditation of Teacher Education (NCATE, 1987), Gollnick (1992) found that preservice teacher education programs do not prepare teachers adequately to work with linguistically and culturally diverse students. In a study that focused on how teacher education institutions were doing in respect to NCATE's accreditation standards, only 1 of 59 institutions had a preservice program in bilingual or multicultural education, and only 8 institutions were in compliance with its multicultural education standards. Many of the teachers who work with ESOL students in all-English classrooms are underprepared and even resentful and fearful of ESOL students (Penfield, 1987; Simons & Connelly, 1997).

Secondary Teachers' Preparation

At the secondary level, teachers tend to think of themselves as content area specialists, and many feel that students should know English before they are permitted to take regular core curriculum courses. Teacher preparation programs are very slow to include ESL teaching strategies in their curriculum for preparing regular K–12 classroom teachers. Most secondary teachers assert that ESL instruction is solely the responsibility of specialized teachers, and should be taught in pull-out classes, rather than integrated into academic content instruction. These teachers also appear to believe that ESL teachers can teach ESOL students sufficient English to do well in academic content courses in a short period of time, and that given ESL instruction, students who fail do so because they are "lazy" or because "their parents just don't care about education" (Constantino, 1994; Simons & Connelly, 1997). Some teachers, therefore, have low expectations of ESOL students and blame the students themselves for their low academic performance, downplaying the significance of students' prior knowledge and cultural experiences in facilitating language and content area learning. Teachers' expectations of student performance and their criteria for assessment of students are culturally derived from their own experiences (Diaz-Rico & Weed, 1995). Without staff development and support to improve teacher awareness of the impact of their own cultural background on their impressions of ESOL students, we can assume that ESOL students will not receive equal educational experiences and opportunities.

A recent study by Simons and Connelly (1997) indicates that regular classroom teachers do not understand how first- or second-language development occurs, cannot delineate strategies for adapting curriculum and instruction to promote academic content learning and English-language development of ESOL students, and do not feel that the English-language development of ESOL students is their responsibility. The 274 teachers included in this study expressed concern that they were not prepared to meet the needs of this population, and that when responsibilities for meeting the needs of ESOL students are combined with responsibilities related to including special needs students, they felt overwhelmed and unable to even meet the needs of the so-called normal students in their classrooms. Other researchers assert that even expert classroom teachers are not necessarily effective with ESOL students (Enright, 1986; Lucas, Henze, & Donato, 1990). According to Cummins (1989), teachers' beliefs and behaviors disable ESOL students. Handscombe (1989) asserts that every teacher is essentially an English-as-a-second-language teacher whether assigned that specific task or not. It is clear that any district with a population of ESOL students must develop a strong staff development plan for teachers at all grade levels. Teachers themselves assert (Simons & Connelly, 1997) that workshops or even intensive class sessions are not sufficient, and that they need follow-up to these sessions consisting of classroom observations and feedback as they attempt to implement new strategies and materials with ESOL students. Teachers who are successful instructors of ESOL students exhibit the following characteristics:

1. They maintain positive language, attitudes, and behaviors toward their L2 students with high expectations for their performance.
2. They activate students' prior knowledge and help them develop the language necessary to express it.
3. They use current instructional strategies in the language arts.
4. They embed learning in a context that fosters mutual accommodation and respect.
5. They engage in reflective practices (Zuniga-Hill & Yopp, 1996).

Parameters Defining ESL Programs Today

To develop programs that truly meet the needs of a district's ESOL students, we must recognize that our ESOL children and youth are first and foremost just that—children and adolescents with all the cognitive, social, emotional, and physical characteristics of their native-English-speaking peers; and, second, that they are native speakers of a language other than English. ESOL students' needs must be considered in relation to their developmental level. Our experiences with many ESL programs indicate that this important factor tends to be forgotten, sometimes through misguided political correctness and sometimes through the parameters that relate to compensatory education. The ESOL student will acquire use of the language and language varieties around them to the degree that educational, political, social, and psychological experiences require them to do so. What kind of experience do schools provide to promote this growth?

The authors have witnessed ESOL students placed two or more years behind their chronological age cohorts, as if speaking a language other than English was some sort of cognitive deficiency that prevents them from learning the same concepts that other children are readily learning. To our horror, we have listened to insensitive teachers discussing ESOL students in a negative manner in ESOL students' presence, presumably assuming that the student does not comprehend sufficient English to understand and be harmed by this unprofessional behavior. More alarming, we have observed that ESOL students are sometimes simply ignored by teachers who assume that ESOL students' needs are met in the 45 minutes a day or less in the ESL classroom. Such attitudes do not lead to equal educational opportunities. Instead, we recommend that administrators and teachers consider the following tenets adapted from those of Minicucci and Olsen (1993):

1. ESOL students must develop high levels of English language proficiency for both communicative and academic purposes, and it is the responsibility of all staff to foster this development.
2. We must plan programs that recognize that academic achievement of ESOL students is contingent on the interaction of sociocultural factors manifest in the context of school, home, and the community.
3. We must accept the fact that regular classroom teachers have a professional responsibility to meet the education needs of all learners, and we must provide these teachers with the training and support they need to meet these needs.
4. We must recognize that bilingual and ESL programs cannot function successfully in isolation, and teachers with specialized ESL training cannot, by themselves, meet the needs of these students. A team effort among regular teachers, ESL teachers, administrators, and support staff is critical to effective programming.

5. We must provide ESOL students with access to the same academic subject matter as monolingual students with appropriate support so that they can learn with this material.
6. We must integrate ESOL students socially into regular classrooms and school contexts, and not segregate them until they learn some arbitrarily determined level of English. Students need experiences in the mainstream to successfully acculturate, and consistent opportunities to use English in meaningful verbal interaction with native-English-speaking peers.

Matute-Bianchi (1991) asserts: "The remedy is to discontinue creating special programs to fit stereotypic perceptions of ESOL students and their problems, and to begin changing the school climate, structures, and practices to ones that are more broadly sensitive, responsive, and challenging to diverse student clientele" (p. 243). The information in this book enables administrators to provide leadership in facilitating just what Matute-Bianchi prescribes. The authors contend that programs that integrate ESOL students into regular classrooms with opportunities for both pull-out ESL and push-in ESL support (see chapter four) are the most educationally sound, culturally and linguistically sensitive, and cost-effective approaches to meet the diverse needs of ESOL students. Adaptive and support strategies can be used to assist ESOL students in these settings and help them gain control of academic, social, and cultural institutions (Trueba, Cheng, & Ima, 1993).

Cummins (1989) states that programs with the following characteristics empower students, so programs with these characteristics provide a context that ensures the success of ESOL students: (1) minority students' language and culture are accepted and incorporated into the school program; (2) minority community participation is an integral part of the school program; (3) instructional interactions encourage students to use language to construct their own knowledge; and (4) educators become advocates for minority students by focusing on the effect of the school context on achievement instead of viewing the student as the problem. These characteristics should become integral features of all programs serving ESOL students and should be considered in the program design and evaluation process.

Tikunoff, Ward, van Broekhuizen, Romero, Castaneda, Lucas, & Katz (1991) conducted a study for the U.S. Department of Education's Office of Bilingual and Minority Languages to determine the

In the Allentown School District, the authors observed a first-grade classroom teacher who told us he was attempting to empower his students and, by doing so, to foster their independence and responsibility. Mr. Lopez had high expectations for his largely Spanish-speaking students most of whom were non-English-proficient when we made our first observation in October of the school year. Children in this class who spoke some English were encouraged to clarify for their non-English-speaking peers in Spanish, and the teacher also explained concepts, facts, and processes in Spanish when he noticed that the students were confused. This strategy was very successful in facilitating the students' English and content learning. Children had plenty of opportunities to play with both languages and engage in active hands-on activities. When we revisited this classroom the following June, we could not identify which students had been non-English-speaking the previous fall. This is just one example of what a difference a teacher sensitive to the needs of ESOL students and trained in strategies for working with these students can make in a single school year.

significant features of exemplary programs for ESOL students from elementary through secondary levels. This study moves beyond the typical language-of-instruction obsession that consumes much of the earlier research evaluating programs for second-language learners, and focuses on identifying administrative, instructional, and program features of exemplary programs in which content area instruction is conducted in English. Several significant administrative features are noted: the presence of an individual who assumes an instructional leadership role for planning, coordinating, and administering the program; availability of expert teachers; a history of staff development for all teachers, not just ESL teachers; and willingness to allocate limited resources to support the program. All of the exemplary programs are integrated into the overall curricular structure of the district, so students have access to core academic and advanced placement courses and opportunities to foster social integration into the school and the larger community. Specific characteristics of successful instruction strategies are discussed in chapter eight.

The Administrative Support Variable

Diaz-Rico and Weed (1995) assert that school administrators and, in particular, principals can support quality instruction of ESOL students in many ways: (1) by advocating for increased funding at the district level; (2) by working with teachers to configure class environment and size to the benefit of ESOL students and all students; (3) by appointing a mentor teacher to help new teachers and frustrated veteran teachers adjust to meeting the needs of ESOL students; and (4) by providing opportunities for building-level professional staff to showcase accomplishments of ESOL students. Principals can begin to develop a climate of acceptance of linguistic diversity by working with staff to design policy that ensures that all students can receive high grades through culturally fair grading policies, by developing schedules that provide time for staff members who have expertise in working with ESOL students to assist other teachers by peer coaching, and by serving as models of respect for and encouragement of diversity.

If districts are to develop and implement successful programs for ESOL students, administrators should attend professional conferences and training that provide them with opportunities to develop their own expertise on linguistic and cultural diversity issues so that they are qualified to provide true leadership for staff and parent groups and can serve as advocates for ESOL students in their communities, especially those where there is hostility or bias. Leadership means active involvement. Over the past four years, we have frequently observed regular classroom and ESL teachers express frustration and even anger toward administrators who did not understand the needs of ESOL students, and therefore failed to provide the type of infrastructure and support necessary for truly successful programming.

This book provides school administrators and school board members with the knowledge of second-language development, language and culturally sensitive program design, fair student assessment, program evaluation, and staff development that will enable them to meet their challenges as leaders in developing, administering, and evaluating programs to ensure the equal educational opportunity of students who are speakers of English as a second language.

Chapter Two

Who Are ESOL Learners?
Assumptions and Profiles

Because of the longstanding and commendable efforts of national organizations such as TESOL, National Association of Bilingual Educators (NABE), and others, ESOL community has received much theoretical and practical attention as educators and linguists seek to understand the nature of second-language learning and ways of improving pedagogy accordingly. Administrators concerned with establishing solid ESL programs or improving existing ones are buffeted at times by competing pedagogical emphases and styles that are rooted in differing conceptions of how a student learns English, or any second language, in contemporary schools. Although progress in theory and practice results from a process of hypothesis and evidence, revised by qualification, counterclaim, and counterevidence, we do well to review the recent history of two related questions— How do students learn a second language? and What pedagogies best promote learning a new language?—if the tasks are to evaluate the needs of a population of ESOL students in a given district and work with faculty and program staff on finding ways to affirm or improve pedagogical practice. Furthermore, teachers manifest different training and different assumptions about second-language learners and learning, and, while no one approach is required or advocated, the following overview may help teachers, administrators, and program directors to identify assumptions and set goals and objectives accordingly. We look at the various answers proposed to two related questions: What goes on when one acquires or learns a new language? How may this process be encouraged and directed by pedagogical choices? While the first question has largely been the concern of linguists, and the second of educators, the two are inseparable in practice and require collaboration of specialists in both disciplines.

Background to the Questions

How does one learn a second language, and what is the best way of doing so? Much of the earlier theoretical discussion engendered by these questions took place within a wider debate in psychology and linguistics between those adhering to a rationalist (sometimes called mentalist or innatist) viewpoint on the one hand, or an empiricist (behaviorist) viewpoint on the other. The debate often posed the question: Is second-language learning primarily a matter of nature or nurture? Does the learner start with an innate set of abilities or schemata that ground first- and second-language learning, or does the learner have to develop a new set of automatic behaviors and suppress behaviors that interfere with the task at hand? Is the process of language acquisition somewhere in between the poles of innatism and behaviorism? These questions have always influenced pedagogical methods and choices. It is the responsibility of the administrator, or the ESL program director, to establish a dialogue among teachers regarding these assumptions and practices, and for this purpose, a brief overview is provided here.

The Behaviorist Legacy

Any linguist or educator profits from reading *Language*, a seminal work in American linguistics by Leonard Bloomfield (1993). Bloomfield's goal was to establish linguistics as an autonomous and scientific discipline: autonomous in method and content from classicist approaches to the study of language, and scientific in the sense of empirical. The linguist is to observe and record real speech in ordinary contexts, and to formulate or describe the patterns observed in the language at every level—phonological, morphological, syntactic, and lexical. Much of *Language* is devoted to establishing a clear descriptive method for linguistics, which in turn allowed a revision of the comparative method, or ways of comparing and contrasting structures of two languages at each level. This effort enabled linguists and educators to compare and rank the difficulties in moving from a knowledge of one language (L1) to the acquisition of a second (L2) (Lado, 1957). This process assumes that delineation of systematic differences in language structure, and explicit awareness of such differences, is of immediate usefulness to teachers and students. Contemporary readers of this assumption may question whether awareness of structural differences, as part of overall metacognition of language, is of use to all learners of a new language.

Bloomfield was influenced by events in psychology, which was also reevaluating its methods and standing as a scientific enterprise. The work of J. B. Watson and A. P. Weiss appealed to Bloomfield in that linguists might benefit from careful observation and description of human linguistic behavior within a stimulus-response (SR) formulation. Linguists need to (1) note the events preceding speech, (2) record and analyze the speech itself, and (3) note the events subsequent to speech. If humans operate in an environment that provides stimuli that produce responses, we may think of language (speech) as a substitute stimulus and substitute response that allow humans to manipulate the environment in various ways.

Bloomfield might not be concerned with the question, What happens when we learn a new language? because his methods allow no reference to mental events or a theory of human "grammar-making." But Bloomfield has much to say on the methods of second-language instruction, as found in his *Outline Guide for the Practical Study of Foreign Languages* (Bloomfield, 1942). Language learning is seen as a matter of establishing new habits, and to this end practice and drill are required. Many American linguists, while not concerned directly with the merits or disadvantages of behaviorist theory in general, nonetheless took to heart the practical matter of reshaping habits by oral drill when learning a new language. In *Teaching and Learning English as a Foreign Language* (Fries, 1945), the oral approach was advocated, whether one's goal was speaking or reading a second language. This approach relied on oral drills of preselected patterns or structures that were graded in complexity:

> Constant practice and use of language forms being learned with free and complete mimicry of the speaking habits of native users of the language must be contributed by the student if he is to make really effective use of the materials that are scientifically chosen and arranged for the efficient mastery of a foreign language. More than that, the oral approach—the basic drill, the repeated repetition of the patterns produced by the native speaker of the foreign language—is the most economical way of thoroughly learning . . . the structural methods of a language. (Fries 1945, pp. 6–7)

From this and similar works (Lado, 1957, 1964) we may conclude that (1) language is all about speaking—that is, language is a set of oral habits, both for native speakers and language learners; (2) these oral habits begin in mimicry and develop in repetition or drill of graded materials; (3) the structural patterns of a language (the grammar) may be discerned and learned in the oral practice rather than by a presentation of grammatical rules; and (4) this learning of grammar can be promoted by controlling grammatical variation (i.e., singular/plural agreement, tense variation) within the drill.

These variations often take the form of transformations or manipulation of one grammatical variable within the sentence frame. Extended practice of the language was conducted largely in a speaker-listener format or simple (to more complex) dialogues. These may be memorized at first, then gradually used to expand on structures embedded in the dialogue.

This kind of drill became the foundation of the audiolingual method (for good contemporary exposition of the method, consult Brooks [1964] and Lado [1964]) and shaped the training of language teachers, the design and function of language labs, and the production of language texts and workbooks for about three decades, beginning in the 1940s. Teachers were encouraged to develop the following pedagogical repertoire (adapted from Brooks, 1964, p. 143; and Chastain, 1971, p. 72):

1. Model, introduce, and teach the language behavior the student is to learn by requiring the student to hear and imitate the material offered (often by way of student/teacher or student/audiotape dialogue). Student responses may take the form of dialogue partnering, choral response, or pattern (transfomation) practice.
2. Once a modicum of structure is imparted through these techniques, have the individual student talk, allowing only the target language and rewarding appropriate effort.
3. Establish the rules of the classroom quickly and enforce them. This point sounds a bit ominous, but language classrooms are cultural and linguistic islands, where only target language use and appropriate cultural responses are rewarded.

The audiolingual method met with considerable early success, especially as incorporated into the Army Specialized Training Program taught at the Defense Language Institute in the 1940s. During the 1950s and 1960s, with the help of funds from the National Defense Education Act (NDEA) and with the encouragement of specialists in linguistics, the audiolingual method became the basic training of a large number of language teachers in the United States and, by extension, of teachers working to teach English as a second language.

Evaluation of the Audiolingual Approach

Is the audiolingual method the approach of choice in contemporary language classes? The answer depends on the approach of the individual teacher and, quite often, on the success (or failure) the teacher may have had in learning new languages under the audiolingual method. Recall that the audiolingual method has a structuralist underpinning: the outline and comparison of L1 and L2 is intended to provide both the teacher and student with a basis for understanding language similarities and differences. Although audiolingual texts did not always insist on making these comparisons an *explicit* part of lessons (relying instead on pattern drill, memorized dialogues), the comparisons were still the underpinning of the graded complexity of the lessons. In this sense, good language students (who may have become language teachers later) most likely discerned the patterns and were helped by ferreting out the comparisons. The danger is in the fact that relatively few language learners may use or rely on these kinds of metacognitive strategies when learning a new language. Furthermore, the method of audiolingual instruction, pattern drill, and memorization, may be of limited appeal. While language classes may still employ drills and other exercises to good effect, the teacher cannot overrely on these techniques when considering the variety of student learning styles. As the study of language learning progressed in the 1970s and 1980s, this variety became apparent.

The Direct Method

Although the audiolingual method was prevalent for some time, it was not the only method available. Another approach, often called the direct method, was promoted by educators such as Berlitz in the 19th century. The method was similar to the audiolingual in that speaking in the native language is primary, and classes are conducted only in the target language. But the underlying assumption about what happened in the learner is different. Berlitz held that the goal was to recapitulate the natural way in which a child learned the first language by speaking in the target language and associating the speech with particular contexts, actions, or performative results. There is a direct connection among speech, objects, and actions, and the learner pieces together the sense of the utterance (and, presumably, object and action parts of speech) from the direct connection to context. This method did not derive from or include behaviorist tenets, but it might be termed rationalist in that an active, meaning-constructive ability on the part of the learner is assumed.

Pedagogical approaches within the direct method start with simple utterances connected to ordinary objects and to actions performed in the classroom. As the situations move beyond classroom life, visual aids establish new contexts for a question/answer engagement with the student. Teachers work only with vocabulary appropriate to the situation and paraphrase definitions in the target language. Translation is considered inappropriate. Correct native-like pronunciation is demanded at the start, and grammar rules are not taught explicitly but illustrated and repeated in context (and, to this extent, the method has much in common with the imitation/drill of the audiolingual method). It is assumed that the learner can formulate a hypothesis about the rules of grammar at work in the lesson. If a rule of grammar must be introduced, it is presented in the target language only.

This approach assumes that second-language learning is essentially the same as first-language acquisition, and that methods and situations appropriate to second-language learning may recapitulate the processes by which a first language is *naturally* learned. The direct method did not have empirical study available to confirm or correct this assumption, if only because the necessary investigative tools and formalism of what human grammar is and how grammar is learned were not developed and disseminated until the advent of generative linguistics in the late 1950s and early 1960s. In fact, the work of Noam Chomsky and others (below) raises some serious question about whether the two events, first- and second-language learning, are essentially the same. While the direct method has the advantages of close engagement between teacher and learner, and while the level of engagement is intended to be contextually appropriate and interesting, the practitioner must allow for a range of student interests and abilities. Some students profit from more explicit attention to grammatical detail, others profit from close integration of useful content. It is the instructor's responsibility to link context, content, and culture to the engagement and style of the direct method, while remembering that linguistic adults (anyone over the age of 6) do not have the time or effortless ability to acquire a second language in the same way as they did the first.

Chomsky and the Rationalist Resurgence

Noam Chomsky reworked and redirected the theory and research agenda of linguistics, beginning with the appearance of *Syntactic Structures* in 1957. His work has undergone several major reworkings, but central to all of them is the idea that the ability to acquire a first language is innate, or is an active faculty of the human species that is both instinctive and structured, not simply a set of developed reflexes or habits. With partial, fragmented, or minimal evidence, a child acquires grammar without difficulty; physical or mental disabilities aside, a child could no more avoid talking than crawling or walking:

> By studying language we may discover abstract principles that govern its structure and use, principles that are universal by biological necessity . . . that derive from mental characteristics of the species. . . . A human child acquires [language] on relatively slight exposure and without specific training. He can then quite effortlessly make use of an intricate structure of specific rules and guiding principles to convey his thoughts and feelings to others, arousing in them novel ideas and subtle perceptions and judgments. (Chomsky, 1975, p. 4)

This quotation contains the terms key to Chomsky's thought:

1. Language is more than speech (or performance); language is also cognitive structure (or competence)—that is, language is a system of systems that comprise in part universal (abstract) principles and parameters. The set of language universals may include grammatical categories (noun phrases, verb phrases, subjects, objects), relations, rule types, and other structures and constraints that languages employ. Other structures and settings are specific to a given language.
2. The learner (here, a child) is disposed to setting these principles and parameters based on limited and partial evidence. Ordinary social exposure to language is sufficient data for the child to establish the correct settings for his or her grammar. For the child to do so correctly in a limited time, linguists assume that the child is equipped with both a universal grammar (an innate ability to have and use linguistic universals) and a language acquisition device, or mechanism, that filters the evidence and sets parameters appropriate for the ambient language.
3. The child is able to use the language is an entirely generative way; from a limited number of structures and settings, a child may create an infinite number of appropriate and effective novel utterances.

Chomsky rejects behaviorist assumptions and methods because these do not account for the basic fact of language acquisition and use; both children and adults (and language learners) are able to produce or generate entirely new utterances that cannot be linked to stimulus/response conditioning. Children and language learners in general also produce grammatically plausible (if incorrect) and novel utterances that could never have been heard or used in the environment. Chomsky established a framework for research in language acquisition that shows that language acquisition is an irrepressible activity of the human species. Children cannot help but learn a language, or more than one, as their ordinary socialization permits.

Chomsky marvels that the child is able to do this "grammar-making," given the variety and incompleteness of the language used with the child, and presents linguists with the problem and challenge of developing a model of innate ability that provides a basis for language learning. The assumption is that the child does not learn by imitation or by repetition, but from limited evidence. Parents do not typically sort out grammar for the child; the child abstracts the necessary grammatical information from the available language. This learning is made possible by a predisposition to build a possible human grammar and a method whereby the child may select and establish a particular grammar compatible with the ambient linguistic data.

Language Is an Instinct

Descriptive and explanatory adequacy in a theory of grammar are more often desired than realized, but Chomsky's work over the past four decades has mapped out a fruitful field of inquiry and provided a developing formalism, or way of representing grammatical facts and theory. Although the formalism within generative linguistics is at times impenetrable to the casual reader, and has undergone several serious reformulations since the 1957 publication of *Syntactic Structures*, the formalism used to describe grammar may be likened to a language with several dialects: researchers using one generative model generally work with other models. Chomsky's theories of the structure of a possible human grammar, and his formal representations of human grammar, have given linguists the tools and impetus to test and refine models of (child) language acquisition. Linguists (Pinker, 1996) are able to identify the processes of acquisition and the developing structures acquired by children. It is possible to map out, for purposes of research and emendation, a child's emerging grammar. It is true that children acquire a grammar in a relatively short period (roughly the first four to six years of life), but what antecedent conditions make this rapid acquisition possible?

As in any branch of cognitive science, linguists have to posit some procedure or mechanism for language acquisition on which more complex procedures are built. A human learner must start somewhere, with some given abilities that are engaged in a social context. Many linguists agree that there is some language acquisition device (LAD) available to children that does not depend for its operation on any other higher-order, or more basic, cognitive structures.

To the extent that LAD can be shown to operate independently of other cognitive structures, and likely has biological (and, to that extent, common to the species) foundations, we may say that the ability to acquire a first language is innate to the human child We may also say that much of the stuff of language acquisition (grammatical categories, semantic relationships, grammatical constituent structure, implicational relationships among grammatical structures, parameter setting) is universal and thereby allows the description or formulation of a *universal grammar* (UG) available to all humans. It is probably incorrect to say that first languages are learned; these are more accurately "invoked" or "engaged." A child is not born speaking English or French, but as soon as the LAD is invoked, the child begins to set the parameters of his or her ambient language. Unfortunately, the LAD does not operate for long, not even for all of childhood. In fact, we may speak of linguistic adulthood as reached at age 6 or so. By then, all the necessary basic linguistic facts of the ambient language are set. What remains is vocabulary growth, flexibility in use of register, style, the learning of reading, writing, and so on. In fact, what remains is the growth of the child into literacy and the *socialization* of literacy, which is the task of the schools.

Pedagogical Implications

Chomsky's influence on pedagogy varies, in part because a great deal of work remains to be done in applying and testing foundational work in the fields of first-language acquisition and second-language learning. It is premature to say that specific, immediate pedagogical approaches can be derived from this framework, largely because the precise overlap and similarity between acquisition and learning requires further research and interpretation. And yet, teachers do well to consider how first- and second-language learning both converge and differ.

If one teaches a second language, it is frustratingly clear that second language-learning is no easy task for the typical adult (anyone over the age of 5 or 6). How do the two processes, acquisition and learning, differ? If researchers in the Chomskian camp hold that there is a critical period for language acquisition, wherein the language-acquisition device is active, the question remains: What happens when this device is no longer active? Some researchers believe that *some* of the ability to learn a grammar as demonstrated by a child is still available to the adult, or that other generic possibilities suggested by UG are available to the adult learner (so that we may say there is a similarity in kind between first-language acquisition and second-language learning). Other researchers stress the notion that adults have other cognitive mechanisms that impose order and structure on data encountered in learning a new language (see Larsen-Freeman, 1993, for a helpful summary). Is the assumption of the direct method, and other "natural" methods, justified, that the two are alike in some significant way? If there were significant overlap, a researcher needs only to identify where the two processes converge, and indicate specific pedagogical methods. If there is no significant overlap in the two processes, or if the processes are divergent, then L2 learning is a different kind of cognitive task, an adult learning task, and pedagogical methods may derive from cognitive theory alone. Let's consider first how the processes converge.

How Is Language Learning Natural?

Chomsky's work allowed researchers to assume that language acquisition is innate to the human species, and focused attention on ways of describing and theorizing about children's language acquisition. Work concerned with doing the same for second-language learning soon followed, but assumptions about language learning, and concomitant notions of how to promote language learning, began to diverge and multiply. We cannot derive pedagogical insights immediately from a reading of Chomskian theory, largely because the theory poses interesting questions about language acquisition and learning, but the research agenda is still very much in progress. Still, if first-language acquisition is natural to the species, is second-language learning natural in any related sense? Do the strategies of first language acquisition replay themselves in the process of learning a second language, or do other cognitive abilities come into play? The following positions (and methods) take up this issue.

The Monitor Hypothesis

Stephen Krashen (1981) proposes that adults employ two separate systems to learn a second language: subconscious language *acquisition* and conscious language *learning*. The former operates in a manner similar to first-language acquisition: to cast the model in Chomskian terms, adults are also capable of resetting UG principles and parameters in the course of learning a new language. At some unconscious level, the acquisition process allows L2 learners to establish new L2 parameters correctly without explicit training or procedural (grammatical) awareness. Furthermore, language acquisition requires meaningful interaction in the new tongue, a kind of natural communication (Krashen, 1981) in which the speaker strives to be understood and is not overly concerned with grammatical precision.

In contrast, language *learning* is very much an "adult" activity. The learner is concerned with correct expression and may be helped by learning explicit grammatical rules. Krashen stipulates that adults are capable of monitoring their behavior in learning a new language; learners may (a) edit or emend their speech when this does not interfere with communication; (b) improve accuracy over time by using the monitor; and (c) distinguish between correct output and casual errors (Krashen, 1981). Language learning is accomplished differently by different students, and no one method of language teaching necessarily addresses all of these differing learning styles. Nonetheless, all methods benefit from explicit integration of comprehensible input into instruction, which links the processes of acquisition and learning.

The Comprehensible Input Hypothesis

Krashen (1981) maintains that acquisition is fundamental to natural, fluent achievement in the target language, and conscious learning operates primarily as a means of monitoring output to conform to overt grammatical rules. Both processes are at work when adults learn a new language. Acquisition is fostered by exposure to what Krashen calls comprehensible input, or that level of the target language that approximates what the learner already knows, while also containing just enough unfamiliar structure to push the learner to distinguish new meaning and new structures. Here, extralinguistic cues and background knowledge may fill in the intended communication and promote acquisition of new grammatical structure. Comprehensible input keeps learning and acquisition integrated.

Too much explicit focus on structure fosters learning structure, but not necessarily application of structure in context. This is all too often the lament of adult learners who can conjugate verbs correctly, or memorize dialogues in L2, but have difficulty accomplishing ordinary language tasks in the L2 environment. On the other hand, L2 structure that is acquired successfully is available to the L2 learner as a basis for communication in context.

The Affective Filter Hypothesis

Krashen (1981) also points out that acquisition is promoted by the learner's desire or motivation to understand, and by a natural communicative setting in which the learner is affectively motivated and confident that the tasks at hand are manageable. The environment and means chosen to convey the acquisition or learning goals should also encourage acquirers to communicate meaning in the target language. This encouragement lowers the *affective filter*, or degree of resistance to the process of acquiring a new language. On the part of the learner, a low affective filter may be brought about by (1) integrative motivation, or the desire to be like the users of the target language; (2) instrumental motivation, or the desire to learn the target language for a specific purpose (although Krashen points out that this motivation may weaken if enough of the target language is acquired for the given purpose); (3) self-confidence, or an ability to tolerate making mistakes; (4) empathy, or the ability to see several points of view at once; and (5) a positive attitude toward the classroom and the activities taking place there. According to Krashen, some students may appreciate, and benefit from, occasional explicit reference to the rules of the target language. Discovering these rules may lower the affective filter for these students.

Pedagogical Implications

If Krashen's hypotheses are accurate, the teacher will have to choose accessible material that is presented in an encouraging environment where affective filters are lowered. The first task implies that teachers will have to spend time developing and presenting material that balances the demands of comprehensibility and meaningfulness. Explicit grammar instruction has a role, but the classroom is primarily an occasion for comprehensible, interesting, relevant input, and a text that relies on the presentation of graded, increasingly complex grammatical structure will have to be modified or adapted. Although Krashen's ideas have not gone unchallenged (McLaughlin, 1987), many educators welcome the insistence on meaningful,

Exhibit 2.1
Key Differences Between First- and Second-Language Learners

First-language acquirers	*Second-language learners*
Have the biological advantage— that is, the LAD.	Generally have no such advantage.
Communication is important but not vital to survival, and their communicative needs match their communicative abilities.	Communication needs are more complex and pressing, but their linguistic skills are not adequate to meet these needs.
The acquisition abilities of a child are engaged by the local language, and the child easily sets the first-language parameters accordingly.	The second-language learner also did this as a child with a first language, but this internalized grammar may be viewed as a a filter or source of interference in learning a second language.
Children learn the social functions of their language as they learn the language.	The sociocultural norms learned with the first language may not match those used by the new culture.

engaging materials and communication-based technique that his theories entail.

Addressing the Needs of the Linguistic Adult

Although many school districts are faced with the task of establishing or enhancing English proficiency in a percentage of ESOL students, these students have already had the successes described in learning a first or native language (NL), and are full-fledged linguistic adults in the NL (within the limits discussed above). What advantages or disadvantages do these students bring to the task of learning English as a second language? Linguist Dan Slobin (1993) has summarized the key differences between first- and second-language learners (see Exhibit 2.1).

And yet, despite these hurdles, second-language learners show a range of success, from the acquisition of near-native ability all the way to minimal acquisition—that is, an improvement to a point beyond which further instruction is of no use (the language ability is said to be *fossilized* at this point). Expanding each of Slobin's points helps to describe ESOL learner. The points include biology, motivation, interference, and socialization.

The Biological Boost

A typical child reaches linguistic maturity in the broad sense by age 6 or so. During this critical period for language formation, the brain selects and uses certain structures to process language. Research indicates that early bilingual children actually use the same area of the brain to process both languages; the area of the brain used for L1 is identical to the area used for L2. On the other hand, those who learn a second language later in childhood or in adolescence develop new regions that likely process L2, and these regions may be near L1 regions or distributed throughout the brain. It seems that very young learners of a second language (who are likely to become bilingual) have a more plastic, economical neurology designated for language functioning. Pinker (1995, p. 293ff.) suggests that this early economy promotes rapid L1 acquisition, but that the brain, engaged in a multitude of developing tasks, shuts down or curtails this rapid acquisition at some point.

Early learning is critical for achieving a native-like pronunciation in L2. The neurobiology of speech is probably fixed at an early stage, and learning a new set of pronunciation skills at a later age is never accomplished with the same efficiency of L1. Traces of a non-native pronunciation will likely persist (for a lifetime) as L2 learning is undertaken later in childhood. On the other hand, older children and adolescents (and mature adults) bring other problem-solving skills to bear when learning syntax and new lexical material. Throughout the population of language learners, some students demonstrate a particular aptitude for learning L2. Whether these students have the advantage of (1) a longer period of neural plasticity in language acquisition, (2) a more varied repetoire of problem-solving skills or higher levels of verbal intelligence, (3) more exposure to situations that demand or promote L2 development, or any combination of the above, is open to debate and further research (see Larsen-Freeman & Long, 1993).

Motivation

Much of the research and literature regarding successful L2 acquisition centers on placing or defining successful acquisition as a cognitive ability. Not all successful L2 learning among linguistic adults hinges on cognitive factors alone. Motivation for learning a second language plays a large role in successful learning (see Ehrman, 1996, for a good introduction to these variables). These motivations range from personal to external, such as the role of teachers, community, family, and ethnic identity, to good programs and curriculum. Some of these motivational variables are closely connected to larger issues such as the stated (administrative) rationale for learning English in a particular setting, and the students' own motivations for learning English. A successful ESL program integrates these motivations by granting all parties—administrators, teachers, and students—the opportunity to express their motives for working (or not working) within a given program.

Interlanguage

A great deal of research has followed on earlier structuralist notions of the interaction of first- and second-language structures during L2 learning. In an earlier period, structuralist or descriptivist linguistic research mapped out and compared L1 and L2 structures at every level of the grammar, phonology, morphology, and syntax, and showed where L2 learners were likely to have difficulty in learning new structures. This work continued throughout the 1970s and 1980s, where researchers used the term *interlanguage* to describe moments of interference between L1 and L2, and to describe intermediate structures used that were not present in either L1 or L2. This kind of comparative research stands or falls depending on the comprehensive power of the model or theory of grammar being used in the comparison. Recent developments toward understanding a universal grammar, and a principles/parameters model of grammar, have provided researchers with more powerful investigative tools.. Researchers again take up the questions of *markedness* within the grammar (a notion of what is common, or unmarked, among grammars, and what is structurally more complicated, or marked) that shed light on points of interference between L1 and L2. Not only does this kind of research still provide a notion of relative complexity, but it also allows for a more realistic assessment of what learners may or may not be expected to accomplish at different points of L2 learning. Interlanguage comparisons may be useful in mapping out the relative complexity of L1 and L2 structures, and thus serve as a guide in assembling and grading L2 instructional materials. Still, explicit presentation and awareness of L1 and L2 structural differences may or may not assist the student directly in promoting L2 communicative success. Mapping out points of L1 and L2 convergence and divergence must be integrated into an overall means of instruction that takes into account a range of factors, particularly the linguistic *socialization* of the L2 learner.

Socialization

Lily Wong-Fillmore (1985) delineates three essential components for effective L2 learning: the learners, the (native) speakers, and the *social* context that brings these two together. At this point, social, linguistic, and cognitive processes all play a role in promoting successful communication. The key themes here are (1) context, (2) meaningful interaction, and (3) range of opportunity to work with L2. Rapid and successful L2 learning is fostered and enhanced by providing a context for the learner to use L2 in a meaningful way. This is a central challenge and opportunity for the L2 teacher today. In essence, grammar cannot be isolated from a context in which native speakers use the structures in question. The task is to use the language in a way appropriate to a situation or context. Ideally, L2 learners have the opportunity to use the new language for self-expression whether in a stand-alone ESL classroom or a (mainstream) content classroom.

Range of opportunity to use L2 in a meaningful context is also critical to L2 success. Children in the elementary years have the school itself as a means of ordinary L2 socialization and growth, but the task is more difficult for the older learner or adult who is newly arrived to the school and culture. Ordinary, interpersonal socialization in elementary schools is a key factor in rapid L2 growth (one need only visit a first-grade class of L1 and L2 learners in September and again in March to see this growth), but as the student progresses into the middle-and high-school years, language use becomes not simply a function of socialization, but also the necessary vehicle for academic success. In sum, the student faces the added task of L2 learning for mastery of academic content. The ability to master the language-of-instruction is a challenge for the native speaker as well, because the goal of instruction is literacy, and the English to be learned is the English of literate self-expression.

Language Expresses Communicative Competences

The focus on the role of socialization in L2 learning success has allowed researchers to redefine means of achieving L2 success. Language may be perceived as communicative competence (not just grammatical competence, which is just part of overall communicative competence). Communicative competence is the ability to express arange of communicative intentions appropriately. Communicative competence includes at least the following, according to Canale and Swain (1980):

- *grammatical competence*: command of the components of a grammar;
- *sociolinguistic competence*: mastery of style, register, and appropriate use of language in context;
- *discourse competence*: ability to coordinate language into a useful whole for particular purposes; and
- *strategic competence*: ability to retrieve errors and breakdowns in communication.

Communicative success is promoted if all of these factors are incorporated into the instruction and assessment of L2 learners. In fact, much effort has gone into defining what appropriate communicative competence might look like at every level of L2 instruction. The pedagogical effect is far-ranging: Rather than placing undue emphasis on one mode of competence (i.e., grammatical), the whole performance of the student may be evaluated at each level by considering other forms of communicative competence. At all levels, negotiation of meaning is foremost. The focus on a range of communicative competences has prompted a national effort by several professional organizations to redefine what it means to be *proficient* at different levels of L2 instruction.

Proficiency in a second language can be defined as knowing how to use L2 appropriately and accurately at a given level and for a certain set of purposes. Proficiency is a working, developing competence in L2, not a once-and-for-all accomplishment. Proficiency is a manifestation of knowing a language at a given point or level. A student can be proficient at a novice level of L2, and still have some way to go before full proficiency is attained. The American Council of Teachers of Foreign Languages (ACTFL) scale for interpreting proficiency (Buck, Byrnes, & Thompson, 1989) distinguishes four general levels of proficiency—novice, intermediate, advanced, and superior—that are matched with the following variables: context, content, accuracy, and text type. That is, a novice-level learner may be expected to express himself or herself in a context of ordinary settings, with content that includes the key points of simple routines. The novice's accuracy level may still be low, even difficult to understand, and the grammatical and discursive expression (text type) may include only elementary sentences, phrases, and words. Proficiency gradations allow for assessment of progress, and show how a student succeeds over time at mastering the elements appropriate to a given level. Note that these criteria match success to context and content variables. Proficiency-based instruction must always keep context and content integrated into the method of instruction.

The ACTFL standards have served well as a measure of progression in second-language competence throughout the country, but the shift to a proficiency-based classroom, in content, method, and style, is still in progress, as second-language teachers work with and implement ACTFL suggestions. In a similar way, ESL professionals seek to keep the content and style of delivery in line with proficiency-based expectations, and, to this end, TESOL recently provided guidelines for establishing and evaluating quality instruction.

TESOL Standards

TESOL takes up the assumptions of proficiency-based L2 instruction in its recent publication, *ESL Standards for Pre-K–12 Students* (TESOL 1997), which sets goals and standards for ESL instruction. The standards recognize that "language acquisition occurs through meaningful use and interaction" (p. 7) and point out that content be meaningful and challenging and the classroom context interactive. Furthermore, TESOL standards recognize the gap between earlier acquisition of language appropriate to ordinary social contexts, and the extended process of acquiring the language of academic contexts. Full proficiency, which bridges this gap, may take five to seven years in school. The ESL goals are straightforward: (1) to use English to communicate in social settings, (2) to use English to achieve academically in all content areas, and (3) to use English in socially and culturally appropriate ways (p. 9). The standards on which these goals are based insist on (1) interactive social, academic, and cultural contexts; (2) use of English for social, academic, and culturally appropriate expression and construction; and (3) use of appropriate learning strategies to achieve communicative competence in all areas.

The TESOL document also states that these standards will not be effectively realized unless school districts with ESOL students (1) design entire curricula and programs with all students, ESOL and native speakers, in mind; (2) promote collaboration among all educational professionals who teach ESOL students; and (3) encourage continued professional development of these educators in issues relevant to ESOL population, including methodology, assessment, and community-school relations.

Theories of first- and second-language acquisition and learning provide as comprehensive a view as possible of what goes on when one learns a new language, but these theories need continuous testing and refinement, often in the classroom itself. While the cognitive underpinnings of second-language accomplishment are varied and at times remote from application, linguists and educators alike are working to forge the vital links between cognitive theory and methodological posibilities. In addition, research has expanded beyond the cognitive concerns alone, as studies now demonstrate the importance and centrality of socialization and motivation as factors in successful second-language acquisition. The authors believe that it is the responsibility of educators, supported by administrators, to understand the similarities and differences in first- and second-language acquisition and in learning academic content. Furthermore, these similarities and differences can be understood in a way that suggests changes and refinements in educators' teaching approaches and styles. It is clear that ongoing teacher education, to keep abreast of developments in acquisition theory, is central to a successful ESL program. In addition, educators are encouraged to research the social and cultural variables that promote or hinder ESOL students' success in the classroom. Finally, we suggest that it is the task of the *entire* faculty and administration at a given site or group of schools to identify means of integrating ESOL students' language and content needs, based on the pertinent ecological variables (Bronfenbrenner, 1979).

Chapter Three

ESL Programs and
Legal Responsibilities

This chapter outlines the legal context and direction of language equity issues in the United States in recent years. It provides information, but in no way substitutes for competent legal advice in situations where advice is required or advisable. There are at least three broad areas of legal involvement regarding language issues in the United States: (1) English-only legislation, which centers on the establishment of English as the official language of government (such legislation does not translate directly into the language of the schools); (2) the language of the workplace (Do private industries have the leeway to use English to conduct ordinary business and deal with employees?); and (3) the language of instruction for schools and the concomitant choices by which all students are granted equal access to programs and educational opportunities in such a way that language does not constitute a barrier.

Language equity issues of concern to the administrator under the third point above include (1) the status of language minorities as a legally protected minority; (2) the scope and nature of remedies to identified imbalances or inequity in educational opportunities and achievement that result from language differences; and (3) the exact responsibilities of the school districts in providing means to correct such inequities. These issues are very much in flux and reflect the workings of a legal system based on precedent. Educational law, to paraphrase former Speaker of the House Tip O'Neill, like politics, is local. While it is primarily the responsibility of the state, county, local school boards, and administrators to establish policy, this effort is shaped by the legal concerns that affect the nation as a whole, and issues of language equity are no exception. Exhibit 3.1 cites key developments at the federal level that have shaped the language-of-instruction controversy in the schools.

How are language minorities recognized under the law? The broadest identifier of language minorities' rights is not language per se but national origin. As such, rights to equality access and oppor-

Exhibit 3.1
Key Developments in Language-of-instruction Controversy

1964 Civil Rights Act, Title VI, prohibits any discrimination by race or national origin in federally sponsored programs.

1968 Elementary and Secondary Education Act, in particular, Title VII, or the Bilingual Education Act, establishes federal guidelines for bilingual education to be offered to language minorities and supports new educational program development through grants.

1970 Office of Civil Rights director Pottinger issues memorandum (May 25 Memorandum) outlining district responsibilities for national origin minorities and educational opportunities.

1974 Supreme Court ruling on Lau vs. Nichols establishes the right of language- minority students to a meaningful education; barriers rooted in language difference are to be addressed at the district level. Later in 1974, Congress passed the Equal Educational Opportunity Act (EEOA), which extended the Lau decision nationally.

1975 The Lau Remedies, prepared by the U.S. Department of Health, Education and Welfare (HEW), but never officially formalized as policy, approves specific remedies for mainstreaming LEP students, which are applied to a variety of cases and districts.

1978 Title VII is amended, expanding coverage to limited-English-proficiency students and allowing two-way bilingual programs. The amendments also point out that remedies that allow primary-language-instruction are by nature temporary; the goal of such instruction is not necessarily maintenance of L1, but transition from L1 to L2 competency. Additional amendments in 1984 and 1988 continue to diversify program approaches, place limits on participation in Title VII programs (three years), and encourage teacher training.

1978 Castaneda v. Pickard devises a three-part test to determine whether districts are taking appropriate action to allow full participation of language minorities.

1979 Supreme Court ruling on Plyler v. Doe prohibits states from excluding children of illegal immigrants from a public-school education.

1994 National educational reforms (Improving America's Schools Act, or ISEA, reauthorizing the Elementary and Secondary Education Act of 1965) include revision and updating of Title VII programs.

tunity in education and in the workplace are guaranteed by the Civil Rights Act of 1964 and, to a lesser extent, by the 1st or 14th Amendment guarantees (freedom of speech and equal protection under the law). Speaking a language other than English in the United States does not confer rights or special treatment, but the inability to enjoy ordinary civil, social, and legal benefits by reason of a language barrier, or language difference, is grounds for remedial action and correction. We may speak of language minorities or national-origin language minorities, as the beneficiaries of these corrections. The scope and nature of the remedies, however, is very much the point and the problem.

All children in the United States have a right to equitable public education offered without barrier, impediment, or special preference. Free access to all programs and the opportunity to excel are given to all. In fact, equitable education may not be equal education in several respects; access to the same programs, curricula, materials, and teachers is not sufficient if language differences in fact function as an impediment and consistently produce differing rates of academic success. If language difference is determined to be a barrier for specific national-origin groups of students, then schools have the legal responsibility to provide the means for overcoming these barriers.

Are national-origin language minorities a protected class under the law? The short answer to the question is no, they are not, in that language minorities are not considered a suspect or quasi-suspect class under the Equal Protection Clause of the 14th Amendment. This clause allows courts to uphold different (or preferential) treatment of suspect classes of citizens (suspect in the sense that the Supreme Court is suspicious of classifications and laws based on race, national origin, or gender) if there is a demonstrable and compelling interest to do so. It has been the practice of the courts so far not to reach for protection of language minorities under the 14th Amendment, relying instead on legislation (such as the Civil Rights Act) to guarantee equal educational opportunities for language minorities.

A Context for Remedies

The term *remedy* as used here indicates a cluster of changes in practice that schools are required to adopt in the aftermath of several decades of court and government decisions. These changes include principally (1) identification and assessment of language-minority students in a given district; (2) devising a set of instructional strategies for providing equal access and participation for ESOL students; and (3) devising appropriate methods to determine progress and exit criteria for these programs: and (4) establishing ongoing program evaluation. Although instruction in public and private schools was not exclusively in English during the first century of the nation's history, use of English as the only language of instruction in public schools grew in the latter decades of the nineteenth century and the beginning of the twentieth, coincident with the arrival of immigrants from many different countries and the rise of nationalism which peaked at the beginning of the World War I. From then until the early 1960s, monolingual education was practiced in the nation's public schools. It was within the power of the states to require English-only instruction in public and private schools (although only a few states had such provisions) until *Meyer v. Nebraska* (1923) struck down such legislation in Nebraska, Iowa, and Ohio. The Supreme Court did not question the practice of delivering instruction in English; the point was that the state could not prohibit teaching some materials in a language other than English. Only in the early 1960s did some districts begin to experiment with bilingual education.

In 1968, the Elementary and Secondary Education Act contained provisions under Title VII (often called the Bilingual Education Act) that allowed for distribution of competitive grant monies to establish innovative bilingual programs. The act was crafted largely through the efforts of Senator Ralph Yarborough of Texas and was more limited in approach and scope than the title suggests. In no way could the introduction of the Bilingual Education Act be construed as a mandate or requirement for the nation's schools to review or change their current practices toward language minorities. Nonetheless, HEW was aware of the implications of Section 602 of the Civil Rights Act, which required that all federal agencies responsible for awarding and administering grant monies also ensure that these funded programs prohibit discrimination. HEW issued guidelines in 1968 that required federally supported school systems to be "responsible for ensuring that students of a particular race, color, or national origin are not denied the opportunity to obtain the education generally obtained by other students in the system" (33 *Federal Register* 4956, as cited Lyons, 1992, p. 7).

In 1970, the director of the Office for Civil Rights (OCR), J. Stanley Pottinger, whose office was contained within HEW, issued a memorandum to all school districts whose constituency comprised more than 5% national-origin (language) minorities. The memorandum (often cited as the May 25 Memorandum) outlined four responsibilities for the concerned districts. The schools were to (1) take affirmative steps to correct language difference where this difference barred students from full participation in instructional programs; (2) assess students properly and not solely by means that assess primarily English language ability; (3) teach English to minority students as soon as possible, and to avoid any grouping of students by language ability if that translates as "limited" ability; and (4) inform minority parents of school activities, if need be, in languages other than English. The memorandum did not look further than the Civil Rights Act to establish these requirements, and linked the import of that act to the task of taking affirmative, proactive steps to integrate national-origin language-minority students (at this point, simply *language-minority* students) into mainstream academic and social activities in the schools.

It should be emphasized that monolingual education at times amounted to a sink-or-swim approach to instruction, which was no doubt the concern of educators and administrators at the time. Such

---

The Office for Civil Rights is obligated to enforce federal civil rights legislation by investigating and helping to resolve formal complaints that fall under the following: Title VI of the Civil Rights Act (discrimination based on race, color, or national origin, which includes language minorities); Title IX of the Education Amendments of 1972 (discrimination based on gender); Section 504 of the Rehabilitation Act of 1973 and Title II of the Americans with Disabilities Act of 1990 (discrimination based on physical or mental disability); and the Age Discrimination Act of 1975 (discrimination based on age). If an administrator must respond to a complaint filed on behalf of a language-minority party, the OCR will facilitate in reaching (1) an early complaint resolution, (2) an agreement based on appropriate fact-finding and proposed corrective action on the part of the school district, or (3) any combination of the above. Readers are encouraged to visit the OCR Web site (http://www.ed.gov/offices/OCR/ocrexpec.html/) for a helpful overview of the process of complaint resolution.

approaches are a kind of immersion so complete as to be termed *submersion*. There may be a range of reactions to this kind of immersion, from the off-the-cuff "it was good enough for my ancestors" to the reasoned account of success within a monolingual approach detailed by Richard Rodriguez (1982). However, the reaction of language-minority parents to monolingual education forced the courts to look at the situation. In the *Lau v. Nichols* (1974), a suit brought against the San Francisco public schools by the Chinese-American community charging inequality of treatment and access in the schools was upheld, reversing the findings of the federal district and appeals courts.

The San Francisco schools were integrated in 1979 following *Lee v. Johnson* (404 U.S. 1215). In the time between integration and the Lau case, some 1,000 Chinese-American students received instruction support in English, but another 1,800 did not. These students were represented in a suit charging unequal educational opportunities. In deliberating the case, the Supreme Court pointed out that these 1,800 students were being deprived of *meaningful* schooling and that the numbers were sufficient to warrant remedial action. The fact that the students were denied a meaningful opportunity to participate in public education constituted a violation of Section 601 of the Civil Rights Act and the corresponding HEW regulations banning discrimination based on race, color, or national origin in any program or activity receiving federal financial assistance. The Court did not need to invoke the Equal Protection Clause. The justices pointed out that equality of treatment in the schools is not defined by providing the same facilities, textbooks, teachers, and curriculum when students who do not understand English cannot make full and fair use of these opportunities.

While affirming the right of language-minority students to a meaningful public education, and the corresponding duty of the school districts to provide such education, the Court did not specify any particular method of remedial action; both bilingual programs and ESL programs were possible approaches. To clarify the obligations of districts following the *Lau* decision, HEW's education commissioner appointed a task force that drew up a working document entitled *Task Force Findings Specifying Remedies Available for Eliminating Past Educational Practices Ruled Unlawful under Lau v. Nichols*. These findings are called the Lau remedies or Lau guidelines. These remedies were never published in the *Federal Register*, so they do not actually have the import of official regulation, but they nonetheless provided direction for remedies within the schools. The Lau remedies presented procedures for (1) assessing and remediating English language skills; (2) determining the skills needed for entering mainstream classrooms; and (3) establishing professional standard for teachers of language-minority students.

Although the Lau remedies did not directly specify methods of remediation or specific types of programs, the burden of proof was placed on acquisition programs to show that these were as effective as bilingual programs in achieving the overall academic success of ESOL students; the operating assumption was that properly implemented bilingual programs were preferable. Arguably, this decade (1970s) could be considered the high-water mark of bilingual education, especially in the primary grades. The key court decisions, namely *Serna v. Portales Municipal Schools* (1974), *Cintron v. Brentwood Free School District* (1978), and *Rios v. Reed* (1978) had the cumulative effect of requiring that schools devise means of determining students' language abilities and establish the content and design of a course of instruction to meet the needs of the students to provide them with fair and successful access to all educational opportunities. In addition, as a whole, these court decisions *required* districts to find or train bilingual educators. Nonetheless, the courts (see *Guadalupe Organization v. Tempe Elementary School District No. 3*, 1978) stopped short of mandating bilingual (or bicultural) education, indicating that the 14th Amendment's Equal Protection Clause does not impose such a requirement.

The Lau remedies were directly challenged in *Northwest Arctic School District v. Califano* (1978) when an Alaskan school district claimed that the remedies were not adequate or uniformly appropriate to determine school compliance. As a result, the Department of Education filed a *Notice of Proposed Rulemaking* (1980), a set of proposed regulations that, when enacted, would have the force that the Lau remedies lacked. These regulations repeated the main themes: assessment, provision of appropriate instruction, and evaluation and exit standards. The definition of *appropriate* instruction proved controversial in these proposals, and in response to criticism from constituents and congressional figures, the proposals were suspended in 1979 and withdrawn in 1980, when Ronald Reagan took office. The OCR did develop another set of Title VI (Lau) standards that reiterated the themes of assessment, programming and evaluation (exit standards), and incorporated the results of *Castaneda v. Pickard* (1981), a three-part standard to determine whether the schools took adequate remedial action on behalf of language minority students. In *Castaneda*, the court defined its own responsibilities to determine (1) whether a program is structured according to a recognized, sound educational theory; (2) whether a program actually has the resources and capability to implement the theory, and (3) whether the program actually achieves the intended results. Although the federal government did not specify a program type or approach as appropriate remedial action, the states are free to do just that. In the wake of these court decisions, some states opted for primarily bilingual programs, and others chose a mixture of approaches.

This is, in effect, where we stand today. Having identified language-minority numbers and needs, administrators are legally mandated to devise a comprehensive approach to ESL programming that is based on sound theory (i.e., shows clear progress from accepted theory to educational praxis) and has adequate resources to accomplish its stated goals. The program must demonstrate what the authors call a *praxis/reflection* approach—that is, the program must be evaluated continually to determine whether stated goals are met and program changes, or fine-tuning, are required. In summary, program design, resourcing, and evaluation are the immediate responsibility of the adminstrator.

Legal issues in this area continue to develop. The nation's schools still face the need to determine what constitutes appropriate remediation, and how appropriate remediation can best be achieved. In April 1998, U.S. Secretary of Education Richard W. Riley delivered an address (*Helping All Children Learn English*) in which he summarized the problems and successes of English-language programming and goals to date. Most of his themes are reiterated here, including (1) setting a three-year goal for English acquisition, but allowing for individual needs in this regard; (2) local design and monitoring of programs, and amelioration or change of program designs if needed, whatever the program type or model; and (3) finding ways to secure trained bilingual and ESL teachers, using Federal funding for this purpose.

Secretary Riley considered the content and direction of an initiative in California (the Unz initiative, or Proposition 227, passed in June 1998) which, in effect, bypassed the option of bilingual education in favor of a one-year acquisition requirement. The secretary cited five objections to this initiative, noting that (1) a one-year requirement cannot take into account the needs and requirements of all learners; (2) each district should be given the chance to allow its own teachers to determine what program is suitable and workable; (3) the chances for litigation are increased, not diminished, if such a requirement fails to achieve the intended effects; (4) the initiative takes program choice and control away from local districts; and (5) the initiative might not be in accord with the direction of federal and legal requirements established in the past decades.

While recent voter decisions in California may not affect other states in quite the same way, the Unz initiative illustrates the ongoing difficulty of determining what is or is not appropriate instruction. The controversy hinges largely on the choice and scope of the "language of instruction" as a key factor: In the case of the Unz initiative, the implicit or explicit claim is that bilingual education slows down the process of English acquisition, particularly academic or content English. The issue arises again and again: Is the language of instruction, be it English or another language, a barrier or the precise means to equal access to and success in academic programs? The administrator faces the daunting task of identifiying what appropriate education is at a time when the language-of-instruction controversy is receiving national attention. The following chapters may help the reader sort out the claims and counterclaims of this controversy as part of the process of identifying and implementing what works in program design and content.

Part Two

✑

Policy Decisions Influencing Program Development

The first step in the development of high-quality programs for ESOL students requires careful examination of at least seven policy issues. Decisions about to these policy issues largely depend on the specific context of the school district, the community, and characteristics of ESOL population that the program will serve, but they are also important to each school district's leadership. District administrators and program design teams must begin their quest for a quality program by answering the following questions:

- Should all, part, or none of ESOL students' academic experiences take place in their native language?
- What program model will be most effective in at the same time facilitating students' academic achievement, English-language development, acculturation, and social integration?
- How can we ensure that the educational experiences of ESOL students have the same academic rigor and access to academic core curriculum available to native-English-speaking students?
- How can we structure school environments and implement district curricula to allow all students to benefit from ESOL students'cultural and linguistic diversity?
- How can we structure school environments and implement district curricula and assessment to foster ESOL students' appreciation of their native language and culture?
- How can we integrate *ESL Standards for Pre-K–12 Students* (TESOL, 1997) into district curricula and/or national content standards?
- How can we validly assess the effectiveness of our program in providing equal educational opportunity to ESOL students?

The second part of this book focuses on using theory, research, and experiences of school districts currently implementing high-quality programs for ESOL students to provide district leaders with the information they need to make policy decisions and design programs that are appropriate for their own particular context. Over the past 30 years, experience has demonstrated that no single prepackaged program or model meets the needs of all districts or their ESOL students. The complex array of variables that negatively affect the lives and academic success of mainstream students (poverty, abuse, homelessness) interact with the characteristics of students with limited proficiency in the language of academic content instruction, and result in a special challenge for school districts. One should remember that accommodating ESOL students' special needs that are the result of linguistic and cultural differences does not protect ESOL student from all the issues and problems that impede the education of native English speakers (e.g., personal or family mental health problems, teenage pregnancy, divorce, physical or sexual abuse, personality conflict with teacher(s), or behavior disorder). Instead, the two types of variables seem to interact, often compounding the difficulties that prevent ESOL students from reaching their full potential.

Decisions about the policy questions outlined above help in developing specific program goals and program models that become an integral part of the district's general curriculum, rather than a parallel program that runs at the same time with the mainstream program. TESOL recognizes the importance of this integration in its recently published, *ESL Standards for Pre-K–12 Students* (1997): "The role of ESL standards can only be fully understood in the broader context of education for ESOL students" (p. 3). Before presenting the specific standards themselves, the authors of this book outline an "overarching" vision of effective education, including: native-like levels of proficiency in English, maintenance and promotion of students' native languages in school and community contexts, the need for all educational professionals to assume responsibility for the education of ESOL students, comprehensive provision of first-rate services and full access to all services by all students, and the recognition that knowledge of one or more languages and cultures is an advantage to all students.

Programming for ESOL students has been the target of considerable tension among community members, school district administrators, regular classroom teachers, ESL teachers, and parents. Such programming is the victim of biased and inaccurate reporting by the media and of generally poor-quality research and theory that lacks integration across disciplines. However, there is one single point of agreement among all constituents: the belief that we must design and implement programs that will enhance the educational achievement, English-language proficiency, acculturation, and social integration of ESOL students to help them develop to their fullest capacity. Our nation's track record with certain groups of ESOL students has been dismal. Our inability to accept definitive recommendations of how to best meet the needs of ESOL students is largely because of three decades of experience with a variety of program models, most of which were not systematically evaluated, although there were federal government mandates and support to do so. In cases where evaluation research of program model effectiveness was conducted, unacceptable research designs and methodology frequently resulted in ambivalent and inconclusive results.

At the same time, the widespread tendency in the 1970s and 1980s to devalue qualitative research resulted in a lack of studies affording us descriptive data and almost no longitudinal data on models that may be successful in providing ESOL students with equal educational opportunity. To make matters more complicated, researchers and practitioners have yet to develop an operational definition of what constitutes a "successful program" or a "successful ESOL student" that has been widely, much less nationally, accepted. The majority of studies have defined *program effectiveness* in terms of scores on standardized tests of English-language vocabulary or grammar or reading and mathematics achievement. Few studies have focused on these students' successful social integration into the mainstream population, or the degree to which they successfully acculturate and manage to at the same time maintain their own cultural and linguistic heritages. Yet, some ESOL students are successful in doing just that. To the best of our knowledge, no studies have examined college acceptance or completion rates of ESOL students, or their success in gaining employment after high-school graduation if they do not go on to college or vocational schools. These factors, combined with the emotional and sociopolitical bias of professional educators and the general public, have resulted in the *language-of-instruction controversy*, a product of our collective inability to provide ESOL students with the multiple services they need to succeed. School administrators face a considerable challenge in making program-related development decisions that will be scrutinized by their constituents solely on the basis of emotional and political perspectives.

The next three chapters of this book outline the issues, policy decisions, and program models that school leaders must consider when designing and administering programs for their ESOL students. Relevant research that provides some direction for policy decisions and program development is reviewed, and generic program models are presented, along with insights from the program development experiences of the Bethlehem Area School District. Chapter four provides an in-depth analysis of the language-of-instruction controversy, a debate that most administrators will face at some point as they develop a program for ESOL students. Chapter five presents generic programming models for ESOL students, including the strengths and weaknesses of each model and the relationship of the models to policy issues. Also included is a detailed description of one effective model that has been implemented in a medium-size school district in eastern Pennsylvania with a substantial ESOL population. Chapter six discusses the importance of reaching out to parents of ESOL students and to resources in the community as an integral part of any ESL program and demonstrates the advantages of an integrated service model in meeting the needs of ESOL students and their families.

Chapter Four

The Language-of-
Instruction Controversy

This chapter examines the *language-of-instruction* issue. The first decision to be made in designing a context-appropriate program for ESOL students is whether academic content instruction and learning will take place in English or in the students' native language (primary language). This policy issue is likely to reveive the most attention from the general public and/or community members. Considering the program model decision solely from the perspective of language-of-instruction is not in the best interests of ESOL students or the school district, but arguments for and against the use of the native language as the language for academic content instruction have been the impetus for major controversies surrounding the education of ESOL students in the United States for more than 30 years. Language-of-instruction is a policy issue that is often fueled more by history, emotionalism, and sociopolitical struggles than by research, much less consideration of the students' long-term welfare.

Unfortunately, less time, money, and effort has been focused on determining the specific conditions, strategies, and materials essential to facilitating ESOL students' success than on measuring the success and failure of a variety of program models of language-of-instruction. In fact, researchers have yet to define what behaviors, skills, or outcomes constitute success for ESOL student. The misplaced desire to be politically correct and an ambivalent body of program evaluation research results lead many educators to frustration in their effort to decide whether all, some, or none of the curriculum should be delivered in ESOL students' first language.

Adding to this confusion is the fact that *bilingual education* is used as a generic term, and refers to a wide variety of program models that may have very different goals and objectives, and that vary even more in terms of implementation (including the degree to which the L1 is used in academic content instruction). At the most basic level, programs for ESOL students are classified in research studies as one of two types: *additive models* or *subtractive models*. According to TESOL's national standards, *additive* is the term used to refer to programs in which the addition of a second language and culture (e.g., the English language and American culture) is unlikely to replace the native language and culture, while *subtractive* refers to educational program models in which the first language and culture of students are given low status, and learners are encouraged to replace their L1 and native culture with the second language and culture (TESOL, 1997). Unfortunately, the terms *additive* and *subtractive* have come to have different connotations when used by many advocates of native-language instruction.

Additive programs are used frequently to refer only to those programs for ESOL students that use native-language instruction for all, or a major part of the school day. *Subtractive* programs refer to all programs that use English as the language of instruction, regardless of the manner in which these programs are implemented and, in many cases. oblivious to how program components are designed to foster ESOL students' pride in their native culture and appreciation and maintenance of their native language. The unfortunate restriction of the term *additive* to refer only to those programs in which all or at least the major part of the academic instruction and learning occur in the native language conflicts with TESOL's definition, and results in lumping together all programs that use only English for academic content learning into the *subtractive* category, regardless of the degree to which these program models provide opportunities for celebrating and maintaining ESOL students' first languages and cultures.

Thus, programs for ESOL students that deliver curriculum content in the English language, provide content-oriented ESOL classes, and foster social integration are placed in the same category as programs that place ESOL students in regular classrooms with only twice-a-week tutoring in English as an accommodation to their LEP population. In other words, the language of instruction has become the sole criterion for measuring program effectiveness. This results in school districts with ill-informed administrators missing out on highly effective programs because they view such programs as culturally insensitive just because they do not use the L1 in academic content instruction. Ironically, some programs described as *subtractive* actively encourage children's use of the L1 to express themselves in class through the use of "buddy translators" (native speakers of the newer ESOL student's home language who are fluent enough in English to translate the newer student's words into English until the new student develops the ability to express

Exhibit 4.1
ESL Program Model Differentiation

Additive Program Models	*Subtractive Program Models*
(Foster L1 maintenance and heritage culture pride)	(No provisions for maintenance of L1 and heritage culture pride)
Dual Immersion Education	Submersion (illegal in U.S.)
Maintenance of Bilingual Education	Immersion
	Structured Immersion
Late-Exit Transitional Bilingual Education	Early-Exit Transitional Bilingual Education
	Pull-out ESL

himself or herself in English). Other programs that use only English for content instruction are termed *subtractive*, even though the use of the L1 is encouraged during informal social interactions with peers in the classroom and on the playground and when clarifying academic content material. A substantial portion of these programs termed *subtractive* may include well-designed multicultural or antibias curriculum components that enable ESOL students to share or teach native-English-speaking peers about their culture and language, and the opportunity to learn about other cultures. Programs with these components encourage social integration and respect diversity on the part of all students. Thus, the additive/subtractive dichotomy is an inappropriate oversimplification of the differences and degrees among program models currently implemented to provide equal educational opportunity for ESOL students. This dichotomy tends to foster poor program design decisions based on inaccurate information. Administrators must first and foremost learn to look carefully and critically at a number of criteria that are more useful in determining a program's effectiveness. Exhibit 4.1 depicts ESL program model differences.

While the majority of experts in second-language development and education of ESOL students agree that demonstrating respect and appreciation for ESOL students' home language and culture is of critical importance in facilitating these students' academic achievement, self-esteem, and social integration into the mainstream culture of the classroom, and while most Americans recognize the cognitive and economic advantages of bilingualism for individuals and the United States, a number of practical factors impede adoption of native-language or dual-language instruction models for educating ESOL students and/or native English speakers toward bilingualism (specific models for ESOL student needs are discussed in chapter five).

Arguments Against L1 Instruction

Arguments against native-language instruction range from historical, emotional, and political perspectives to practical positions, but are sufficiently significant to make native-language instruction impossible in the vast majority of school districts. The staffing dilemma and the heterogeneity of languages in many school districts (and even within individual schools) make it impractical to implement primary-language or bilingual programs in many school districts. A severe shortage of high-quality texts and materials printed in the languages of students and their families is an equally serious problem. Recent research on ESOL parents' attitudes toward instruction in the native language indicates that the majority of parents want their children to learn academic content in English, but want their children to do so in a manner that does not discredit their native heritage (LaVelle, 1997).

The Staffing Dilemma

One of the most pragmatic reasons cited by school district administrators for not using ESOL students' L1 as the language of instruction is their inability to find qualified professional staff for the program models. There is an acute shortage of qualified bilingual teachers in most parts of the country, and data indicate that the number of minority students entering education is decreasing, and that this shortage will continue for years to come. This shortage is especially acute in Asian-language bilingual teacher candidates. If a district is going to adopt a transitional bilingual education model (see Glossary), the teachers who are responsible for each of these classrooms need to be true bilinguals and biculturals, or at least close to it. Bilingual teachers are especially sensitive to the language, culture, and experiences of ESOL students, and have personally experienced or learned strategies and techniques that help ESOL students make the eventual transfer into instruction in English and the mainstream social structure of the school. In addition, they can be positive role models for immigrant children. Very few administrators would argue against hiring certified professional staff who have a thorough knowledge of the language and culture of their ESOL population and who bring cultural sensitivity and diversity to their work. At the same time, hiring a teacher solely because he or she speaks the students' native language or is familiar with the cultural experiences of ESOL students and their adjustment to a new language and culture is not sufficient qualification for working with these students.

Some teachers hired by districts to teach in the L1 are "imported" from other countries and have extremely limited English proficiency themselves. Many districts have actively recruited teachers from students' native countries. These teachers may be excellent models of immigrants who have gainful and rewarding employment and lives in the United States, and they may have firsthand knowledge of culture shock and the trials of functioning in and integrating into a new culture, but these characteristics are not sufficient to ensure high-quality instruction. In some cases these teachers have not yet acquired adequate English proficiency to serve as models for pronunciation and grammar in English for ESOL students. They may be such recent immigrants themselves that they have little to offer in terms of insights into the acculturation process, and, because of their own limited English, they may be unable to use sheltered English or other techniques that facilitate ESOL students' learning. Sometimes these teachers have professional and personal difficulties themselves as they strive to learn the culture of the school and the community in which they live. Some may become isolated and lonely and have little motivation or skills to help their students with English communication when they feel more comfortable themselves speaking in their L1. Administrators must develop clear criteria for all teachers and must prepare a series of interview questions to ensure that these teachers have English-language skills, understand the context of instruction, and know instructional strategies appropriate for working with ESOL students.

The authors repeatedly interact with recent immigrants who teach in the Philadelphia schools with emergency teaching certificates. In some cases, these teachers lack the fluency in oral English necessary to function as competent ESL teachers or regular classroom teachers. Yet, Philadelphia and other districts across the country continue to hire them because of a misplaced sense of appropriateness on the part of the administrators. The reality is that teachers who are not adequately proficient in English and who have not at least begun to acculturate successfully are a detriment to ESOL students' success. These teacher candidates could become excellent teachers for ESOL children, but districts would need help them become truly proficient in English, and to understand the educational policy and practices. A teacher, guidance counselor, or

When one school district changed from a primary-language program to a structured-English-immersion program, it realized it would have to test its non-English native-speaker teachers to ensure their English proficiency. While most of these teachers passed the standardized test, several did not. Fortunately, the particular teachers in question were not tenured, but had they been tenured, the district would have been faced with potential litigation for dismissing them. Therefore, the prudent district may need to establish some measure to be used with all potential teachers to ensure oral and written English proficiency.

school psychologist who has limited English proficiency and who lacks an in-depth understanding of American culture and the educational system is never an appropriate candidate for working with children in schools with bilingual models or structured-immersion programs (see Glossary). These native speakers may be an excellent resource for tutoring more advanced students in content area learning, or for serving as instructional assistants or co-teachers under the guidance of a more experienced bilingual teacher, but they should not be hired with the expectation that they will be able to manage the education of ESOL students if the district's goal is equal educational opportunity. Unfortunately, many of these teachers are hired on emergency certificates based only on their language background, with potentially disastrous results for their students.

Heterogeneity of ESOL Students' L1

Some districts also experience heterogenous language backgrounds of an increasing number of public and private, urban and suburban students. The ESOL population from a single language background must reach a considerable density level for native-language instruction to become feasible. Even in districts where as much as 30% of the student population are ESOL students, there may not be a sufficient density of a single language to warrant separate classes for ESOL students in grades K–5 in a particular language, much less in classes at the secondary level. Providing 10 or 12 students in a building with bilingual instruction throughout the lower grades may be impossible because of cost considerations and mandated ratios, even when a qualified bilingual teacher is available.

Additionally, countless superintendents across the country have experienced the wrath of ESOL students' parents who do not want their children (especially elementary-level children) bused across town for the sole purpose of bilingual instruction. Parents do not approve of the long day such arrangements involve and frequently find it difficult to get to the school for parent-teacher conferences, PTA meetings, or classroom volunteering. At the same time, most principals find it difficult to defend a class structure in which all ESOL students K–5 or 6 matriculated in one class with a single teacher for 5 or 6 years just to have a bilingual teacher. Such an option is not developmentally appropriate and constitutes a burden on the assigned teacher that is far beyond that of the regular classroom teacher.

Another important issue district-level administrators face is the question of whether the district is providing an equal experience for all ESOL students when students from only one language background (usually Spanish) receive primary-language instruction, with ESL support, while others receive only ESL support but have all content-area instruction in English. Administrators of such programs find it difficult to avoid allegations of inequality or favoritism when bilingual instruction is available only for students from one or a couple of home languages and not others, especially in large districts where there may be children representing 5 or more languages in a single school. Even if the district manages to provide native-language instruction programs to students from all language groups—by sending all students speaking one language to one building—there is still the serious problem of finding the qualified professional staff needed to maintain such a program.

Lack of Quality Texts in Languages of Instruction

Hiring competent bilingual/bicultural teachers is only the first step toward establishing a high-quality dual-immersion or primary-language instruction for ESOL students. A lack of academic content-area learning materials, such as textbooks, trade books, and games for classroom and library use may be a serious detriment to using the home language as the language-of-instruction. While there are an adequate number of books and materials available in Spanish, these texts are frequently criticized by researchers and teachers for their lack of quality. It is almost impossible to find appropriate materials to support content-area learning in most languages other than English. Furthermore, some ESOL students come from language backgrounds where the written form of the language was only recently established. In fact, one Massachusetts school district actually spent the money to develop the written form of an obscure language and accompanying reading materials (Porter, 1990). Providing students with equal opportunities to experience literature-based curriculums, to use CAI (computer-assisted instruction) in content-area learning, and to access up-to-date trade books in a language other than English can be an impossible task. Therefore, districts that may have a sufficient concentration of students with like native-language backgrounds may still be unable to provide appropriate materials and texts. A native-language instruction program in which instruction and learning experiences occur in the L1 using texts, videos, and visuals in English cause considerable confusion, not to mention a lack of continuity based on cultural differences.

ESOL Parents Prefer English Instruction

With bilingual/bicultural children, program development personnel should be aware that ESOL students' parents do not always support native-language instruction, and in some cases refuse to permit their children to participate in primary-language instruction classes. When ethnic surnames are the basis for selecting students for testing and participation in special programs, many contacted parents refuse to have their children tested in the hope of keeping them in the English-language mainstream classes. In the BASD, a series of ethnographic interviews during the year prior to elimination of the native-language instruction program (Simons, unpublished data) revealed that most parents preferred that their children attend schools where they are taught in English. In other cases, parents were indignant that a district appeared to believe they, as parents, were not capable of maintaining their child's primary-language and culture. Additionally, the middle- and low-SES parents, in particular, equated English proficiency with economic and social advantages, and all of them were adamant about their children attending classes taught in English, even if this arrangement meant some delay in their children's ability to benefit academically. One mother said, "I want my child to walk like you, talk like you, and be able to compete with you and your children for jobs—good paying jobs—and they can only do that if they speak perfect English. I can't teach them at home, so it must be English in school" (Simons, unpublished data, 1992). Another parent stated, "She is not in Puerto Rico now, so she needs to talk English, especially in school; that is how she will make something of herself."

The majority of parents who supported native-language instruction (sometimes militantly) in the BASD were largely professionals who themselves were bilingual and whose children had been raised as bilingual from birth. Many of the children of these bilingual professionals attend parochial or other private schools in the community. These parents argued that their children were deprived of their culture and their native language if it was not the language-of-instruction in the schools. While bilingual speakers of Spanish and English were far more adamant in their support of primary-language instruction, parents who were bilingual speakers of other languages were in favor of dual-language programs in which their child learned English. One parent, a bilingual program coordinator who insisted on the necessity of having immigrant children learn to read in their L1, so that they transfer those skills to English, acknowledged that it is not fair to treat children from different language groups differently. This parent realized that some students might receive instruction in their home language while others received instruction only in English, but this individual still participated in a campaign to maintain Spanish as the language-of-instruction in her district. Another group of parents who were fluent in English felt, in contrast, that their children were unfairly "forced" into the district's bilingual education program, solely on the basis of their surname rather than on the child's demonstration of a lack of English fluency sufficient for success in a class conducted solely in English.

In the BASD, the language-of-instruction debate attracted the attention of local media that transformed it into a issue of equal rights, empowerment, solidarity, and loyalty, and tended to shift focus from the needs of the children and adolescents in the school system, opening a chasm among some faculty members on one side, and other faculty, the superintendent, and other central office personnel on the other. The school directors who had to make the final language-of-instruction decision listened to hours of testimony that included emotional pleas and research findings. Their decision was to implement a new program that would help ESOL students gain proficiency in English as quickly as possible, so they could participate more readily in all of the services of the school and community. Many of the directors spent agonizing hours considering the empirical evidence, and ultimately decided that there was little overall support for primary-language instruction. Thus, the decision to implement a model with all academic instruction in English was based on these facts: there was no research to justify maintaining a primary-language program; children were not acquiring English within a reasonable time; and, many students were experiencing adjustment problems when mainstreamed into secondary programs because they had few previous opportunities for acculturation and social integration.

The Instructional Segregation Problem

The practice of segregating ESOL students for native-language instruction must also be considered as a valid argument against native-language instruction. The following case study outlines one district's dilemma about this segregation issue.

Case Study: Bethlehem Area School District, Bethlehem, Pennsylvania

In 1992, Superintendent Thomas Dolusio of the Bethlehem Area School District (BASD) mandated replacing the district's primary-language instructional program in Spanish (referred to as the *bilingual education program*) and called for development of a structured-immersion program, which came to be referred to as the *English Acquisition Program*. In a telephone conversation (1993) with one of the authors, the superintendent expressed his concern that the segregation necessitated by the primary-language program in Spanish did not provide ESOL students with regular opportunities for meaningful verbal interaction with their native-English-speaking peers. Dolusio believed that this lack of meaningful communication in the target language not only interfered with ESOL students' English-language development, but also with their acculturation and social integration. Dolusio asserted that failure to acculturate and socially integrate became noticeable as ESOL students moved back into mainstream programming, generally in middle school. Over the years, he had repeatedly observed that when ESOL students exited the primary-language programs, and were back in their neighborhood schools, the majority of the students were hesitant to socialize with Anglo peers. In fact, they tended to isolate themselves socially and to develop close friendships only with other native-Spanish speakers. Dolusio was concerned that many of these ESOL students refused opportunities to take advanced placement courses for which they were qualified because they wanted to remain with their native-Spanish-speaking friends. He also noted that the district's data showed that secondary ESOL students participated in extracurricular activities less frequently than Anglo peers with similar characteristics and were less likely to assume leadership roles. Dolusio felt strongly that, instead of providing ESOL students with educational experiences equivalent to those of native-English-speaking students, the primary-language experience was interfering with the students' development, so he appointed a committee to develop a plan allowing the majority of ESOL students to be integrated into their neighborhood schools.

The practice of segregating ESOL students for native-language instruction may account for some portion of the high dropout rate among Hispanic high school students across the country. Students who matriculate in programs with native-language instruction in all content areas beginning in the early elementary grades, and who attend these programs for 5 to 7 years, may be integrated into mainstream classrooms just as they reach adolescence during the late elementary or early middle-school years, when mainstreamed students have already formed peer groups that remain relatively intact throughout high school. This fact may make it excessively difficult for ESOL students entering a new school in grades 6 through 8 to integrate socially to the degree that they might if given an earlier start with this cohort group.

Another problem with primary-language programs was noted by Ann Goldberg, BASD's coordinator of the English Acquisition Program, who found that teachers tend to maintain students in ESL support programs as long as possible, albeit with good intentions, and felt that teachers might tend to keep students in primary-language programs considerably beyond the period necessary. In fact, these ESOL students might have already reached the point in their English-language development where they would benefit more from a regular classroom setting. Likewise, in the Allentown City School District (PA), director of Minority Language Education Ana Sainz de la Peña found that ESL teachers are often hesitant to reclassify students into intermediate and advanced ESL classes, because the reclassification reduced the amount of ESL instructional support, opportunities for individualized tutoring in academic content, and even consideration for accommodations in regular classroom instruction and assessment. The ESL teacher's decision is often based on his or her realization that the regular classroom teacher does not know how or is unwilling to make an effort to adapt instruction to help ESOL student in regular classes. In addition, Sainz de la Peña asserted that some ESL teachers feel the need to "protect" the LEP student from the negative attitudes of regular classroom teachers who already feel overburdened by the needs of students in their included classrooms.

Research on second-language development supports the potential negative impact of the effects of segregation on native-language instruction. If we accept Krashen's (1981) "comprehensible input hypothesis," which emphasizes the language learner's need for understandable input in the target language, it follows that ESOL students could benefit in several ways from instruction in English as long as teachers present academic content in a meaningful context, and adapt it to match or slightly exceed the learner's level of English proficiency. The more students are stimulated to produce the target language, the more they will receive additional opportunities for verbal interaction from peers and teachers; thus, academic-content learning itself becomes the vehicle for the two-way exchange that increases English proficiency in a well-structured English immersion program.

Additionally, it has been widely accepted that functional use of the language facilitates development of proficiency. Careful collaboration between the ESL and the regular classroom teachers to introduce concepts and activate ESOL students' prior knowledge, combined with adapted instructional and assessment strategies, allows ESOL students to succeed in regular classrooms, which provide multiple ongoing opportunities to learn the nuances of their new culture. These opportunities, in turn, facilitate their comfort in social interactions with peers. Thus, ESOL students in a language-sensitive content-instruction setting with experienced teachers and peers who demonstrate respect for and interest in their native language and culture are likely to acculturate, socially integrate, and develop proficient English without harming their self-esteem or motivation to learn. This condition is not possible when ESOL students are segregated from native-English-speaking peers. Based on our knowledge of early adolescent development and socialization patterns, primary-language instruction for a period of 5 to 7 years may well be a detriment to ESOL students' long-term academic and English-language learning.

If we accept the contention that ESOL students' academic-content instruction should be in English (given that teachers are trained to make the appropriate accommodations in instruction), we may now examine the second policy question—What program model will best simultaneously facilitate ESOL students' academic achievement, English-language development, acculturation, and social integration?—and the third policy question—How can we ensure that the educational experiences of ESOL student have the same academic rigor and access to the academic core curriculum available to native-English-speaking students?

The reality of the world of the non-native-English-speaking children is that at some point in their basic education they will need to make a major transition from a native-language program or ESL support to the regular classroom where English is the only medium of instruction. This transition has been demonstrated to provide the same potential for stress as placement in well-designed and implemented mainstream programs. Ultimately, ESOL children must acculturate and integrate socially into the mainstream if they are to reach their fullest potential, and it may well be the teachers' sensitivity rather than an arbitrary decision about an appropriate level of English-language skills that dictates academic success and social integration when transitions occur.

The arguments mentioned above against native-language instruction are often accompanied by less altruistic and more emotional arguments against L1 instruction These arguments tend to reflect a lack of understanding or appreciation that ESOL student's environment today is far more sophisticated in terms of academic content standards and technology than 10 years ago. Arguments based on the premise that native-language instruction and even special support services are not necessary because earlier generations of immigrants did not receive them and were still able to lead successful and productive lives are not relevant to the situation of of ESOL students today. Nonetheless, many district administrators face these arguments as they design and implement programs that provide ESOL students with equal educational opportunity. In a time when funding is often limited, it is prudent to eliminate unnecessary programs, but such decisions should not be based on historical case studies.

Time on Task and L2 Development

A powerful argument against native-language instruction is the "time on task" research (Doyle, 1983) that demonstrates that students reach higher levels of achievement in tasks and content when they spend more time learning. Therefore, if ESOL students receive daily content instruction in English and daily content-based ESL instruction to support content instruction in English, they are likely to spend more time developing the language than students who are learning content in their L1. Theoretically, these ESOL students should become more proficient in English in a shorter time. Likewise, students who spend more time interacting in English with students from mainstream American culture are likely to acculturate more readily than students whose only instruction in English is during daily ESL classes with other students who are new to the language and culture. Furthermore, students who are immersed in the mainstream culture at an earlier age will integrate socially more easily. We have no research data that delineate the process of social integration of ESOL students in primary-language, bilingual models, or structured-immersion programs, so important questions remain unanswered: Does academic competence achieved by primary-language instruction increase self-esteem and facilitate the acculturation process and social integration? Does participation in cooperative learning groups within an English-language classroom with native speakers encourage ESOL students' social comfort and integration and, thus, provide motivation for more English-language learning and content achievement? Acculturation, social integration, academic achievement, English-language development and self-esteem/self-confidence are so intricately interrelated that even sophisticated statistical techniques are pressed to sort out causal relationships. But we can observe what takes place in classrooms, and we can talk to ESOL students to find out what they experience in a variety of program models if we want to build a grounded theory (Glaser & Strauss, 1967) of what programming is best for ESOL students in a particular context.

Arguments Supporting Native-Language instruction

As compelling as the arguments for English as the language-of-instruction are, there are many equally convincing arguments against using English. For example, native-language instruction allows ESOL students to continue their academic content learning uninterrupted while they develop English-language proficiency. In addition, some contend that children from different cultures have different, culturally dictated learning styles, so ESOL students are more successful and comfortable if they learn in their native language from teachers who are familiar with their expectations regarding the classroom, the role of the teacher, and education in general. Ample data from qualitative studies indicate that children from different cultural groups have very different expectations regarding the classroom social environment (see Au & Jordan, 1981; Diaz, Moll, & Mehan, 1986). Cornell (1995) cites the typical learning styles of students from Latin America as follows:

Teacher Characteristics
- Assumes a role of academic authority
- May be the only one to possess a textbook
- Lectures and writes critical information on the chalkboard
- Provides little or no audiovisual or reference material to supplement lecture
- Expects student to provide specific, detailed information on examinations
- Tends to use fill-in-the-blank and short-answer testing techniques

Student Characteristics
- Depends almost entirely on teacher as source of subject information
- Copies in notebook anything and everything the teacher writes on the board
- Focuses on memorizing material, often word for word
- Is reluctant to question the teacher in class when something is not understood
- Depends on and seeks help from classmates to explain points not understood
- Consults with classmates outside of class to decipher unclear statements by teacher
- Readily shares notes, ideas, and knowledge with classmates
(Cornell, 1995, pp. 132–133)

In contrast, the typical American teacher may assume the role of guide or facilitator of learning rather than that of academic authority; engages students (especially at the elementary level) in individualized or cooperative learning activities, using lecture and blackboard to a far lesser degree; provides extensive access to audiovisual or reference material to supplement learning experiences from students' own textbooks or literature books; and tends to use performance-based assessment, portfolio assessment, and/or essay tests in addition to fill-in-the-blank and short-answer testing techniques.

While still dependent upon the teacher for guidance, the American student is encouraged to become an independent learner.

American students vary greatly in their tendency to question the teacher, but the vast majority are comfortable asking questions when they do not understand the teacher's vocabulary, concepts, or processes, and discussing explanations with their peers.

Teachers should be aware of these differences because when teaching and learning styles do not parallel one another, students may experience overwhelming frustration. However, teachers who are familiar with children's cultural norms and expectations may not be able to accommodate these differences in a structured English-immersion program.

Studies have consistently shown that ESOL students drop out of high school at a rate of 200% to 250% more frequently than their native-English-speaking cohorts (Watt, Roessingh, & Bosetti, 1994a, 1994b), because of the simultaneous effects of language difficulty (Seifeddine, 1994) and culture shock (Levine & Adelman, 1982; Watt, Roessingh & Bosetti, 1996; Waxler-Morrison, Anderson, & Richardson, 1990). ESOL students themselves cite school-related reasons rather than their personal or home lives as their impetus to drop out of high school (Watt, Roessingh, & Bosetti, 1996). However, the students who drop out most frequently and at the highest rate (62%) are beginner-level students who leave within 24 months of enrolling in high school if they have not developed interpersonal communication skills (Cummins, 1989). Cornell (1995) found that good performance by Hispanic students is frequently discounted rather than affirmed by teachers, and that perceptions of mainstream curriculum conflict make the content incomprehensible and often offensive.

At the same time, because many ESOL students do not socially integrate easily, their marginalization makes them more likely to become involved in at-risk behavior (Valverde, 1987), as they seek acceptance after their peers and teachers have rejected them (Cornell, 1995). Cornell (1995) also refers to the "passive survivor" who never participates in class activities and does not complete schoolwork, but who is largely ignored since he or she is not disruptive. Cornell found that this group of students includes a disproportionately high number of ESOL students whose talents are not supported and who are virtually invisible. Few strategies to prevent dropout by ESOL students are in place (Watt, Roessingh, & Bosetti, 1994a, 1994b), so it becomes impossible to determine if native-language instruction or language-sensitive content instruction are more effective models for ensuring the equal educational opportunity of these students.

There is very little evidence that native-language content-instruction models produce statistically significant higher levels of academic achievement than other models. This is largely because of the consistently poor design of evaluation studies and the poor methodology of existing studies that generally fail to define "success," and consistently compare incompletely described program models. Sampling bias is perhaps the greatest problem with studies comparing native-language instruction models with structured-immersion models.

Lily Wong-Fillmore (1991) takes a different approach to the language-of-instruction debate. She outlines the potential danger of ESOL students' isolation and inability to communicate, not only with members of their community but also with parents and grandparents as a by-product of losing their L1 through early-age matriculation in a structured-English-immersion program. Such a loss is compounded by a parallel loss of self-esteem and even personal and cultural identity. While few professionals would argue that the prospect of language loss and isolation is a desirable outcome, positions such as Wong-Fillmore's tend to focus on structured-immersion models that are poorly designed and pay little attention to affirmation of the native language and culture. In effect, she criticizes the worst examples of a particular model rather than examining the likelihood of language loss and isolation in high-quality models delivered in English.

The social-cultural match argument for native-language instruction asserts that it is the mismatch between the home and school environment/culture that presents problems for ESOL students in regular classrooms. Ample data from qualitative studies indicate that children from different cultural groups have very different expectations about the classroom social environment (cf. Au & Jordan, 1981; Diaz, Moll, & Mehan, 1986). However, the evidence is not convincing that teachers who are familiar with ESOL students' cultural heritages and expectations cannot accommodate these culturally dictated needs in a regular classroom environment if they receive appropriate staff development.

Perhaps the most convincing argument for native-language instruction is the research that demonstrates the cognitive, social, and economic advantages of bilingualism (Cummins, 1976; Glick, 1988; Hakuta, 1986; Padilla, Fairchild, & Valdez, 1990). Few educators deny the need to produce American citizens who are proficient in more than one language if the United States is to remain competitive in the emerging global economy. The ultimate solution to this dilemma is to develop and implement more programs that provide elementary-grade children with the opportunity to become proficient in a second language. Models that provide the infrastructure for integrating native English speakers and ESOL students in classrooms that are truly bilingual and bicultural are discussed in chapter five.

Research on ESOL Program Model Effectiveness

Interestingly, both advocates of English-language academic-content instruction and native-language content-instruction contend that research supports their viewpoints on educating ESOL students when, in reality, no such evidence exists. Program evaluations have been mandated by Title VII funding, yet the majority of studies are not helpful in determining if there is a single, most effective model for providing ESOL students with equal educational opportunity. Common sense tells even the casual observer that immigrant children and children of immigrants must develop English proficiency; learn the content and process knowledge recently dictated in national content standards and state and district curricula, and acculturate and socially integrate into the mainstream cohort in their class, school, and community. At the same time, these ESOL students should maintain their first language and culture and a sense of pride in their heritage. Obviously, accomplishing this goal involves a variety of complex variables. Research examining program effectiveness has never outlined these goals as dependent variables; in fact, the vast majority of studies never operationally define "success." Since the studies are not longitudinal, success has usually been defined by one of the following: (1) scores on a standardized achievement test that demonstrate that ESOL students are performing at the average level according to the norms; (2) exit from programs that support ESOL students until they achieve English-language proficiency suitable for successful matriculation in regular programs. Unfortunately, the studies do not examine equally important variables such as graduation from high school, matriculation in higher education or postsecondary vocational training, or employment that might be indicators of successful learning and social integration/acculturation. Nor are there data on ESOL students' success once they are mainstreamed, their degree of social integration, their matriculation in honors programs or advanced placement classes, their membership in extracurricular activities in junior high school and high school, and their leadership in student government or extracurricular activities. Thus, the data that are available are essentially narrow in scope. Common problems with published studies of program effectiveness are the following:

- Samples of the various model groups are seldom equal. In some of the studies most frequently cited as evidence supporting one approach or another, subjects in the sample may have participated in more than one type of program during the course of their schooling. For example, one 14-year-old subject may have attended grades K–3 in a program that provided all-English instruction supported by ESL classes twice weekly, but once he arrived in grade 4, he was placed with a team of teachers who used language-sensitive content instruction. After 4 years in this program, he moved to another district, where he was in a dual-immersion program for grades 8 through 12 in which part of his instruction took place in English and part in his L1. This student might be viewed as a subject in the dual-immersion category, while another student who was in dual-immersion program throughout his or her education might also be in the dual-immersion subject group. The multiple possibilities threaten the validity of the samples in these program evaluations.
- To date, we have no way of knowing if a single program design is most effective across grade levels; after all, it is conceivable that the program that provides the best structure for the second grader might be very different from the ideally designed program for the fifth grader, and still different for the tenth-grade student. Additional research examining model success as a function of developmental level of students would be extremely useful.
- Many of the earliest program designs were narratives with minimal systematic data collection. While qualitative program evaluation can be an extremely important process, especially in program development, without a tighter design and specific causal comparisons, it becomes impossible to interpret data and reach conclusions with any level of certainty they are correct.
- Even when the characteristics of program models are clearly articulated, we can assume that high-quality instructional strategies may be the same in both primary-language programs and structured-English-immersion programs. Instructional strategies, expectations of teachers, and training of

teachers may be the variables that predict success rather than the language of instruction.

- Regular classroom teacher training may be more significant than the program model in determining ESOL students' success.
- Evaluation studies do not examine the possibility that model effectiveness could depend on the native language and culture of the students matriculating in the program.

Appendix A outlines the major program evaluation studies conducted since 1978. We suggest that any administrator or program design team chair read the original versions of these studies if they are experiencing a controversy related to language-of-instruction.

Once the decision of language-of-instruction has been made by the program design team, flexibility is a critical factor in meeting TESOL standards. The high-quality program should have clearly defined strategies for responding to each of these six policy decisions:

1. What program model will be most effective in bringing about simultaneous academic achievement, English-language development, and acculturation or social integration? (see chapters five and seven).

2. How can the administrator ensure that ESOL students' education has the same academic rigor and access to core curriculum courses available to native English-speaking students? (see chapters seven and eight).

3. How can administrators structure school environments and implement district curricula to allow all students to benefit from ESOL students' cultural and linguistic diversity? (see chapters five and seven).

4. Similarly, how can the administrator structure school enviroments and implement district curricula and assessment to foster ESOL students' appreciation of their own native languages and cultures? (see chapters five, six, and seven).

5. How can administrators integrate the TESOL standards for Pre-K–12 Students into the district curricula and/or national content standards? (see chapters five and six).

6. How can administrators validly assess the effectiveness of a program in providing equal educational opportunity for ESOL students? (see chapter eight).

Chapter Five

Program Models for ESOL Students

Organizational models for programs to meet the needs of ESOL students vary widely, and the actual educational experiences of ESOL students vary markedly, depending on the program model selected for implementation by the district and the various components added to the basic organizational models to ensure that the program is appropriate for a particular district. This chapter presents the basic models for ESL programs, including descriptions of their general parameters and specific variations. The Bethelehem Area School District (BASD) program model is outlined in some detail in order to show how programs are tailored to meet the specific ecological variables of an individual district. Finally, the role of the recently published *ESL Standards for Pre-K–12* (TESOL, 1997) is examined.

The program models that follow are presented in generic form. In actual use, each is modified somewhat to meet the needs of the students, district, and community. Descriptions of the program organizational models have been accepted by both ESL scholars and practitioners. Most of these models, however, may vary considerably in actual implementation from district to district, largely depending on the size of the program, characteristics of ESOL population, and training and experience of classroom teachers. It is conceivable that the same organizational model could be used in a large urban district in which language-minority students are actually the majority of students served by the district; in a district where 20%–30% of the student population needs ESL services; or in a small school district in which there are only a few ESOL students in a single elementary, middle, or high school. Therefore, district administrators should dedicate sufficient time and resources to initial model selection and adaptation. Administrators or the program design team will need to consider carefully the need for program variations within the various communities served by a district, and be willing to make changes to accommodate particular contexts and needs in the early implementation stages.

The decision to use a model for ESOL students' primary-language generally necessitates adopting one of three general models: (1) a transitional bilingual-education model (TBE): (2) a maintenance bilingual-education model (MBE); or (3) a two-way or dual-immersion bilingual model (sometimes referred to as developmental bilingual education). Successful implementation of one of these models is generally limited to districts that have significant numbers of ESOL students from one language background. In larger districts, one of these models may be implemented in several different primary-languages at different sites in the district. That is, two elementary schools, a middle school, and a high school may have a program that involves primary-language instruction in Vietnamese, while five elementary schools, two middle schools, and a high school may provide primary-language instruction in Spanish, all within a single district.

Another district might implement a bilingual magnet-school model in which a single elementary and middle school are designated as the site for all ESOL students needing special services because of their limited English proficiency. Other districts in parts of the country where there are high concentrations of ESOL students and bilingual families from a single language background may implement either a language-maintenance model or a dual-immersion model in each of its schools, an especially appropriate decision if the community is bilingual in practice. Relatively few districts develop dual-immersion programs, making the commitment to educate both ESOL and native-English-speaking students as bilinguals. Implementation of a dual-immersion program tends to be difficult because of the need to find a sufficient number of bilingual/bicultural teachers, psychologists, and administrators.

Dual or Two-Way Immersion Model

In the two-way immersion model, academic-content learning takes place in both languages for ESOL students and native-English speakers. The languages are not mixed. Instead, both groups receive language instruction (language arts and reading) in both their native language and in their second language, while the rest of the academic-content learning takes place in one of the two languages. The language of instruction used in a particular content area may vary by teacher, content area, or time of day. For example, Mrs. Smith may be the health and social studies teacher, and she teaches those subjects in English, while Mrs. Garcia teaches science and art in Spanish. Another program may teach content areas in alternating languages on a semester or annual basis so that Spanish may be the language-of-instruction for science in the fall semester, and English is the language-of-instruction for science during the spring semester. A third possibility may be that all morning courses are taught in French, all courses after lunch are taught in English, with the languages alternating time of day each semester.

The exact nature of the academic-content areas split by language largely depends on certification of the bilingual faculty. This type of program can be truly bilingual and bicultural in every sense since it supports not only learning and communication in two languages, but also provides the opportunity for both groups of students to learn about one another's language, culture, and heritage firsthand. This model is also a maintenance bilingual-education model (MBE) since the students maintain their native language and culture, and the two languages are given equal treatment and value. The major premise underlying dual-immersion programs is the belief that bilingualism is a valuable asset for both individuals and society. Dual-immersion programs have high academic expectations and language-proficiency expectations for both groups of students, and students become proficient in both languages through meaningful, relevant dialogue and socialization in both languages. A high-quality dual-immersion program tends to increase the self-esteem of students from both primary-language backgrounds. There is no question that ESOL students are receiving the same academic rigor and access to the core curriculum as their native-English-speaking peers, and all students have equal opportunity. Obviously, this program model lends itself well to bringing about social integration of ESOL students in the classroom and the school. In communities where there are substantial concentrations of ESOL students from a single language background, this model provides equal footing for children of both groups, and students often become a truly bilingual and bicultural learning community where there is a high degree of cooperation, collaboration, and respect for each others' cultural and linguistic backgrounds.

Another type of maintenance bilingual-education model is currently provided to some Native American students. Reyhner (1992) reports that 74 schools and 22 community colleges are operated by Native American organizations under grants or contracts from the Bureau of Indian Affairs. This model, which maintains both English-language development and literacy and the children's Native American language (which is, in many cases, facing extinction), is

The Allentown City School District is developing a dual-immersion model for use in a single middle school. This program will be treated as a magnet and all students who seek a bilingual English and Spanish environment will be eligible to attend the program, in which half of the academic-content instruction is in English and half in Spanish. This program will bring together children from diverse cultural backgrounds and, therefore, will provide a natural opportunity for children to develop an appreciation and respect for each others' cultures and language. LEP students will not be segregated from native-English-speaking students, so this program will have a positive impact on high-school dropout because the students will be socially integrated and interdependent in terms of teaching each other a second language.

sometimes referred to as *restorative bilingual education.* This type of language-maintenance program is also implemented in Hawaii, Guam, and the Marshall Islands. Students are at a disadvantage in acculturating to the mainstream American culture and have fewer opportunities for social contact with native English speakers. Although instruction is always in both L1 and L2, relatively few districts can implement such models because of a lack of trained staff and material resources.

Transitional Bilingual Education Model

Transitional bilingual education (TBE) is an organizational model that has received both acclaim and criticism nationally over the past 30 years. TBE's ultimate goal is to mainstream students into the regular education program of a school district where only English is used in the learning process. TBE programs are generally divided into two categories. In *early exit* programs, there is initial native-language instruction for periods that vary in length, usually depending on the students' level of native-language proficiency. Students generally receive academic content instruction in their native language for 1–3 years, until they exit to a sheltered-English program or to the regular classroom with or without continued ESL instruction. Since the majority of early-exit programs are designed to serve students for only 1 to 3 years, ESOL students who attend these programs become at best proficient only in basic interpersonal communication skills (Cummins, 1989), but they often have not been sufficiently exposed to English in the classroom to develop cognitive academic language proficiency in English. When students exit, they usually have a fairly good command of oral language, listening skills, and developmental reading and writing in their L1, but they now move into a fourth grade or higher where they must learn academic content in English.

Sheltered English is often the model used during the transition into content classrooms. Teachers use English as the medium of instruction but adapt their discourse, instructional strategies, and the language demands of the lessons in a variety of ways. Teachers may modify the rate at which they speak; expand the use of content clues; or use extensive demonstrations, visuals, or graphic organizers to provide a bridge between content and ESOL students' emerging English skills (TESOL, 1997, p. 156). Ideally, early-exit students are given a transition to provide time for them to develop cognitive academic-learning skills in English prior to matriculation in the regular classroom. Early-exit TBE programs usually are categorized as *subtractive* since the native language is not maintained. The early-exit TBE program is probably the most frequently used bilingual education model in the United States, and there are countless variations in its design. Unfortunately, students who experience this model often do not have adequate opportunity for English-language development prior to the transition and ESOL students are often completely isolated or segregated for the program. Therefore, students leaving the early-exit program may have considerable adjustment in making the transition to the regular classroom. More research on the effects of this transition on ESOL students' long-term academic and social development is needed.

Late-exit TBE programs generally dedicate 40% or more of the learning time each day to instruction in the L1. Again, there are numerous variations in late-exit models so it becomes very difficult to compare the outcomes of individual programs. Students generally remain in late-exit programs until the sixth grade, even if they are reclassified as fully English proficient. A significant number of late-exit programs begin with students receiving 90%–100% of their instruction in the L1, and gradually reducing the amount of academic learning and social interaction in the L1 until the class is conducted solely in English. The late-exit model generally also uses *sheltered English* as the transition model. One criticism of the late-exit model is that bilingual teachers tend to focus on instruction in the L1 and often fail to transition to English in some districts, simply because they are more comfortable in the ESOL students' native language. Thus, they compromise ESOL students' development of cognitive, academic-language processing in English. In a few instances, some so-called bilingual teachers in these programs do not have adequate English proficiency and model incorrect English grammar.

These ESOL students are eventually transitioned into classes with native English-speaking teachers and peers and may experience difficulties. In fact, in some school districts it is possible for an ESOL student to arrive in the regular classroom after years in a TBE program without ever having heard a native English speaker except on television or another context in which there was no two-way discourse.

As the result of the inadequate research available, it is difficult to judge whether TBE is effective, and, as with many program evaluations, only careful qualitative research will show whether the model is ineffective or if the manner in which it is implemented is weak. Both TBE models are flawed, however, if they generally provide little or no opportunity for ESOL students to learn English through relevant and meaningful verbal interaction, and to be immersed in the American culture with students who are native English speakers. The TBE models also may involve busing students from their home communities to bilingual program sites, which reduces the likelihood of parent involvement in their children's education.

Immersion Models

Immersion models of instruction also provide language and academic instruction in two languages. The goal of immersion programs is for students to become proficient in two languages. The term *immersion* originated with program models in Quebec, Canada. In Quebec, middle-class children whose home language is English are instructed in French. Canadian-style immersion (Krashen, 1991) incorporates English into the program as both a second medium for instruction and a subject (Lambert, 1984). However, this model is not appropriate for most programs in the United States. In Canada, both French and English have high status as the language of instruction. In the United States, no other language has developed the same status as English. One only has to look at the "English-Only" movement and some of the rhetoric promoting California Proposition #187 to understand how the U.S.

social and political context precludes the high level of acceptance and success of the Canadian model.

A small number of school districts nationally, including expensive private schools, foreign language magnet schools, and public schools largely in upper-middle-class districts, that have made a commitment to a model referred to as *enrichment immersion.* In these schools, foreign-language education is supported enthusiastically, and all learning experiences are implemented in a foreign language to develop students' proficiency in that language.

The academic performance of the children in this program does not suffer, and their achievement tests scores in academic-content areas, including English language arts and reading, are not compromised. Parents enthusiastically support this program and, recently, actively resisted opposed a proposal to eliminate the program. The school directors, whose major concern appeared to be equal educational opportunity across the district, then voted for a FLES (foreign language elementary school) program in Spanish for all district students beginning in the third grade. This program provides regular proficiency-based instruction in Spanish for the largely Anglo student body, which maintains its content-area instruction in English. In the immersion program, the classroom teachers are all bilingual in English and Spanish, but students sign a "promise" to speak only Spanish in their classroom. Unfortu-

The Southern Lehigh School District in Center Valley, Pennsylvania, serves a largely upper-middle-class school district in a suburban area. Several years ago, one of the elementary schools implemented an experimental immersion program. First-grade students and their parents were given the option of enrolling in a Spanish immersion at Liberty Bell Elementary School. Each year an additional grade of Spanish immersion was added, and a student now may attend the Spanish-immersion program in grades 1 through 5 at Liberty, which serves as a magnet school for foreign-language immersion that attracts students from other district elementary schools. In addition, the district middle school maintains students' fluency by providing one content-area class each day in Spanish in grades 6 through 8.

nately, there are relatively few of these programs in the United States. One weakness of this program, however, is that the children in the Southern Lehigh District have little opportunity to interact with children who are native speakers of the language, so the largest portion of language proficiency is in academic language rather than in basic interpersonal communication skills (Cummins, 1989). But it is likely that when these children finally have time for relevant meaningful socialization in Spanish, they will be able to adapt to interpersonal communication with native speakers with few problems. Still, many immersion models with homogeneous student populations fail to provide their students with sufficient intercultural experience to foster true acculturation.

Structured-Immersion Models

The structured-immersion model has many variant formats across school districts. In structured-immersion programs, ESOL students are placed in regular classrooms with their English-speaking peers for academic instruction; however, teaching and learning activities are adapted to accommodate the special needs of ESOL students. Monolingual classroom teachers learn strategies to adapt classroom discourse and engage in instructional techniques that promote comprehension and encourage participation of ESOL students. In this model, which is sometimes referred to as *sheltered English*, and, more recently, referred to as *content ESL* and *language-sensitive content instruction*, teachers accommodate ESOL students' lack of English language proficiency through pedagogical strategies designed to enable them to benefit from instruction in English and, at the same time, experience social integration and acculturation. In many cases, ESOL students receive ESL instruction as an additional program component, and the amount of ESL instruction depends largely on the students' level of English proficiency.

Successful structured-immersion programs are almost always integrated into the general curriculum with a strong multicultural program. Students learn to appreciate and respect linguistic and cultural diversity. Generally, both Anglo and ESOL students attending these programs develop respect and empathy for one another. The ESOL child immersed in the American classroom context is in a social setting where she or he feels safe and accepted and, therefore, is more willing to take risks, speaking English more frequently in both learning and social situations. ESOL student in the structured-immersion program experiences natural social integration that facilitates his or her acculturation into the larger school community and the neighborhood. Students are not bused to schools across the district but remain in their neighborhood school instead and have opportunities for extended interaction in school and after school with their age cohorts. Thus, the structured-immersion model fosters social integration (third policy question), and allows all children to benefit from ESOL students' linguistic and cultural diversity (fourth policy question). Students who experience this model are more likely to have equal access to the district's core curriculum because the teacher adapts the teaching and learning experiences to foster ESOL students' learning and participation, rather than watering down the curriculum for these students. Language-sensitive content instruction requires training teachers not only to facilitate the learning, but also the acculturation and social integration of ESOL students. Teachers must learn to foster the development of learning processes and fix-up strategies (Chamot & O'Malley, 1994).

The structured-immersion model is extremely flexible, can be adapted to meet a variety of school and community needs, and often includes additional components such as native-language tutors to work with students to provide additional support as needed, especially for students who enter the district in the middle of the year, or students who enter in the higher grades. The major drawback of this model is that many districts implement it without sufficient staff development. In other words, if staff do not understand the premises that make this program successful, do not understand how to implement language-sensitive strategies, or how to simultaneously teach academic content and English language, the model will not work. More important, ESOL students may become frustrated and lost if teachers in this model are not adequately trained.

The structured-immersion model is especially appropriate when student populations are multilingual, which increasingly is becoming the norm in many communities. The philosophy behind this model is simple: Students in American schools need to learn English as quickly as possible, and without jeopardizing their self-esteem or cultural heritage, ESOL students must acculturate and socially integrate if they are to become successful adults. It is the schools' responsibility to provide teachers with the skills they need to help ESOL students reach these goals. Thus, the teachers receive training in second-language development and linguistically and culturally sensitive pedagogy. Specific strategies are discussed in a later chapter.

Districts implementing structured-immersion programs may have ESL teachers who work in collaboration with regular classroom teachers. In some districts, the ESL teacher enters the classroom for a period each day to co-teach with the regular teacher or to work specifically with one or more ESOL students in small groups or individually as needed. This arrangement is referred to as *push-in ESL*, as opposed to *pull-out ESL* in which language-minority students are taken from their classrooms for a specific amount of time each day (the amount generally depends on the student's level of English-proficiency—typically, beginner, intermediate, or advanced). These ESL services are used to prepare students for content in the regular classroom, to review academic content learned in the regular classroom, and to develop English-language skills in the context of meaningful content rather than having a separate English-language development curriculum that usually has no connection with the content currently being taught in the mainstream classrooms. Sometimes the ESL class focuses on a topic about to be introduced in the mainstream classroom to provide ESOL students with advanced organizers that will facilitate English comprehension and give them the opportunity to experience success participating in the activities of their whole class.

Exhibit 5.1 lists common variations of the structured-immersion model. While research on the effectiveness of this model is limited, we believe it is important to help all children develop respect and appreciation for cultural and linguistic diversity. If school systems have adequate fiscal and personnel resources, we would like to see all children exposed to a second language in a dual-immersion setting. It is critical that children who live in bilingual communities, with two languages and cultures, should receive an education that fosters biliteracy and an understanding and appreciation of both cultures. Children in bilingual communities have meaningful and relevant experiences in two languages, ideally in school and out, and, while problems such as lack of quality instructional materials in the non-English language are not conducive to high-quality programming, increased motivation to become bilingual tends to make up for this lack. However, homogeneous bilingual communities are increasingly less likely to be the norm. In fact, the vast majority of school districts are finding their ESOL populations becoming more heterogeneous than they were only a decade ago. If dual-immersion programs are impractical for any of these reasons, structured-immersion models, carefully planned and supervised, may serve ESOL students well.

Exhibit 5.1
Typical Variations of the Structured-Immersion Model

Variation 1   Structured immersion with traditional *pull-out* ESL

Variation 2   Structured immersion with *content-sensitive* ESL

Variation 3   Structured immersion with *push-in* ESL

Variation 4   Structured-immersion model with traditional ESL and content-area tutoring as needed by individual students

Variation 5   Structured-immersion model with tutoring

Variation 6   Structured-immersion model with context-sensitive ESL, push-in ESL in Grades 1–4, tutoring as needed, integrated family services.

We believe that carefully designed structured-immersion models taught by bilingual and monolingual teachers who thoroughly understand the process of language acquisition and learning and intercultural communication, combined with a repertoire of learning strategies for accommodating ESOL students through adaptation of classroom techniques, can meet the needs of both ESOL and native English-speaking students at the same time. A strong collaborative relationship between ESL and regular classroom teachers permits ESOL students to participate in core academic-content learning and helps them see themselves as competent and capable in academic settings and the larger community. As a result, ESOL students receive equal educational opportunities. In addition, structured-immersion programs with strong multicultural programming components foster respect and appreciation of diversity through meaningful experiences that foster ESOL students' acculturation and social integration and provide native-English-speaking students with valuable experiences with another culture and language. This approach resolves the fourth policy question because all students have the opportunity to benefit from the cultural and linguistic diversity of ESOL students.

Padilla (1992) states that over the past 20 years, the language-of-instruction debate has become increasingly more sociopolitical to the disadvantage of ESOL students. More time, energy, and money have been committed to determining relative effectiveness over the question of whether all, part, or none of academic content should be taught in the native language than on more promising qualitative studies of specific pedagogical strategies that are effective in fostering ESOL students' academic learning, acculturation, and social integration. Equal educational opportunity is the sum of equal access to core curriculum and advanced placement courses, *and* successful contexts for acculturation and social integration in the school and community. The following case study provides an example of one district's effort to put aside the language-of-instruction debate in order to establish a quality acquisition program.

Case Study: BASD's English Acquisition Program

The Bethlehem Area School District serves the City of Bethlehem, Pennsylvania, and sections of two counties in northeastern Pennsylvania, a community of slightly more than 100,000. The district serves approximately 13,000 students, of whom 23% are Hispanic, 4% are African American, and 1% are Asian. One in four children in the district is from an economically disadvantaged home, with 20% participating in the federally sponsored free or reduced lunch program. Ten percent of the district's students live in federally sponsored subsidized housing, and another 5% in low-income center city housing. There is a significant unemployment rate in the district because of a long-term decline in the steel and garment industries. BASD serves more than 1,300 ESOL students in grades 1–12 with a special program called *The English Acquisition Program.* The home language of the majority of students in this program is Spanish (86%); however, the remaining 14% of the students speak a wide variety of home languages, including Arabic, Chinese, Czech, Farsi, German, Greek, Hindi, Italian, Korean, Polish, Russian, Turkish, and a few African languages.

The BASD had provided bilingual education (in Spanish and English) for almost 20 years, when in 1992, Superintendent Thomas Dolusio concluded that a change was needed to help all ESOL students become fluent in English as quickly as possible to give them access to the same academic, social, and leadership opportunities as native-English-speaking students. Dolusio was disillusioned with the district's award-winning bilingual program that took students from their neighborhood elementary and middle schools and bused them to the bilingual program schools for several reasons:

- After 5 to 6 years in the program, most ESOL students were not English-language proficient enough to qualifiy them for mainstream programs.
- Students who exited the program appeared to have difficulty acculturating and socially integrating into mainstream schools, tending to avoid social interaction with peers other than Hispanics to the extent that qualified students avoided advanced placement classes at the high-school level, and generally did not become involved in the extracurricular activities or school leadership opportunities that involved social integration.
- Hispanic students' dropout rate remained alarmingly high.

The superintendent believed that ESOL students should be integrated into the mainstream population, and have opportunities to achieve success among their peers as a means of affirming their self-worth and cultural heritage. Social integration between language-majority and -minority students in the high school was not occurring, so all students were losing important opportunities to develop an appreciation of cultural diversity. Hypothesizing that this trend was largely because students enrolled in bilingual programming seldom attended their neighborhood school, Dolusio concluded that change was needed if ESOL students were going to have the opportunity to reach their fullest potential.

After extensive controversy, which included a series of presentations defending the bilingual model before the school board, district directors voted to change the bilingual program to one that emphasized English acquisition. The goal of the BASD's new program for ESOL students was "to have all LEP students become fluent in English in the shortest amount of time so that they might achieve maximum success in school" (BASD, 1993). A team of 30 educators, led by the assistant superintendent, developed a new program after reviews of relevant research and site visits to successful structured-immersion programs in Virginia during spring of 1993. The district did not just adopt a program from a demographically similar district, because the administration felt strongly that the probability of success would be greater if teachers and administrators were actively involved in the program design process. Many of the district's faculty and administration had worked with ESOL students for some time and were sensitive to their needs, so they were recognized as the best source of background knowledge and understanding for developing the new program.

The transition to the new English-Acquisition Program was not easy. Many teachers, a number of administrators, and some community members adamantly protested the program change and filed an OCR suit contending that ESOL students, who were not provided with native-language instruction were not receiving equal educational opportunity. Media attention made the program change a subject of public debate that even spread to neighboring Allentown, causing some dissention among its school district staff and community members. Even the Allentown City Council joined the debate with a proposal to enact "English-only" legislation for the city that resulted in major controversy in a second community with a population of just over 100,000 people. Once again, we see the emotional and political power of language outlined in an earlier chapter and by James Crawford (1992).

The program finally designed by the BASD team included a formative and summative program evaluation model and was adjusted to meet somewhat different needs at each level: elementary schools, middle schools, and high schools and the needs of individual schools within the district. This high-quality program is described in detail in the next section of this chapter. Almost immediately after the program was implemented, even the administrators and teachers who strongly disagreed with the termination of the bilingual model began to make every effort to make the program a success. This action was a result of three factors: (1) the high level of professionalism and genuine concern for ESOL students on the part of the administrators, faculty, and support staff; (2) the sensitivity of the administrator of the new program and the central office administration in avoiding a comparison of the two programs; and (3) the encouragement of dissident faculty and staff to provide formative feedback and suggestions as the new program was implemented, which allowed for refinement.

Major Characteristics of the English-Acquisition Program

The characteristics common to the entire BASD English-Acquisition Program viewed by the district administration and program director as the foundations of the model include: ongoing consistent collaboration between regular classroom and ESL teachers; maintenance of high expectations for ESOL students' academic performance with instructional adaptations as needed; use of technology as an integral part of the learning process for both academic content and English; and frequent opportunities for parent involvement. While each of these characteristics is essential for a successful acquisition program, teacher collaboration is key to the success of the whole.

Teacher Collaboration

In order for ESL teachers to provide students with the support necessary for their success in regular classrooms, ESL teachers are kept abreast of learning activities in the regular classrooms, difficulties common to ESOL students as a group and as individuals in these classrooms, and any special events or unit themes of instruction. ESOL students' difficulties are more readily identified by the regular classroom teacher with whom they spend the major part of the school day, so the BASD program design team included a mandate and provision for ongoing scheduled communication between ESL and regular classroom teachers at all levels. Emphasis on this collaboration provides continuity between ESL instruction and academic-content instruction and allows ESL teachers to be aware of their ESOL students' progress in acculturation and social integration with their peers. Since ESL instruction in this model does not focus on teaching isolated grammatical constructions in English or on isolated pronunciation drills, but instead focuses on facilitating students' simultaneous English-language development and academic-content learning, ongoing communication is critical to the success of the overall program. English-language instruction is integrated into the introduction, development, and reinforcement of content-area learning.

Strategies for providing frequent and intense collaboration are somewhat different at high-, medium-, and low-impact schools, and even differ from school to school, depending on other administrative scheduling needs. However, during our initial formative evaluation of the program, it was evident which schools' faculties had more opportunities for collaboration on integration of ESL instruction and academic content by observing both ESL classes and regular classroom instruction. The level of active participation by ESOL students in discussion and other activities was different, and students in the highly collaborative settings seemed to have a better grasp on what was occurring in their class, even early in the school year. The level of active participation by ESOL students in discussions and even manipulative activities was clearly higher in buildings where there was greater collaboration. Ethnographic interviews with ESL and regular teachers indicated that all of the teachers agreed that this collaboration was critical to meeting

ESOL students' needs. In a few cases where the building adminis-trator was not particularly sensitive to the need for collaboration time, we found that teachers made their own opportunities for col-laboration, and not without some degree of annoyance with the principal. Administrators working with structured-immersion programs must be sensitive to the importance of information and idea exchange by these two groups and provide for it on a regular basis.

The actual collaboration meeting involves reviewing any prob-lems ESOL students are having with regular classroom content and planning strategies to activate students' prior knowledge on topics in the ESL class; brainstorming about techniques to accommodate ESOL students' limited English proficiency during content learning in the regular classroom; and proactively considering concepts and content that may be particularly difficult from the perspective of ESOL students' native language and culture. Appendix C is a copy of the written format used by collaborative teams of ESL and regu-lar classroom teachers in the BASD. Our initial qualitative forma-tive evaluation of the English-Acquisition Program, and responses to a survey instrument with open-ended questions after the first and third years of implementation, revealed that both the regular class-room and ESL teachers strongly agreed that collaborative efforts among the teachers clearly contributed to the program's success. Since many of the regular classroom teachers had no experience or training in working with ESOL students, these teachers found the insights of the ESL teachers extremely helpful in pedagogical deci-sions. ESL and regular classroom teachers also collaborated twice a year on assessing the ESOL students' listening, speaking, reading, and writing skills in English. While the collaboration appears to have been implemented more fully at the elementary level because of largely self-contained classrooms, teachers at the middle-school and secondary level also find the collaboration useful. The charac-teristics of the acquisition program at each level follow.

Elementary-School Program for ESOL Students in the BASD

The goals of the program for ESOL students in the elementary level are as follows:

1. to provide an academic setting that accelerates acquisition and learning of English;
2. to integrate ESOL students into all mainstream classes;
3. to increase all ESOL students' oral language proficiency;

4. to coordinate ESOL children's educational program to reduce fragmentation; and
5. to provide native-language support for concept clarification whenever possible.

Each ESOL student is monitored twice a year as he or she moves through three stages of increasing proficiency in oral language, reading, and writing in English. See Appendix D for an outline and description of the stages of proficiency in each of these areas as outlined by the BASD.

Three of the BASD elementary schools are classified as *high-impact schools*. These schools have an ESOL student population that constitutes 40%–50% of their total student body. Student–teacher ratios are reduced in these schools to approximately 20:1. *Moderate-impact schools* with 12%–30% ESOL students have class size reductions when large numbers of ESOL students matriculate at a particular grade level, especially if most of the students are in the beginning stage of proficiency. ESL classes are provided to these beginner students at high-and moderate-impact schools for 75 minutes each day. Intermediate and advanced students receive 45 minutes of ESL instruction three days a week. At the 10 low-impact schools with up to 6% ESOL students, itinerant ESL teachers schedule classes 2–4 times a week for small mixed groups (these students may be grouped by grade level or English-language proficiency level, depending on the configurations in specific schools). Additional support for elementary ESOL students' academic-content learning may be provided by paid tutors for up to five hours per ESOL student per week at the school's request. These tutors speak ESOL students' native language and are called *second-language guides*. They are required to pass a test using materials from the anthology of the reading program before they are hired. Tutors are especially effective with students whose L1 is a language other than Spanish because, while the district has a substantial number of English-Spanish bilingual teachers and support staff, there is an acute shortage of teachers in the local area who speak many of the other home languages of the ESOL students in the program.

The ESL teachers do not work with the students in kindergarten, which has a curriculum based on integrated thematic units that are rich in language activities. During kindergarten registration in April of each year, students are given the *Pre-LAS* (De Avila & Duncan, 1977) test by trained testers from the Center for Language Acquisition (the administrative headquarters of the program in the district located in a high-impact elementary school). A follow-up assessment is administered sometime in May or during the kindergarten year to determine the student's level of oral language proficiency and whether the student will need ESL programming in the first grade. More than 90% of the students who attend these kindergarten programs have demonstrated consistent growth over the school year, often going from an initial score of zero on the test to a score of 50%–70%. Any score below 72% results in a placement as an ESL "beginner" for the first grade, but it is evident that students make substantial gains in this kindergarten program based on developmentally appropriate practices. It is important to recognize that because of the multiple risk characteristics of many of these students entering the district, the documented gains indicate an especially strong program (Goldberg, 1997). How these children gain the basic interpersonal communication skills in English is interesting. During the first week of school, many of the five-year-olds truly do not speak a word of English, but by January it is often difficult to tell which students these were when observing them interacting with their native-English-speaking peers.

Children in grades 1 through 5 from a variety of ethnic and language groups work side-by-side learning mainstream academic content, celebrating each others' cultures, and interacting in meaningful, relevant ways that make ESOL students' acculturation an integral part of their day. ESL and regular classroom teachers strive to become sensitive to cultural differences and are generally able to determine if a particular concept or lesson will be hard for children from a particular language background to understand. Over the course of several months, ESOL children learned many subtle cultural and language variables, such as gesticulation, speech patterns, and pragmatics, and we observed many children adjust their behaviors to the child with whom they were interacting at the moment. Children's natural curiosity is aroused in a multicultural environment, and these elementary students are generally uninhibited in exploring and posing questions about their peers' language and culture. These students are successfully learning to respect differences and even value them. Conflict negotiation can be modeled in a meaningful context as an integral part of the curriculum as students learn to accept and adjust to different perspectives.

Middle-School Program for ESOL Students in the BASD

The middle-school ESL program operates with the *team teaching* philosophy, an integral part of the structured-immersion program at this level. Middle-school students who are at the beginner level of English proficiency attend Broughal Middle School, where an academic learning team provides language-sensitive content instruction through careful collaboration between content and ESL teachers, much the same as in the elementary-school program. These teachers were selected because of their special interest in working with ESOL students and their willingness to explore strategies and techniques necessary to provide the academic rigor of mainstream curriculum to students who, despite their beginning level in English, are generally capable of developmentally appropriate cognitive functioning.

Beginner-level students have two ESL periods a day, language arts and reading periods with both the ESL and content teacher teaming for instruction (push-in ESL). The other content subjects are taught to beginner classes by content-area teachers with the support of a bilingual aide, permitting clarification in the L1 as needed. All beginner students are assigned "buddies" (whenever possible from the same language background), and the pair attend homeroom, art, lunch, home economics, related arts, physical education, and industrial arts together integrated with their native-English-speaking peers. This strategy appears to facilitate both acculturation and social integration of newer ESOL students. Note that the "buddy" in these pairs, who is the more advanced student of English, should receive some training that includes a clear articulation of how he or she can help the newer student. Language buddies are most willing to serve as language and culture guides, but need direction in what types of behaviors constitute appropriate help.

Selected beginner students who complete most of the fifth grade in their home elementary school, and who have demonstrated adequate growth in English proficiency, may apply to attend their own middle schools instead of Broughal. The decision to change schools is based on the student, parent, and teacher input, another example of an appropriate context for parent involvement. This accommodation is used to promote social integration and proactively avoid school dropout at a later date by providing ESOL students with the opportunity to maintain any peer group affiliations they may have begun in the fourth grade.

Intermediate-level ESOL students attend their neighborhood school and take ESL classes taught twice each day. They take mainstream classes in mathematics, science, and social studies with native-English-speaking peers. All middle-school students are eligible for the ESL tutorial program available from 3:00 P.M. to 3:45 P.M. each day. ESL teachers are required to staff this program, which provides peer tutoring, a homework club, and after-school activities. ESL teachers have a later starting time each day than the regular classroom teachers to accommodate this assignment. Students may continue in this program even after they exit the English-Acquisition Program into mainstream programming with no support services, again providing continuity of support and the opportunity for any needed proactive intervention. Collaboration between content-area teachers and ESL teachers continues to be important. One difficulty is that the ESL teacher is now dealing with more than one teacher per child.

High-School Level Program for ESOL Students in the BASD

The high-school program offers two options: (1) EAP, the English-Acquisition Program, designed for students who want a program that will prepare them with marketable skills for business and vocational-technical classes, and (2) TEP, the Transitional Education Program, designed for high-school students who want a more traditional program. TEP allows students to participate in mainstream classes at an increasing level, from 30%–40% of their classes in their freshman year, to 55% in their sophomore year, to 75%–80% in their junior year, and to exit into the mainstream in their senior year. The complete program of studies for secondary students is found in Appendix E. The TEP structure is particularly helpful to students who arrive at high school with good academic preparation in a language other than English.

Teachers and administrators alike admit that the most difficult students to serve are those who arrive at high school with little formal education in their own country. These students receive additional tutoring, but are often quickly frustrated and drop out of school altogether. The district has been examining "school-to-work" program options for these students, for which a considerable number of grants are available. Vocational programming is often not available to students without sufficient English proficiency, especially some of the high-level technology programs. In addition, some of these late-arrival students may be unable to meet graduation requirements, a critical legal and ethical problem in many states. It is important to note that ESOL students request special accommodations for taking the SAT and ACT tests.

In the BASD, a Latino leadership club provides special mentoring and guidance for secondary students who want to become leaders. These clubs at both of the district's high schools are instrumental in providing opportunities for cultural heritage celebrations and ethnic group leadership, and they foster support and encouragement for students who experience challenges in navigating their bicultural status.

Exiting the English-Acquisition Program

The decision to exit a student from special ESOL services is made by a team at each school, organized by the building administrator, that evaluates each student's ability to succeed in the mainstream program without special services. On the "Stages of English Acquisition" form (Appendix D), the level of competence for exit is described for elementary-, middle-, and high-school levels. The ESL and classroom teacher provide documentation for determining the English-language level, reading level, and writing level for each student, as described in "Stages of English Acquisition." For reading assessment, the teacher provides a photocopy of a passage that the student must read and paraphrase successfully, and a photocopy of a sample of the student's written work taken from actual performance in the classroom and added to the student's portfolio (Appendix E).

The oral language, reading, and writing stages decided on by the team are circled on the "Change of English-Acquisition Program Form" (Appendix F), and signed by all team members. One team member (generally the bilingual member) is designated to inform the parents of the change in program. Copies of the form and documentation are then sent to the Center for Language Assessment (CLA) for review by the program coordinator for English-Language Acquisition and Literacy.

The BASD complies with the Civil Rights Act of 1964 by giving all students or parents of students entering the district for the first time the "Home Language Survey" (Appendix G). Students who indicate they speak a language other than English at home or speak a second language are referred to the Center for Language Assessment before beginning classes. The assessment of each student includes the following:

1. *Language Assessment Scales—Oral (LAS-O)* (De Avila & Duncan, 1977) to measure the oral proficiency of students from the end of Grade 1 through Grade 12 in either English or Spanish.

or

2. *The Pre-LAS* (De Avila & Duncan, 1977) to measure the oral proficiency of preschool, kindergarten, and beginning first-grade students.
3. *The Brigance Reading Test* to measure oral reading, word recognition, and reading comprehension.
4. A writing sample in English and the native language.
5. A mathematics test for secondary students.

Results of these tests are used to recommend the student's placement in either the mainstream program or the English-Acquisition Program and designates one of the three levels of English proficiency. Copies of the tests and summaries are forwarded to the student's school for review by appropriate faculty. Assessors are well aware of the numerous validity issues related to the ESOL student's assessment. Anyone who is responsible for assessing culturally and linguistically diverse students must receive special staff development before doing so. Ideally, students should be assessed by someone who is conversant in their home language. In the case of special education placement evaluations, the school psychologist should be bilingual/bicultural in the student's language/culture for the test to be at all valid.

Staffing the English-Acquisition Program

The program coordinator is responsible for administering the English-Acquisition Program in the BASD. He or she is supported by a full-time secretary and a full-time tester. The program design team and the district administration recognized that this particular program needed strong leadership because of its size and the staff's divergent perspectives on the model's appropriateness. The program administrator needed to be capable of assessing and refining the formative phase of the program, which was critical to the program's acceptance and implementation. The BASD program coordinator position is a full-time, 12-month-a-year position.

Fifteen ESL teachers serve the 6 high-impact and moderate-impact schools in the BASD, while 4 ESL teachers serve the 10 low-impact schools. Of the eight ESL teachers serving the four middle schools, four are at the Broughal Middle School (the school serving beginner students). The high school has five ESL teachers. The program coordinator is charged with hiring additional part-time or full-time ESL teachers if the population in a particular school changes during the academic year. Both the ESL and the regular classroom teachers are directly supervised by the principals in the buildings where they work with the program coordinator.

Early Program Effectiveness Data (1993–1996)

An internal district evaluation of the initial cohort of students who entered the English-Acquisition Program in 1992 indicated that 83% of these students were eligible for free or reduced-cost lunches, suggesting that the SES level of this cohort highlights the majority of the students as at-risk. Originally 181 students were classified as beginners in this cohort. By June 1996, 130 of the students classified as beginners in the original cohort remained and were classified as shown in Table 5.1.

Table 5.1
Status of the EAP 1992 Beginner-level Cohort (130 students) in 1996

Exited	12 (9%)
Advanced	32 (25%)
Intermediate	59 (45%)
Beginner	24 (18%)
Special Education	3 (2%)

Of the 34 students in the original cohort who were classified as intermediate level, the distribution was as shown in Table 5.2.

Table 5.2
Status of the EAP 1992 Intermediate-level Cohort (34 students) in 1996

Exited	15 (44%)
Advanced	13 (38%)
Intermediate	6 (18%)

The 17 students who had originally been classified at the advanced level had all exited with only one exception. Data indicate that the typical student who enters the program with low levels of oral, reading, and writing proficiency in English may need two years at the beginner level, one to two years at the intermediate level, and one year at the advanced level before exiting the program. A limited number of students moved quickly through the program levels, and others remained at the same level throughout the three years; however, staff are directed to respond to the needs of the individual student rather than using a prescribed formula for exit (Goldberg, 1997). It would be interesting to conduct case studies of the students at the two extremes to explain their variation. However, so many sociocultural variables both in and out of school affect the rate of second-language development that the validity of such an analysis would be suspect unless significantly more studies were conducted and the original cohort was followed over a longer period.

Parent response to the English-Acquisition Program conducted as part of this internal evaluation indicated that they were satisfied with the program: 88% of the responding parents thought the schoolwork was appropriate for their child's grade level; 73% reported that they felt their child's spoken English had improved, 63% felt that their written English had improved, 54% felt that their independent reading had improved, 41% felt that their child's study skills had improved, and 46% of ESOL students' parents felt that their child's social skills had improved. Parents had been given the opportunity in the original survey to add narrative responses to the survey, and the most common comment was *adelante*, "keep going."

This initial internal program evaluation discovered that, at the elementary schools (where the major program change had been from the bilingual program), two-thirds of the students are within the average achievement range in grades 1–6. At the middle-school level, more ESOL students were moved into the regular classroom courses with support from ESL teachers. The internal evaluation determined that, at the high-school level, the greatest need was to extend programming to improve performance of students in the vocational or business track through a school-to-work model. Teachers at all levels voiced a strong need for staff development. Overall, the BASD is an example of a district that successfully designed a context-sensitive program that is well on its way to meeting the needs of its multilingual/multicultural student population. While longitudinal data will provide documentation of success and perhaps additional focus for refinement, the district serves as a model for other communities. Paramount to the success of the program has been so many teachers' interest in and commitment to the welfare of ESOL students. At the same time, administrative support for the BASD program is exemplary and necessary.

Administrative strategies of importance exhibited in this district include the following:

- open, honest communication among administrators in integrating the different aspects of the program;
- the central office's decision to involve all interested professional staff in the program design process, and

- commitment to quality staff development as an integral part of program implementation and the dedication of fiscal resources to this end.

Note that it is qualitative research on programs such as the English-Acquisition Program in the BASD that will ultimately provide researchers and, more important, practitioners with the documentation of outcomes that will allow for more valid program decision making. Not every district has the same contextual needs as Bethlehem. Additional districts with very different structured-immersion programs include Arlington, Virginia; Dearborn, Michigan; El Paso, Texas; and Seattle, Washington. Districts seeking to design a high-quality program for their ESOL students should review as many program designs and visit as many programs in operation as possible to get a perspective of a variety of program designs. Even when such data is available; a design team should explore carefully its own context demands and all options before adopting a model.

ESL Standards for Pre-K–12 Students and Program Design

The purpose of the new ESL standards recently published by TESOL (1997) is to identify characteristics of excellent programs for ESOL students, regardless of the specific model selected to prepare ESOL students for life in the new century. The ESL standards describe the language skills necessary for social and academic purposes, achievement in grade-level-appropriate academic instruction, and, ultimately for productive, satisfying lives. These new standards provide a bridge to general education standards expected of all students in the United States, and, as such, are sufficiently flexible to be integrated with the district curriculum or state or national content standards to: (1) articulate the English-language development needs of ESOL students, (2) provide direction about how to meet ESOL students' unique needs; and (3) emphasize the central role of language in the development of competencies in other standards. The ESL standards also attempt to help teach educators about effective education for ESOL students, including development of native-like proficiency in English, maintenance and affirmation of students' native languages in school and community contexts, the need for all educational personnel in a school or district to assume responsibility for the education of ESOL students, and recognition that knowledge of more than one language and culture is advantageous to all students. The ESL standards are a valuable resource for regular classroom teachers and for administrators working on program design or evaluation and refinement.

The standards are organized by grade-level clusters (Pre-K–3, 4–8; 9–12), and by English-proficiency levels (beginner, intermediate, advanced, and limited formal schooling). Districts developing a new program or making major changes in an existing program would do well to adopt these operational definitions of English proficiency as their own. In addition, the standards publication includes vignettes to help administrators and teachers learn how to translate goals and standards into actual classroom practice. The vignettes illustrate the concepts and procedures articulated in the standards document through use of multiple examples. TESOL (1997) outlines the goals for ESOL learners in pre-K through Grade 12 as follows:

Goal 1   To use English to communicate in social settings.
Goal 2   To use English to achieve academically in all
         content areas.
Goal 3   To use English in a socially and culturally
         appropriate way.

The document breaks down each goal into specific standards. For each standard, descriptors of behavior are described and sample progress indicators are outlined, making it easier to apply these standards to integrated thematic instruction and ensure simultaneous development of academic content-area knowledge and English language. For example, descriptors of Goal 1, Standard 1 are

- Sharing and requesting information
- Expressing needs, feelings, and ideas
- Using nonverbal communication in social interactions
- Getting personal needs met
- Engaging in conversations
- Conducting transactions

Sample progress indicators include:

- Engage listener's attention verbally or nonverbally
- Volunteer information to respond to questions about self and family
- Elicit information and ask clarification questions

(TESOL, 1997, p. 31)

Thus, the standards can be used by both ESOL and regular classroom teachers in collaborative planning to ensure integration of ESOL standards into the more inclusive content standards or outcomes, and as a guide for lesson or unit planning.

A copy of these standards should be available to any ESL or classroom teacher who works with ESOL students, and is particularly helpful for monolingual teachers working with students in a multilingual classroom who have little prior training in second-language learning or simultaneous teaching of content and language. The standards can also be used to help plan balanced content-area instruction since the teacher can examine each of the standards under each goal, integrate them directly into the teaching process, and develop a checklist or rubric for assessing student progress. Administrators are encouraged to visit the appropriate Web sites (chapter 9) for follow-up studies. In any case, districts are likely to profit from using the standards as an integral part of the program design process.

Chapter Six

Reaching Out to Families and Communities

An effective approach for family and community outreach and participation is a key factor in developing quality programs for ESOL students, regardless of the specific model implemented. This chapter examines potential strategies and paradigms for developing a model that will support family and community involvement. Numerous research studies have demonstrated that parent involvement has a positive impact on the academic achievement of children and youth in general, and ESOL students are certainly no exception. In fact, specific research on ESOL student population indicates that family and community involvement may be even more important for these students (Ada, 1989; Bermudez & Padron, 1987; Epstein, 1992). With regard to ESOL students in a district, family and community involvement has the potential to contribute markedly to almost every aspect of the students' education. ESOL students who interact with members of the community who are themselves native speakers of English or who are true bilinguals have invaluable opportunities to facilitate their acculturation and social integration. Community members may also serve as role models and mentors, which is especially valuable if the community members are from ESOL students' own cultural backgrounds and have become successful members of the greater community. Elementary- and middle-school ESOL students benefit from regular contact with successful high-school and/or college students for whom English is a second language.

Programs that provide comprehensive or integrated services at school sites affect students' lives beyond the classroom walls in many planned and unplanned ways. Active participation of ESOL students' parents in the same activities and functions as mainstream students' parents provides ESOL students with a sense of belonging and unity with their peers, while at the same time affirming ESOL students' language and cultural identities. The district that provides opportunities for expanded involvement of ESOL families provides mainstream students in the district with increased opportunities for interactions with other languages and cultures, and provides at least a partial strategy for the third policy question: How can we ensure that all mainstream students benefit from the linguistic and cultural diversity of ESOL students? Reaching out to families and the community will enrich the lives of all students and professionals in the district in numerous ways.

This chapter examines multiple strategies for reaching out to ESOL students' families and fostering the empowerment of families who are new to the community or country. Some of the endless opportunities for community and business partnership are outlined. In addition, this chapter suggests program components for a school-centered comprehensive services model. Once again, we use a model from the BASD ("Family Centers") to show how a medium-sized school district can improve the availability of services to ESOL students' families.

Family Involvement

Fine (1993) contends that school districts should encourage the more realistic model of "family involvement" rather than the more limited "parent involvement" if the goal is to gain active participation of children's caregivers in the education process. In many cultures, the entire family is responsible for caring for the family's children and supporting the children's learning. It is not at all unusual for entire immigrant families to arrive at a school to enroll a single child or to come to a parent conference if a child is experiencing academic or behavioral difficulties. In fact, many principals and teachers have shared with us their belief that the likelihood of anyone in the family attending a parent day or other activity increases markedly if the entire family is invited. They believe that family members provide support for one another in the strange and somewhat intimidating context of the school. For a variety of reasons ranging from immigration patterns to work schedules to cultural mores, grandparents, older siblings, other relatives, and even trusted neighbors who care for a child while parents work may become allies in helping ESOL children (and their parents) navigate the often stressful maze of communication, policy, and procedures of the school and the learning process.

To involve families in the school and in their children's learning, professional staff must overcome language and cultural differences, a wide variety of perspectives on the purpose of education, family members' own negative experiences with education, and more pragmatic considerations such as transportation if they want to build a truly collaborative partnership. In many instances, staff need to overcome their own stereotypic thinking and perspectives, and sometimes they even need to face their own prejudices and preconceived notions of parents and families associated with various ethnic and language groups.

ESOL students' parents may have markedly different views of their appropriate role in their child's education. Typically, these parents' perspective of what constitutes a so-called good education vary considerably from that of mainstream parents who believe that they are responsible for tutoring their children at home; helping their children with homework; attending conferences; helping with fund raisers, PTO, and field trips; and attending class plays (Leitch & Tangri, 1988). Most parents of ESOL students have little understanding of how American schools work (Olsen, 1988). They are unlikely to become active in unfamiliar and uncomfortable school environments. Even if they acquire considerable fluency in English, they may discover or believe erroneously that their views on education are not applicable to the American system and/or that American teachers and administrators are not interested in hearing what they have to say about their children and about education. Often lacking confidence because of limited English proficiency and limited knowledge of and experiences with the mores of the American culture and school, or embarrassed by their welfare status or their inability to purchase school supplies requested by the teacher, parents of ESOL students may be intimidated by or even angry at school personnel, but never express their views. This lack of voice may reflect a cultural tradition of respect for the teacher. Therefore, the teacher, support staff, and administration of the district need to reach out to parents and families of ESOL students to encourage their more active participation.

The parents' or family's initial contact with the school or district is generally during the enrollment process. Initial enrollment may take place at a "Welcome Center" in a district with a large ESOL population or, more typically, at the neighborhood school. Frequently, parents who do not speak English bring along a family member or friend to facilitate communication who has little more knowledge of English than the parent. Whatever the point of initial contact, the district should make the family feel welcome. Signs in a variety of home languages common to the district's students, identifying the main office, testing center or whatever offices the family will need to visit, provide a sense of welcome and comfort before personal contact is ever made. A sign announcing an open-door policy for parent visits also shows parents that the school respects them and their heritage, and wants them to participate in their childrens' education. Whenever possible, a translator should be available if the parents schedule an appointment for enrollment. Frequently, however, parents simply show up at the school speaking no English and having no idea of what to do to enroll their children. Some ESOL parents quietly drop off their children without a word to anyone! In the case of older students, some are sent to school alone to enroll themselves because they speak some English and the parents don't speak any. It is hard to even imagine the amount of courage this takes on the part of the parents and the children!

It is helpful if the school or district secretary who is responsible for receiving new families speaks the language of the majority of ESOL students who enroll in a particular district. If that is impossible, or if the district or school has no one language that is spoken by a majority of ESOL students, the receptionist or someone quickly available to the reception area should learn basic greetings in a number of languages common among the children who already live in the district. What is really important, however, is not so much being able to greet the parents and children in their native language, but that this first point of contact be someone who is comfortable with foreign-language speakers, and who is at least

We have seen fear and disappointment on parents' faces as secretaries and even administrators literally scream at them in English, as if speaking loudly will make them understand. Annoyance or displeasure is also a clue to ESOL student's parents that they are not truly welcome. Imagine having to leave your child with someone who reacts to you in this manner. Respect and politeness are cultural givens in the lives of many immigrant families. Most of the families we have worked with over the years view the U.S. education system as the most important key to their children's success. They all want the best possible education for their children, and the vast majority of immigrant parents respect teachers and will go out of their way to do everything the school or teacher asks of them, if they understand what that is.

aware that he or she should avoid body language, facial expressions, or other indicators of displeasure or annoyance on learning that the family does not speak English.

Some districts with ESOL populations have one day a month when a translator is available at a particular school for enrollment and parent conferences. Once the schools advertise this arrangement, parents and family members are willing to wait until the "right day" to enroll their child or meet with their child's teacher. Other districts provide each school with a short publication describing the enrollment process and necessary documents in as many as 12 languages to be given to the family spokesperson. These pamphlets describe the enrollment process, how to make an appointment at the testing center to meet with a guidance counselor, attendance, and other policies and procedures. Reaching out means above all not pushing parents away. If the parent or spokesperson hands the pamphlet back to the secretary, it may mean that the pamphlet is written in the wrong language or the family has no one who is sufficiently literate to read it. We have spoken to ESOL parents who left a school believing their children had been denied entrance when, in fact, the secretary had just been unable to make the parents understand that they would have to come back at another time, or that they would have to go to the "Welcome Center," or that they needed documentation and/or a completed medical form to process the student.

One proactive strategy is to develop a "Newcomer Video" in a variety of appropriate home languages to serve as a guide, not only to enrollment, but also to other basic services that can be accessed via the school or district. The videos can even be checked out in some districts, and this approach helps the family with no literate members. Some districts have handbooks translated into numerous languages. Through strategies such as these, families who arrive at the school or district office speaking no English still have immediate access to important information regarding the enrollment process or requesting a translator. Videos and handbooks should address the information outlined in Exhibit 6.1.

The manual or video should be comprehensive yet simple, and include a clear rationale for parent involvement in their children's educational process.

Bronfenbrenner (1979) asserts that effective partnerships can be established between schools and families that foster development of mutual trust. ESOL students' parents appreciate efforts to establish an initial exchange of information that can form the foundation for

Exhibit 6.1
New ESOL Student Orientation

*Outline of Basic Information to Include
in Newcomers' Handbook or Video**

GENERAL INFORMATION

- Welcome
- How and where do I enroll my child in this district?
- Statement about parents' role in their child's education
- Which school will my child attend? (simple maps are helpful here)
- What special programs are available to help my child gain English proficiency?
- What special programs are available to help my child on academic-content grade level while learning English?
- How is my child's grade level determined? How are grade levels divided among schools?
- What are the names given to the various levels of education in the district (elementary, middle school, high school)?
- Will the school district accept credits earned toward graduation from other countries?
- Can the district help me access previous records from other schools?
- What are the expenses related to my child's education?
- Who can participate in free/reduced-cost lunch programs?
- What do I do if my child will be absent from school?
- What transportation is available to and from school? What happens if my child misses the bus?
- How do I sign up for transportation?
- Are there special procedures for nonfamily members picking up the child at school?
- How are children assigned to a classroom or teacher? How are they grouped for instruction?
- Is there anyone available in the school who speaks my child's native language?
- What is special education? Inclusion?
- What are the hours of the school day?
- What subjects are taught in each grade level?
- What high-school graduation requirements or promotion requirements will my child be expected to meet?
- How does the school determine my child's level of English-language proficiency?
- What program options are available for my child? Do I have the opportunity to voice my opinion about my child's placement?
- How long does an English learner typically remain in a special program?

- What are advanced placement courses? Gifted programs?
- What alternative education programs are available (charter schools, vocational schools)?
- Are there extended day services available for working parents?
- Is there a Head Start or other preschool program available?
- What is "summer school"? How do I know if summer school would help my child?

INFORMATION ON GRADING, PROMOTING, AND TESTING STUDENTS
- What is a report card? What does the parent do with a report card? What do the report card symbols mean?
- What is a _____ grade? (citizenship, work habits, attitudes)
- What procedures are followed if my child is having an academic or behavior problem? If the teacher wants to retain my child?
- Are there alternative ways to obtain a high-school diploma or equivalent?
- How is student progress assessed?
- What tests are given every year? What do the scores mean?

INFORMATION ON FAMILY INVOLVEMENT IN THE SCHOOLS
- Why should I become involved in my child's education?
- Who else in my family should become involved?
- How can I help my child at home with his or her learning?
- Should I speak only English at home?
- How can I learn about American culture and/or schools?
- What legal rights do I have as a parent?
- What do I do if I disagree with something the school is doing with my child?
- What are some of the ways I can participate in my child's education?
- How do I access a translator if I need help communicating with a teacher or administrator?

INFORMATION ON THE STRUCTURE OF THE PUBLIC SCHOOL SYSTEM
- What is the structure of the school system?
- Is the system the same in every state? In every school?
- What major agencies have an effect on what the public school does?
- What is the role of the various professional members of staff (teacher, IST teacher, ESL teacher)?
- What is the structure of elementary, middle, and high schools?
- Who controls the schools in this district?
- How are the schools financed?

INFORMATION ON WHAT TO DO IF THERE IS A PROBLEM OR CONCERN
- Who can answer my questions?
- If I am not satisfied with the teacher, principal, guidance counselor, bus driver, etc., what are my options?

- What is an IST?
- What is an MDE?
- What is an IEP?
- What is cooperative learning? Integrated curriculum? Whole language? Block scheduling? Looping? Flexible grouping?

*Adapted from Faltis, 1993, and Diaz-Rico, 1993.

a multilevel outreach effort. Faltis (1993) proposes an approach to home-school relationships in which teachers assume the primary responsibility for getting parents and/or other family members involved by focusing on balancing opportunities for teachers to learn about the home environment of the students while parents and family members learn about school programs, activities, and policies. Rasinski and Fredericks's (1989) models served as the foundation for Faltis's approach, which begins with the teacher taking the initiative to learn about the ESOL student's parent and family community support systems and the sources of stress they face in order to empower the parents of ESOL students. Exhibit 6.2 depicts four levels of involvement.

While only a few parents are likely to reach Level IV, a substantial proportion of parents, with patience and encouragement, should reach Level III. Generally, ESOL parents can be encouraged to participate in their children's learning if the approach taken considers their cultural background and makes it comfortable for them to do so. This participation can serve as an important part of their own acculturation and social integration. Teachers who acquire strong intercultural communication skills can frequently help parents bridge the gap between home and school culture and language.

Faltis's (1993) Level I necessitates considerable homework by the classroom teacher, especially when the language and culture of ESOL student is new to the school or district, because the teacher must learn about the newcomers' culture, language, and constraints without the benefit of former teachers' insights. Teachers who learn the circumstances of immigration, home environment, and English-language knowledge of the parents and other family members gain important insights for guiding the students' learning and for encouraging the parents' participation. There are several excellent sources of general information regarding cultures that may help teachers in this first level, but home visits are probably the most im-

Exhibit 6.2
*A Multilevel Approach to Family Involvement**

Level	Teacher	Family/Student
I	Learns about family's experiences in community Initiates contact with parents and family with home visit Works with caregivers of child to demonstrate importance of child's progress Learn basic cultural information about child's home culture	Enrolls children in school or Welcome Center Makes provisions for placement testing Reads newcomers' manual Interviews teacher or family liaison
II	Keeps parents informed of child's progress via notes, newsletters, and telephone calls	Provides feedback on child's adjustment and other sharing
III	Invites parents to observe/participate in classroom: information observation Provides parents with opportunities to learn how to foster/reinforce child's learning	Informal involvement in class, school, community Helps with activities, special events; activities by family/caregivers Participation in family literacy programs Parent/older sibling GED programs Parent groups
IV	Assists parents to involvement in school/community at decision-making level	Organize work groups, Parent Advisory Councils; become advocate for children

*Adapted from Faltis, 1993.

portant activity at Level I. Some districts use a native-speaking paraprofessional who works with teachers on Level I goals. In other instances, community members are trained to serve as family liaisons. The home visit permits the teacher or liaison to obtain firsthand knowledge about the living conditions, other residents living in the family home, part-time caregivers, parental and family attitudes toward education, family work schedules, and resources (Delgado-Gaitan, 1990; Olsen, 1988). The purpose of the visit should be communicated clearly to ESOL family before the visit.

Sometimes parents experience unnecessary stress and fear because they assume that visitors from the school are trying to get information about the family's alien status or home conditions, to take sanctions or encourage investigation by public welfare. Other parents may assume that their child is in terrible trouble for the teacher to take the time to visit the parents in their home. Home visits should never be related solely to severe problems. Family members should expect the visit as an integral part of the school enrollment process. Before the visit, the teacher or liaison should make a special effort to learn about protocols or taboos, including greetings, leave-taking rituals, and politeness formulae. (Delgado-Gaitan, 1990; Wong-Fillmore, 1990). Teachers/family liaisons should outline a plan for each home visit, but it is especially critical to do so for the first visit (see Exhibit 6.3).

Teachers should also investigate community-based resources that provide information and support to CLD families prior to the visit. In districts with comprehensive or integrative service models, teachers should compile a list of services or bring along a booklet on the services in the family's L1 if available. The home liaison of a friend or relative may translate if the publication is not in English, and may also help the family access the services.

If the family has no adult member who can serve as translator and a family liaison is used instead, Faltis (1993) points out that a clear working relationship should be established between the family liaison serving as translator and the teacher. The family liaison must provide the teacher not only with a literal translation of information shared by the family members, but also with insights on parents' reactions to the visit, the school, and the teacher. Most important, the liaison must feel comfortable sharing perceived cultural nuances. Newcomers to the community always appreciate information on places to shop for ethnic foods and to attend church services in the L1. Some districts include this type of information in their hand-

Exhibit 6.3
Sample Home Visit Plan

Family Name: _____

Student Name: _____

Teacher Name: _____

Family Liaison Name: _____

Date: _____ Time of Visit: _____

Type of Visit (Circle): Welcome Visit
Scheduled Visit
Conference Visit
Intervention Visit

Introduction Activity:

Structure of Visit:

Materials Provided:

Date of Next Visit: _____

Comments or Visit Evaluation (to be filled out after the visit):

books for newcomers; others prefer to mention this information during the first visit. Moll, et al. (1988) refer to this information as *funds of knowledge* information, which is essential to the family's adjustment and sense of well-being, and recommend that teachers integrate this information into thematic units on community in the classroom.

Family liaisons may assume responsibilities well beyond translating. The scope of the position depends on whether the position is voluntary or paid, part-time or full-time, professional or paraprofessional. In some districts, ESL teachers become the liaison; in other districts it is the domain of a bicultural/bilingual school social worker. All family liaisons must be active listeners with strong interpersonal skills who are willing to collaborate with classroom teachers and parents. Liaisons frequently serve as sounding boards for parents and teachers alike and as guides for families. It is critical that they speak, read, and write the L1 of the families to which they are assigned.

The knowledge derived from the prehome visit learning process of the teacher is especially useful to districts that are just beginning to experience enrollment of ESOL students from a variety of cultural backgrounds. Teachers who develop a stock of information about customs, culture, and community resources for particular language backgrounds or ethnic groups may become excellent sources for staff development as the district's ESOL population grows. The knowledge derived from the visit itself will also help the teacher design individually appropriate strategies for parents to monitor their student's school work. For example, the local YM/YWCA's Homework Club may have a Vietnamese-speaking counselor every Wednesday from 3 P.M. to 6 P.M. who can work with ESOL children until their parents arrive to escort them home. At this time the volunteer explains the students' assignments for the rest of the week to the parents, or suggests to the parents books that they may want to check out of the public library, for example.

A modest approach at the first home visit might be to ask the parent(s) or other family members to spend at least three minutes every evening discussing schoolwork with their children in their home language. Parents should be encouraged to use their home language with their children. Many parents attempt to use only their own limited English to communicate with their children, either to model the importance of English to the children, or because they believe or have been told that it will help the child if only English is spoken at home. Unfortunately, speaking broken English limits the quantity and quality of conversation between family members and children. Instead, teachers should encourage preservation of the primary language in ESOL students' homes by suggesting that parents, grandparents, and older siblings work with the student on a variety of activities related to their schoolwork in their home language. Furthermore, teachers should find ways to demonstrate their respect for the home language.

The second level of parent/family involvement (Faltis, 1993) increases the kinds of communication between school and home. Parents should receive consistent communication by means of notes, telephone calls, informal conferences regarding their children's progress, classroom activities, and upcoming school and community events. Information sharing should become increasingly more of a two-way exchange of information as trust grows. Teachers can encourage this two-way exchange initially by asking questions, opinions, or advice of the parents. Whenever possible, these communications should be translated into the home language, a strategy that demonstrates respect for linguistic background of the parents.

Level III (Faltis, 1993) participation in the classroom and school activities should begin as soon as the teacher senses that family members are responding positively to the two-way communication and information sharing. Getting parents or other family members, such as grandparents, aunts or uncles, to observe informally in the classroom or help with a class or school activity is a major step in fostering parents' understanding of American education. The observations also provide models of adult-child interactions that parents can readily use in their own interactions with their children at home in supporting and monitoring their studying and work habits. The teacher should encourage the parent or family member to ask questions and offer opinions about strategies used in the classroom. It is not unusual for parents who respond to Level I and II activities to resist Level III activities for a variety of reasons. Often work schedules make participation during the school day impossible. When this is the case, the teachers need to maintain contact and solicit family members' insights or ideas about alternative strategies for their involvement and that of other working parents. Parents' ideas may result in new avenues for involvement, not only for parents who provide the idea but for others, as well. It may also be an important beginning in taking a leadership role for the parent who shares an idea that is implemented. This type of interaction tends to empower the contributor.

The teacher who senses that a parent or other family member is hesitant to come into the classroom to observe because of fear or lack of confidence may invite the family member to observe for "just five minutes" when dropping off the child in the morning. Sometimes parents who are extremely uncomfortable with the idea of becoming involved in a classroom activity need to pay many five-minute visits before they are comfortable remaining in the classroom for a whole activity. Other times the family member is simply integrated into an activity by their child's or another's enthusiasm. Frequently, adults who speak English as a second language are more comfortable speaking in English with children than adults, and cannot resist being led by a child who requests their help or asks them to take a look at a new project or accomplishment, even when the adults do not understand exactly what it is that the child wants them to do. Family members who work may be willing to become chaperones, participate in, or organize Saturday field trips or projects. Classroom or schoolwide programs such as potluck dinners may bring other family members to the school, especially if they are encouraged to share something from their native culture. It is often helpful if family members who attend such functions are introduced to other ESOL students' parents. Some schools have been successful in initiating this third level of involvement by having a "Culture Breakfast," a program where a different culture is featured each month and family members just drop by on their way to work for the day.

As family members become more comfortable observing in the classroom, the teacher can point out strategies that might improve their participation in their child's learning at home. Even parents who speak no English will acquire skills through observation, and if a translator is available or a child becomes their translator, they will learn even more quickly how to support their student's learning. ESOL parents participating in the work of the classroom also provide mainstream students with the benefit of their cultural and linguistic diversity. Native-English-speaking students learn that teaching and learning can take place in any language. They also learn strategies for intercultural communication, words and phrases in a second language, and how people are alike in many ways despite their cultural and linguistic differences. Children who are from the same cultural and linguistic background as the participating parents

One ESL teacher in Freemansburg Elementary School has developed a program model for encouraging not only parent involvement in their child's education, but parent participation in a learning community that includes parents, their children, teachers, and preservice teachers from a neighboring college. Rita Hatton's "SOS" (Sharing Our Stories) model has received national attention (Education Week, 1997,7(16)) and a grant from the National Foundation for Improvement of Education. It has fostered parent involvement and children's pride, not only in their cultural heritage but also in their parents, and at the same time has helped teachers develop an understanding of culture that would not be possible with most traditional staff development programs. The "SOS" program is initiated in the fall of the school year as students begin exploring their own cultures and those of their classmates with a focus on how cultures are different and alike. They begin the process of producing a multimedia autobiography, and, during the second semester, parents are invited to class one night a month to help their children expand these autobiographies. After parents and children work together on the autobiographies at classroom computers, the entire group shares their stories. Parents have an opportunity to communicate in English with other non-native-English-speaking parents, which reduces communication stress and fosters new friendships in the community. Parents have participated readily and enthusiastically in these sessions, which focus on a variety of topics such as autumn holidays, weddings or other traditional rituals, and food. At each session, more parents bring artifacts from their own culture, talk more to explain their children's comments, and ultimately recognize the positive impact they have on their children's learning and enthusiasm for school activities. Several parents who lacked literacy skills in English sought ESL classes after a positive experience in this nonthreatening classroom environment. For one parent, the sessions introduced technology that gave her new direction in her career decision process. The teacher noted that parent participation in the classroom increased markedly after the "SOS" experience, and that parents also began socializing with and participating in some community groups as the result of their experiences with "SOS."

have their native culture confirmed, and family members of ESOL children may experience satisfaction at being present in the classroom and able to contribute to their child's education. Subsequently, parents and family members may also volunteer to make bulletin boards, prepare class materials, or serve food at schoolwide events, all without much more than a basic understanding (Beginner Level) of English.

Each experience the family member engages in serves to expand the immigrant's social interaction beyond the ethnic community, and provides the family member with a greater understanding of school programming, the educational system, and the greater community, thus helping his or her acculturation and social integration. Many parents begin to view the school as a genuine resource for acculturation and recognize that they have valid contributions to make to their child's education, the school, and the community in which they live despite their limited English proficiency. The parent is affirmed as a member of a new community and culture and, in some cases, becomes active at the community level.

This realization by parents and other family members that they have valuable contributions to make and that their ideas, opinions, and concerns are valid and valuable helps to move them to Level IV

Pajaro Valley parents worked with teachers to implement a highly successful family literacy program (Ada, 1988), while other ESOL parents established escuelitas for after-school tutoring of their children (Padilla, 1982). In the BASD, parents support the Latino Youth Leadership Group's "Puerto Rico Day" celebration in a variety of ways. Other ESOL parents may initiate a Parent Advisory Council to represent their views on the education of ESOL students to school directors and local government officials. Parents may ultimately become involved in a variety of community activities as the result of their empowerment, and, in doing so, expand their own and their children's social integration and cultural and linguistic knowledge of the greater community. Level IV parent involvement is highly rewarding and generally results in higher levels of acculturation, English-language development, and social integration into the greater community for the entire family.

(Faltis, 1993), where they begin to take an active role in decision making and policies related to their child's education. Rasinski and Fredericks (1989) refer to this type of participation as the *empowerment level*. This level is reached only after trust and a collaborative relationship have been established. Parents now assume a leadership role and work with other parents of ESOL students or with mainstream parents in organizations such as the PTA or on committees related to curriculum, community building, and other concerns. These empowered parents may recognize children's needs that have gone unnoticed by professionals and work cooperatively with other parents to meet the needs.

Outreach efforts of teachers and administrators are critical in helping children and youth adjust to their new country and to maintaining nurturing, caring relationships with parents and other family members. Some districts with more homogeneous language backgrounds of ESOL students are offering teachers the opportunity to study their students' home language. When families learn that teachers and administrators are making an effort to learn the language of ESOL families, they sense the sincerity of the district's welcome to newcomers.

While a plan for welcoming new ESOL students and their families is critical to a full-service program, and while a plan for parent and family involvement will go a long way toward fostering a partnership between the school and the home, which has been demonstrated to improve student achievement, many children's families need more intensive services if students are going to succeed in school.

Family Centers and Integrated Service Models

Many school districts are developing "family centers" as an integral part of their services for ESOL students. The family center philosophy is that the most effective way to ensure the healthy development of children is by supporting the families and communities in which children live. Family centers allow all segments of the community, including parents, Head Start, local government, schools, public and private agencies, and businesses, to collaborate as equal partners in identifying and achieving mutual goals. These collaborations serve and empower families, their children, and entire communities. The centers provide integrated services that any family can access easily. Duplication of services is eliminated, and service providers work together so that no child or family "falls through the cracks." Thus, families are supported in their efforts to care for themselves. Typical family centers provide services such as:

- Parent support and parent education programs
- Home-based early childhood education
- Health care information and assistance in accessing health care services
- Child development activities or programs
- Toy and resource libraries
- Comprehensive access to information about access to services provided in the community

Most family center services are provided at school sites to families through referral to other service agencies in the community. Pennsylvania is a national leader in the development of family centers. In collaboration with the Pennsylvania departments of Education and Health and Public Welfare, family centers integrate and provide effective services to help families and children to become and remain healthy, economically independent, and educated. One of the advantages of family centers is that they are located in or linked to schools and offer programs, activities, and services designed to meet the unique needs of families and their communities.

In the BASD, three elementary schools serving substantial ESOL student populations have family centers. The philosophy of these centers is grounded in the following principles:

- Families are individually unique and enrich communities with diversity, so support for families needs to respect these differences.
- Nothing in a child's life has more impact than his or her family, so when families are supported, their capacity to meet the needs of the children is expanded.
- Every community has resources that may be combined into a unified, systematic effort to support families more effectively.
- Every child has the capability to learn, but primary health care and child development knowledge on the part of parents are essential to fostering this capacity.
- The integrity of the family must be preserved, and convenience and access to services should support family priorities over system priorities.

Not a new component of the school system, family centers are a community process in which all members of the community are equal partners in identifying and achieving mutual goals and objectives. Such centers provide community-driven service integration that identify and remove barriers to services and develop and administer the most effective practices and use of resources of various agencies.

Family centers in the BASD are a place where parents can share and support one another, learn about community resources, and receive services. Center activities are not limited to the center's physical boundaries, but involve many interagency partnerships that evolve from the parents' input, social service agencies, government agencies and officials, and community leaders. These centers do not usually provide new programs so much as they link already existing services at the local and state levels. They are also an important step forward in moving schools from a reactive model of social services and intervention to a proactive, preventative mode. This model seeks to empower families to care for themselves and their children. See Exhibit 6.4 for a comparison of reactive and proactive social services models.

Family centers in the BASD have active governing boards made up of parents and key stakeholder groups in the community. The governing board has authority over the actions of the family center and collaborates with other community planning committees to map community and family assets, assess community needs, identify service gaps, and influence local policies. The governing board has three standing committees:

1. Consumer and Resource Partnership
2. Planning and Evaluation Committee
3. Steering Committee

These committees meet twice a month. The BASD family centers offer the services listed in Exhibit 6.5, but services offered vary based on community, school, and family needs.

The "Parent as Teacher Program" is the State of Pennsylvania's required parenting program used in all family centers in the state. It is based on parent instruction carried out in the homes of families with children up to age 5. This program teaches parents that they are their child's first and best teachers and provides classes in parenting based on the child's developmental level. The Family Center at the Marvine School (a high-impact ESOL elementary school) has over 100 participating families.

Exhibit 6.4
Family Centers Compared with the Traditional Social Services Model

Family Centers	Traditional Models
Proactive	Reactive
Emphasize early intervention	Crisis-oriented services
Cooperative, collaborative, coordinated service delivery Pooled resources of many agencies	Individual agency agendas
Focus on family unit	Focus on individual
Build on strengths	Emphasize weaknesses
Family as active participant	Family as recipient of services
Respect for individual and cultural differences	One approach for all
Ease of accessibility to a wide range of services	Inflexible hours of operation Waiting lists for services
Home-, school-, neighborhood-based	Office-based
Effectiveness measured by improved outcomes	Effectiveness measured by use of services

Family-to-Family Foster Care Reform Initiative

One cooperative venture that originated through the family center model is a cooperative effort between the Northampton County Department of Human Services and the BASD Marvine Family Center designed to prevent foster care placements, avert disruption of foster care placements, facilitate the return of children already in foster care to their families, and recruit culturally and linguistically diverse community-based foster families in the Marvine-Pembroke neighborhoods. Two staff members provide individual and family counseling, education about foster care to all family members, assistance with life-management tasks, resource liaisons, foster parent recruitment, development of mentoring relationships between foster care families and birth families, and service referral for each family.

Exhibit 6.5
BASD Family Center Services

Health
Two pediatric clinics
Free immunizations and lead screenings
HIV/AIDS testing and counseling
OB-GYN, diabetes, and family health referral information

Social
County children, youth and family information
Women, Infant, and Children Services (WIC)
Resources and referral for child care information services
Substance abuse support groups
Youth clubs
Parenting support groups
Legal Aid referral and information services
PTO technical support
Foster care training and referral
Vision screening
Family counseling services
Cancer caregiver support groups
Parent workshops ("Budgeting," "Domestic Violence," "Menopause and Women's Health," "Child Abuse and Safety Issues")

Education
Adult GED programs
Adult ESOL programs
New Choice programs for displaced homemakers

After-School and Recreational Programs
Boy Scouts
Girl Scouts
Girls, Inc.
Dance class
Teen conferences
College visitations

The Wraparound Model

The wraparound model is based on individualized, needs-driven service planning. Its goal is to create services for children on an individualized basis to provide inclusive options for meeting the needs of students and their families. An individualized plan is developed by a "Child and Family Team." The service plan is family-centered rather than child-centered because the family is generally a constant in the child's life while the service system and its personnel fluctuate. The parent is the owner of the plan and is an integral part of the planning team that works collaboratively. This model focuses on strengths rather than deficits, with the team committing to services adapted to the needs of the family and the children. Services are community-based, culturally appropriate, comprehensive, and flexible. The team encourages family-to-family support and networking as another way to empower community members and affirm the skills of CLD parents Deciding whether a family needs a wraparound plan reflects several of the following criteria:

- Several systems are already involved in meeting the needs of the child.
- The child is dually diagnosed.
- The child's current arrangement is collapsing.
- The child has been referred for services out of his or her neighborhood, county, or state.
- The child is at risk for separation from his or her family.
- The child is pregnant.
- Local agencies have rejected the child.
- The child has severe disabilities.
- The child is medically fragile.
- Other children in the family are also at risk.
- The child is returning from an out-of-home placement.

The child and family team consists of the parent or surrogate parent, the child, the appropriate representative of the state, a lead teacher or vocational counselor, the child's therapist or counselor, any other person who is significant or influential in the child's life or the parent's life (neighbor, counselor, physician, coach), and a resource coordinator. The resource coordinator is responsible for ensuring that services are coordinated and accountable. Regular meetings are scheduled during the first six months of the plan, which are held in settings in which the family and child are comfortable.

The programs in the BASD were designed specifically to the needs of their context and local and state mandates, so they probably cannot be adopted directly by another district. Since these programs are relatively new (1994), there are no longitudinal records of their success, but related research on child development and school success document that this district is at least moving in the right direction toward dealing with the many noncultural and nonlinguistic variables in a child's life that may have a major impact on the child's academic achievement and life in general.

Part Three

꿵

Program Administration

Part three of this book carefully examines the processes and concerns related to ESL program administration, including program development, supervision, and evaluation. These three processes are totally integrated in nature and purpose. School directors or administrators evaluate the demographic information they have and decide whether ESL programming must be developed or revised to meet the needs of ESOL students. The ESL program administrator and principal make decisions based on this needs assessment and design a program that meets the needs of ESOL children to maintain and further their academic background, facilitate their English-language development, and foster their socialization and acculturation. The program is implemented and supervised by building principals and the program administrator, and it is developed further as it is practiced. The process is essentially that of a *praxis-reflection* approach, whereby structures and processes are evaluated "by the doing" as much as by the results.

Chapter Seven

Program Development, Administration, and Evaluation

This chapter focuses on the actual process of developing a high-quality program for ESOL students that meets state and federal mandates to provide equal educational opportunity to ESOL students. Appendix B lists state mandates and statutes related to programming for ESOL students, and the name and telephone number of the state official(s) responsible for CLD programs within each state's department of education. However, state requirements change frequently, so the program designer(s) should contact the state department of education representative for language-minority education for specific information. The same representative should be able to provide information on districts with high-quality programs already in existence that the designer(s) may want to contact or visit. State contacts are also an excellent resource for information on staff development opportunities, instructional resources and materials, and consultants and, in many cases, can supply technical assistance for grant writing and follow-up.

Before continuing, we want to remind administrators of the importance of recognizing that special services designed for students classified as CLD or LEP on the basis of language testing only may not provide equal educational opportunities for all bilingual/bicultural students because the definition of an "advanced" or "exited" student in most programs does not necessarily equate with "success." These students may well need continued support on a regular or periodic basis to allow them to reach their academic potential and facilitate their becoming truly bilingual and bicultural. Even students who exit high-quality ESL programming need continued support to further the process of acculturation and social integration and, in most cases, also need academic support to deal with highly abstract or culturally loaded content.

While all U.S. public schools ideally would have bilingualism as a desirable outcome for all students, scarce resources may dictate that districts focus on fostering bilingual/bicultural students primarily among their ESOL population. Unfortunately, some professionals still advise parents of ESOL students to avoid speaking their home language to the students and not to allow these students who may already be literate in their L1 to continue reading for enjoyment or learning in that language because it 'interferes" with their English development. Some may even punish students for using their native language in the school. We strongly recommend that districts seriously examine the context of their community in terms of home languages and determine if a dual-immersion program might be appropriate. However, the majority of districts will find staff resources for such a program very difficult to provide and may need to limit dual immersion to one magnet school setting to which parents may choose to send their children.

A successful magnet program could easily lead the way to a more extensive dual-immersion model over a period of time if administrators provide proper resourcing and encourage media coverage of the program. Positive public relations and media coverage sometimes facilitate obtaining high-quality bilingual/bicultural staff members necessary for program expansion. But what is the district's ultimate goal: dual-immersion programming, maintenance-bilingual education programming, or structured-immersion? Ultimately, this question returns us to our list of policy questions at the beginning of part two.

- Should all, part, or none of ESOL students' academic experience take place in their native language?
- What program model will be most effective in simultaneously facilitating ESOL students' academic achievement, English-language development, acculturation, and social integration?
- How can we ensure that the educational experiences of ESOL students have the same academic rigor and access to academic core curricula available to native-English speaking students?
- How can we structure school environments and implement district curricula to allow all students to benefit from the ESOL students'cultural and linguistic diversity?
- How can we structure school environments and implement district curricula to foster ESOL students' appreciation of their native language and culture?
- How can we integrate *ESL Standards for Pre-K–12 Students* (TESOL, 1997) into the district curricula and/or national content standards?

- How can we validly assess the effectiveness of our program in providing equal educational opportunity to ESOL students?

In answering the above, certain steps or directions may become clear. Regardless of the program type, all programs should seek to achieve the following goals:

- ESOL students will develop English-language proficiency at an appropriate level for successful social interaction and academic achievement.
- ESOL students will at the same time achieve academic-content standards of the district at an appropriate level for the students' chronological age while developing English-language proficiency, and content-area and ESOL instruction will be provided in a manner that is integrated and logical, regardless of the language of instruction.
- ESOL students will engage in experiences that will facilitate acculturation and social integration into the school and larger community through matriculation in mainstream educational experiences that at the same time validate their home culture and language and provide opportunities to ensure acculturation and social integration.

We believe that the policy questions outlined previously are an excellent starting point for administrators or district directors to consider within their own perspectives and beliefs regarding programming for ESOL students, prior to appointing a districtwide program designer or design team. Administrators will benefit from considering the complex questions and will probably face division among their ranks with regard to several of them. If no one in the district has experience in educating ESOL students, or in districts where a major controversy exists over any of the issues related to educating CLD children, it might be advisable and less expensive in the long run to hire a consultant or a consultant team to develop a program based on the program development team's needs assessment or to provide leadership for a program design team. Three possibilities exist: Turn the design of a program over to a preselected person or team within the district, hire outside consultants, or work out some combination of the two—consultants working in direct conjunction with designers.

Program Design Team Options

To develop a context-sensitive ESOL program, or to redesign an already existing model, the district administrator may want to consider developing a program design team, whose membership represents the shareholders in the project: central office administrators, principals, teachers, professional support staff, parents, and, if possible, members of the wider community. Under the heading of professional support staff, representatives from special education, guidance, and school psychologists must be included. The administrator, if supervising or conducting this preliminary step of gathering the shareholders, may serve as chair of the group, or, if local circumstances dictate otherwise, may allow some other shareholder to chair the group.

Among the first decisions the design team needs to make are these: (1) Does the team include sufficient expertise? (2) What expertise can the team provide, and is this expertise appropriate to identified needs? (3) Are there enough shareholders, and are they adequate to the task? If the answers to these questions are sufficiently affirmative, the team may then consider the policy questions formulated above. If doubts remain, call in outside professional help.

In a district such as BASD, where many staff members have extensive experience working with ESOL students over an extended period of time, an internal team is appropriate. However, in a district that is new to the issues, research, and policy related to providing ESOL students with equal educational opportunity, it makes more sense to hire outside consultants. The amount of time required to familiarize a design team with the intricate program, learning, political, and social issues and research related to program design would be extremely prohibitive for staff with other responsibilities. In fact, a thorough mastery of this integrated and often technical information (linguistics and cognitive science) would take a minimum of 2 to 3 years of full-time reading and analysis. The type and number of variables affecting the success of the program may be presented more quickly and holistically to the program design team in summary form by a consultant who can then provide additional specific information as the design team requests.

At all times, the more honest reflection the shareholders engage in, the better the chances for a realistic and high-quality program.

Consultancy Options

Administrators and the program design team first and foremost need to accept that no single approach guarantees success, that the design team will from time to time feel its task is impossible, and that the process will take more than a year considering the policy issues related to programming to training professional staff to implement the program. An experienced program consultant will take the design team through the process described in Exhibit 7.1.

A consultant should have a thorough grounding and experience in program development and evaluation design, an understanding of second-language development including the psychosocial factors that affect second-language development, program models and the research related to each model, characteristics of effective programs, and the variables that affect the model selection process. The consultant needs to be well informed about the community's

---

Variations in Consultant Roles

District A: Consultant trained program design team members for three days on the following topics: Second-Language Development, Intercultural Communication Skills, Research on Program and Instructional Models, Program Evaluation Options, and ESOL Student Assessment and Needs.

Then consultant reviewed and critiqued program designed by program design team. A second consultant was hired to conduct formative program evaluation, and the first consultant was responsible for a two-day training session for ESL teachers and teaching staff.

District B: Consultant conducted needs assessment with input from design team and staff; then design team worked with consultant to design program and program evaluation.

District C: No consultant was used for program design, but consultant was hired to train teachers to improve teaching strategies for ESOL students in regular classroom settings.

demographics, the district's ESOL student population, the language(s) and culture(s) of the community, and the sociopolitical context of the community. In the absence of this knowledge, the consultant must conduct a needs assessment before beginning the design process. Once policy decisions are made, the program consultant is hired (if needed), and a needs assessment has been conducted and analyzed, the program design team is ready to make decisions about the program model itself.

Additional Points to Consider: Clearly Stated Goals

Carter and Chatfield (1986) report attributes present in effective elementary schools serving Mexican-American, African-American, and Asian-American students in California, which suggests that structures of pedagogy, administration models, and classroom organization are not as closely related to effectiveness as processes. They divide their analysis into two parts. Part I of the report focuses on specific characteristics that are crucial to the development of effective schooling and, thus, to a positive school, including a safe and orderly environment; positive leadership; a strong academic orientation; clearly stated goals, objectives, and plans; and well-conceived methods for monitoring faculty input and student outcomes. Part II of the report focuses on the establishing a positive social climate and high staff expectations for children and the instructional program, a strong demand for academic performance, denial of the cultural deprivation perspective and its supporting stereotypes, high staff moral—which is the result of strong internal support and consensus building, job satisfaction, sense of personal efficacy, sense that the system works, sense of ownership, well-defined roles and responsibilities, and beliefs and practices that resources should be expended on shareholders rather than on educational hardware and software. These studies were closely aligned with studies on effective school programs in a more general evaluation.

Program Design and Curricular Considerations

Carey (1997) has cited four key elements that characterize a workable curriculum for ESL instruction in all program types: (1) integration of content areas and language instruction; (2) accessibility of information and concepts; (3) student-centered learning; and (4) a challenging curriculum. The standard integrated curriculum, in which explicit connections are made among subject matter in math-

Exhibit 7.1
The Program Design Process Model

Policy Model Decisions
(Central Office Administration and School Directors)

Needs Assessment
(Central Office Administration)

Program Consultant Hired
(Consultant may need to be hired to help with Needs Assessment.)

Program Design Team Develops Model
1. Reviews state mandates and regulations
2. Conducts research review and summary
3. Explores existing programs, visiting when possible
4. Using policy decisions, needs assessment, research and evaluation studies, context requirements develops draft of program
5. Program draft reviewed/critiqued by faculty, staff
6. Program changes based on faculty, staff input

Program Coordinator Appointed or Hired
1. Training
2. Provides input on program
3. Meetings with site principals and staff
4. Plans staff development based on input from principals and staff
5. Develops program operations procedures

Policy and Procedures Developed	Program Model Designed
Program Administration Procedures Developed	Staff Development Plan Developed

Program Evaluation Design Developed

Initial Staff Development Implemented
(Program Orientation)

Program Implementation Begins

Program Formative Evaluation Begins

Program Refinement Begins with Input from
All Stakeholding Constituencies

ematics, science, language arts, social studies, and the arts, must be integrated further to include English-language development opportunities in all formal and informal learning. This involves, among other tasks, developing the vocabulary and grammatical structures associated with basic interpersonal communication skills and the academic skills required by the curriculum. This integration may require a thorough review of curricular materials and content delivery so that the curriculum is appropriate and relevant to all students.

Students need access to information and concepts found in the curriculum; this accessibility is fostered by a variety of practices, including supports such as language pairs (language buddies), primary-language instruction, and language classroom aides, while keeping in mind that ESOL students should be exposed to the same content as native English speakers. These practices should not undermine efforts to integrate ESOL student socially at every appropriate occasion.

Learning is student-centered in that all students' native languages, cultures, interests, and experiences are valued and incorporated into the curriculum as feasible and practical components of learning. This does not imply or permit the curriculum to be watered down for the so-called benefit of language minorities, nor does it imply that the curriculum should overwhelm or prove completely inaccessible to ESOL students. To this extent, a curriculum that is challenging for native speakers should look much the same as one for ESOL students, provided that some thoughtful and practical adjustments have taken place, in the spirit of Carey's four points.

Carey (1997) has also asserted that the effective administrator makes provisions to help faculty develop the skills needed to keep these points integrated into their own teaching practice. By extension, the design team must also be aware of the goals at each stage of planning, and should remember what is necessary to support these practices.

Administrators Need Training Too!

Integration of these four attributes depends on overall district operations and strategic planning, the specific training provided for district teachers and administrators, and the attitudes of the professional staff in the district. Our experience has been that successful programs do not emerge without administrators having a thorough understanding of what constitutes a high-quality program for ESOL students, and, therefore, we recommend that administrators receive extensive staff development related to programming for these students, and that building-level administrators are at least represented on the program design committee. In our conversations with teachers committed to high-quality programming for their ESOL students, we have heard them mention the principal's understanding and involvement as one of the key factors of program success.

A consultant who works with the district should provide in-service training for the program design team and serve as a facilitator to the design team during the decision-making process after the inservice training. The district may opt to have this consultant design and implement program evaluation or hire another outside consultant for this task. The advantage of using the consultant involved in program development as the evaluation consultant is that this person has gained an in-depth understanding of the context in which the program is implemented and the program goals, so he or she would spend less time developing an understanding of the program.

As if the above were not enough to occupy the harried administrator, we recommend reading Tikunoff, et al., (1992), which reports the findings of a three-year study to identify and describe successful programming for elementary- and secondary-level ESOL students. In the study, 70 programs were identified as exemplary by a total of 147 educators who have had experience in ESL education. Indicators of program excellence include (1) relative gains in English-language proficiency; (2) relative gains in academic performance; (3) the amount of time needed before full mainstreaming of ESOL students; and (4) the extent to which ESOL students met or surpassed grade promotion requirements. This study is unique in that the administrative features and techniques in the exemplary programs are reported along with the expected comments on instructional features and characteristics. Two significant administrative features were noted in all of the exemplary programs, including contextual features and administrative resource allocations. Contextual features include: (1) the presence of an individual who is responsible for instructional leadership in planning, coordinating, and administering the integration of ESL instruction; (2) the presence of expert teachers; and (3) a history of intensive staff development for all teachers in ESL programming issues, not just for those directly or predominantly involved with ESOL students. Last, exemplary programs were characterized by adequate administrative support in resourcing and supporting ESL instruction and programming.

Additional Important Steps

With or without a consultant, the administrator and design team will need to have a knowledge base on which to begin their deliberations about policy and programming decisions. Absolutely basic to a successful undertaking is an understanding of the following:

- Federal and state legal mandates related to the education of CLD students
- An understanding of second-language development from the viewpoint of modern linguistics and cognitive science
- An understanding of the process of acculturation and social integration by ESOL students familiarity with the ESL standards (TESOL, 1997)
- Projections of district demographics for at least a 10-year period program design options
- An understanding of the need to encourage maintenance or development of pride in one's first language and culture

A two-day workshop generally can provide design team members with the information they need to make informed programming decisions. It is also helpful if the design team can visit one of more districts that are contextually similar to their own district, and meet with teachers and administrators from the district(s) to hear about their reactions to and reflections on programming for ESOL students. If visiting a district is not practical, the district administration should consider bringing in a team from a district with a successful operating ESL program, or using video conferencing to communicate with such a team. The opportunity for give and take with experienced colleagues is extremely valuable to avoid reinventing the wheel or perpetuating mistakes. If videoconferencing is feasible, it would be extremely helpful to have a second conference with an experienced district team to review the team's program design before it is voted on and implemented.

After initial training of the design team, policy questions should be discussed and positions on them resolved. Decisions made with regard to these policy questions will shape the program. Once policy decisions are made, the design team can develop a program as a group effort or have the consultant develop a program design that is then reviewed and revised by the program design team. The next step is staff development. Teachers and principals working in the program should be provided with initial staff development that covers the same basic topics as the program design team experienced, but this training should also outline the rational for the program decisions that have been made.

It is helpful to allow some latitude for program changes recommended by the faculty and principals who were not on the design team at this time. As in the case of all curriculum or policy change, involving teachers and other staff who will be charged with implementing the program in the development phase of the program is a valuable factor in getting staff and administrators to make the model their own. Needless to say, it also provides staff with a deeper understanding of what they will be doing and why.

The vast majority of school districts facing the challenge of meeting the needs of ESOL students have ESOL students with heterogeneous language backgrounds. A district that is making a decision regarding language-of-instruction and attempting to decide between an English-immersion and native-language instruction program must assess the likelihood of demographic change. A district that has a homogeneous native-language ESOL student population in a particular school district may have substantial enrollment of students from one or more other native-language backgrounds five years later. The well-designed program for ESOL students needs to consider the following components, regardless of the program model implemented:

- initial assessment of English proficiency and academic-content achievement
- levels of English-language proficiency
- criteria for student exit from the program
- strategies for English-language development
- assessment strategies
- strategies for encouraging parent involvement
- strategies for providing ancillary services needed by ESOL students and their families
- strategies to ensure opportunities for social integration at the school and community levels
- curriculum coordination

Curriculum coordination is particularly important and must occur between ESL and regular classroom teachers in English-only programs, and across languages in TBE programming. Content themes at each grade level should be coordinated between mainstream classrooms and primary-language classes so ESOL students

School District D has both structured-immersion and primary-language programs in its neighborhood elementary schools. Careful attention is given to ensure that the curriculum content across all schools in both models in consistent so that these children will all have had parallel studies before they reach middle school. In addition, there is special emphasis on the transition process of students who participate in the primary-language programs. The program focuses not only on the transition in language-of-instruction but also on opportunities for social integration of primary-language students with the native-language students through frequent extracurricular activities, and cultural celebrations throughout the elementary grades.

will have access to the same core curriculum as native-English-speaking students.

Program Design for CLD Students with Special Needs: Some Problems

Gonzalez, Brusca-Vega, & Yawkey (1997) point out that "virtually all students who have historically fallen outside the mainstream in American schools are at risk for poor treatment in a system that is only beginning to adapt to their needs" (p. 4), but ESOL students are at particularly high risk if they have disabilities, since they tend to be over-, under-, or misidentified. It is not unheard of for ESOL students to be identified as disabled based on their lack of English proficiency rather than a true disability, resulting in inappropriately reduced teacher expectations for that student. Some ESOL students are at risk of being identified as having speech problems or pathologies that may be a by-product of a particular stage in language learning or development. Conversely, some genuinely disabled students are not identified as such because of a presumed English-language deficiency. This last group of students often fails to receive legally mandated services to which they are entitled. Even CLD students who are correctly identified may have individualized instruction programs (IEPs) that do not provide for services appropriate to both their learning disability and their language or cultural differences. ESL instruction or services are frequently not available to special education CLD students, mainly because of a lack of trained personnel. Finally, all administrators, teachers, and specialists look for more studies and more information to help distinguish between learning problems rooted in language difference and those rooted in genuine disability.

Districts with moderate to high numbers of ESOL students need to (1) decide whether to provide integrated ESL or native-language services, and on the context in which these services are rendered, and (2) determine which baseline services are needed and available. In addition, the district administration has to determine staffing needs and qualifications for those who are called on to diagnose and educate learning-disabled ESOL students. In any case, the goal should be a coordinated and holistic approach to identifying and working effectively with disabled students among the ESOL population (Hodgkinson, 1989). Specialized, adapted curricula for the disabled, including bilingual or ESL services and special education, should be planned and delivered, when needed, as an integrated support to the general curriculum goals and outcomes.

Legally, the IDEA (see Glossary) does contain some strong mandates regarding CLD students, but Gonzalez, Brusca-Vega, & Yawkins (1997) point out certain omissions that compromise the act's effectiveness:

- Special education administrators (SEAs) are not required to provide information on the number of CLD students with disabilities who receive or are eligible to receive special services.
- SEAs do not have to report training of persons for working with these students in their state plans.
- IDEA requires provisions for CLD-appropriate assessment but not for instruction, which may result in IEPs that address disability but not proficiency in the L1 or in English.
- Most important, many administrators fail to integrate federal and state legislation and case law to develop policies that meet the needs of the CLD special-needs population.

Schools have a legal and moral obligation to identify CLD students with special needs, to see that these students matriculate in the appropriate programs, and to monitor their progress in annual IEPs and three-year evaluations. To provide an assessment that rules out the confusion of L2 learning issues and disabilities, testing has to be administered in the child's first language, by qualified personnel, using instruments that assess all areas related to the suspected disability. Finally, the teacher, appropriate administrators, and testing personnel discuss the assessment, including in their consideration any pertinent environmental, cultural, and economic factors. Wider consideration of program development and the inclusion of CLD special-needs students is beyond the scope of this book, but we recommend that administrators make every effort to consult (Gonzalez, Brusca-Vega, & Yawkey, 1997) as an introduction to the issues.

Adapting Special Education Services for ESOL Students

Professionals with expertise in the education of ESOL students should serve on referral teams to assess students' linguistic and cultural behavior as part of an overall special-needs assessment. The ESL professional may also assist in obtaining information from, or giving information to, the parents of students under referral to special education assessment. The ESL teacher is in a good position to compare and contrast the behavior and achievement of a given student with that of others from the same linguistic and cultural group who are achieving the program's goals. All involved in CLD special-needs assessment should be aware of the following recommendations (Yeats & Ortiz, 1995):

Students should be assessed in the dominant language. If this is not possible, administrators should document attempts made to secure the services of a bilingual professional capable of such an assessment.

If interpreters are used in the assessment process, they must have at least adequate proficiency, and should have or receive training in the techniques and goals of assessment, the eligibility criteria for special services, and the roles and responsibilities of interpreters. Accuracy in determining the responses of students during assessment is vital. Additionally, school psychologists should be alerted and trained to secure the services of expert interpreters as needed.

Instruments and testing procedures should be selected to provide comparisons of students' academic achievement and language proficiency in both L1 and English, using formal and informal tools.

Students' scores should not be reported when standardized administrative format is violated or if norms are not appropriate. Instead, patterns of performance should be used diagnostically. When performance on formal and informal assessments correlates highly, investigators can be more confident of results.

As mentioned above, individuals with expertise in the education of CLD students should be included on teams when making decisions about special education eligibility.

If these considerations are included from the start, proper assessment for special-needs eligibility can be an integrated part of the program from the beginning, rather than an add-on should the need arise later.

Conclusion

Once the administrator has developed the appropriate personnel into a design team, and secured any needed outside consultation, plans for ongoing administrative and staff needs necessary for instituting and maintaining a quality program are just beginning. The next chapter describes the day-to-day administration of a program and the resourcing requirements for it. Typically, the program is under one administrator (program administrator) who reports to the overall administration. The design team's responsibilities include considering the characteristics and requirements of the program administrator.

Chapter Eight

Program Administration
and Staff Development

This chapter explores the responsibilities of the person selected to administer the program(s) for ESOL students, and the preparation of teachers and support staff to implement a high-quality program for these students. Characteristics of a successful program administrator/coordinator are outlined, and the critical nature of the position is discussed. After presenting the research to date on teachers working with CLD students, the second part of the chapter focuses on the scope and content of preparing teachers and support staff (guidance counselors, special education supervisors, content area supervisors, school psychologists, and principals) who work with ESOL students and programs to meet the needs of ESOL students. We contend that implementation of the "study support group" model at each building site is a viable approach to providing ongoing staff development and support.

As the program design team makes policy decisions, it becomes the responsibility of the consultant to ensure continuity and alignment between policy decisions and program characteristics. Some districts may opt to offer more than one program design at different schools within the district. That is, a dual-immersion magnet school may be offered at one or more sites for both native English speakers and ESOL students who learn content and a second language at the same time throughout the K–12 years. The district may also offer an English-acquisition (BASD or another structured-immersion model and traditional English-only programming for native speakers. Other districts may actually pilot two programs for ESOL students in different contexts within the district. For example, a bilingual-maintenance program may be implemented in Chinese in a school district serving only Chinese immigrant students, while a structured-immersion program may be offered in schools where ESOL students come from heterogeneous home-language backgrounds. If the district decides to have a maintenance model in one language only when serving more than one language group, the design team and administration must be prepared to deal with allegations of unequal opportunities from members of other language groups. In some states this multiple type of programming may be discouraged because of the potential for litigation by parents or community members. Regardless of the policy decisions made and the program model ultimately selected by the program design team, it is important to select a program administrator for the ESL program early in the process.

The ESL Program Administrator

A district with any ESL program implemented in multiple sites benefits immensely from appointing a program administrator. The staff member coordinating ESOL students' program may be assigned sole responsibility, or may be asked to assume responsibility for ESL programs as part of a more encompassing job description. In school districts with negligible ESOL student populations, the responsibilities of the ESL coordinator are subsumed under a variety of positions, depending on state requirements and individual expertise and interest. For example, in some districts this administration position falls under the auspices of the Director of Student Personnel Services. In others it is the domain of the Curriculum Supervisor for Literacy and Language Arts, or it may become the responsibility of the Foreign Language Supervisor or a Vice Superintendent for Curriculum. It may even become the responsibility of the Director of Special Education.

In practice, building principals are generally responsible for supervising the program and its staff at the individual sites. Districts with larger ESL programs generally find it advantageous to appoint a district director for the ESL program so that the program administrator can coordinate services and serve as an advocate for the program and to supervise ESOL teachers in cooperation with the site administrators. Regardless of who assumes official responsibility for the ESL program, whenever possible this person should be actively involved in designing the program model. Across the United States, certification requirements for professionals working with ESOL students vary widely. Check with your state department of education to ensure that the person selected will be in compliance if there is no certification specific to supervisors of ESL/bilingual programs. States vary widely on the matter of certification, from Pennsylvania which has a rapidly growing number of ESOL students and yet no certification for teachers and program supervisors who work with ESOL students, to California and Florida where the density of ESOL student population has resulted in a greater degree of attention paid to preparation and credentialing of all staff who work with CLD students.

Again, always remember that even when students are exited from a program, they remain culturally different, and mainstream classroom teachers need training on this point. Of course, a school district in a state with no credentialing requirements will benefit from hiring a seasoned administrator and staff members who are certified by another state. In many districts, however, a sudden demographic shift in the population served by a district, rather than an increase in the total district population served by the district, may make the hiring of additional faculty impossible because tenured faculty are already in place, albeit with little or no experience with ESOL students. In most districts, the teaching staff must then develop the background knowledge and instructional facilitation skills that will allow them to provide high-quality programming. In this case, it is of paramount importance to assign responsibility for the ESL program to a staff member who at least exhibits a willingness to become the program administrator, has the motivation to become knowledgeable about second-language learners, and has the self-confidence to oversee a program that may be highly visible.

A supervisor certificate in the language arts or reading is generally not sufficient preparation for planning and administering programs for CLD students. In contexts where no one is suitably trained for the position, school districts are wise to use the services of a consultant who should support the neophyte administrator in staff development. We encourage support for this administrator to obtain a certificate in K–12 TESOL or attend a variety of workshops and courses that would provide him or her with a thorough understanding of second-language acquisition, program options for ESOL students, and instructional strategies. The summer institutes sponsored by TESOL are an excellent place to start.

The staff member who is assigned responsibility for administering an ESL program is key to the program's success. As with any administration position, interpersonal skills are of the utmost importance. The program administrator serves in a multifaceted capacity—s the supervisor who ensures the integrity of the program as designed, as liaison between the central office and the principals and teachers in the field who actually implement the program, as the coordinator for ancillary services for ESOL students and their families, as the person who is responsible for ensuring that the program remains an integral part of the district's overall curriculum rather than an isolated separate "add-on" entity, and as the coordinator of program evaluation.

Ideally, the candidate selected for the administration of the program is a professional who has taught ESOL students. The particular capacity does not matter as much as the fact that the person has worked with ESOL students and their families, and ideally, with staff who are responsible for serving ESOL students. This firsthand experience helps the administrator until he or she can arrange for more systematic formal self-development. Excellent communication skills are also a must, because this person must clearly articulate the goals and features of the program to staff and the general public and to parents and ESOL students themselves. Since ESL programs are under heavy scrutiny, as they should be by the OCR, the program administrator should be willing to develop a system for record keeping to demonstrate compliance.

A background in applied linguistics, second-language learning, and previous supervisory experience is also highly desirable. Candidates for the position should recognize the unique characteristics of the job, which involve the complex task of ensuring implementation of a program staffed by personnel who all report to other supervisors. The responsibilities of the program administrator fall into four categories (Exhibit 8.1):

- curriculum development, supervision, and evaluation;
- staff development and supervision;
- communication and public relations; and
- record keeping and financial management

Exhibit 8.1 lists typical responsibilities for ESOL program administrators; of course, specific contexts require variations in this position's responsibilities.

Curriculum Development, Supervision, and Evaluation

The program administrator is responsible for aligning and re-aligning the ESL model with district curriculum standards. Using TESOL's Pre-K–12 program standards (TESOL, 1997), the administrator develops specific strategies for ensuring students are identified appropriately for inclusion in the program, changes in services based on level of English-language fluency, and exit from the program. The administrator is also responsible for a strategy to orient new ESOL students to be implemented at each school, in

Exhibit 8.1
Responsibilities of ESOL Program Director

Curriculum
Development, evaluation, and refinement
Integration of TESOL, state, and national standards
Grant writing to support program development

Program Development
Member of design team
Hires consultants as needed
Chairs internal evaluation

Program Communication
Public relations/media
Community/adult education

Staff Development
Needs assessment for staff
In-house development
Hires consultants as needed

Program Administration
Collaborates with administration to ensure compliance with legal and
    educational mandates
Budget planning
Collaborates with special education personnel and other supervisors
Communications with office/building staff

addition to any districtwide orientation that may be developed (Appendix K). The coordinator also collaborates with curriculum coordinators and textbook selection committees or other committees related to implementation of the district curriculum, such as a report card committee, or graduation requirement committee, as the advocate for consideration of ESOL students' special needs with regard to the core curriculum. This administrator is also responsible for developing and implementing program changes to parallel changes that occur in the district's general policies, curricula, or standards. The administrator is notified of any problems related to ESOL program and the general curriculum or programs, context issues resulting from variables of a particular program site, or major concerns with a particular student or students, and participates in the resolution of these problems.

When an internal program review in the BASD documented the need to improve motivating and engaging ESOL students who were not in the academic track, the program coordinator researched successful programs. After a series of biweekly meetings with interested colleagues and a local hospital, the St. Lukes Hospital/Liberty High School Health Career Program was initiated in the fall of 1997 as a pilot program serving 16 English-Acquisition Program students. These students currently spend two afternoons a week at St. Lukes Hospital with mentors who assist the as they rotate through 41 different departments to learn about careers. Classroom curricula in English and science at the high school were developed by two teachers to tie core curriculum content to students' hospital experiences. This program is sponsored by a grant written in collaboration with the program administrator and the district grant writer.

The program administrator is also responsible for the design, implementation, and reporting of internal program evaluations, as deemed appropriate by the central office administration, and for engaging outside consultants for external program evaluations. With a team of colleagues, the administrator typically reframes the program based on evaluation results or a change of context at a particular site or districtwide. In his or her role as program designer, the administrator seeks, writes, and administers grants to support a pilot program, staff development, or other additional services that have been identified as advantageous for ESOL students.

The program administrator also assumes responsibility for arranging or conducting staff development experiences related to program goals. Staff development is covered in considerable detail later in this chapter, but it is often through supervision and support of the program administrator that classroom teachers get feedback on their efforts to implement what they have learned from staff development sessions. To make the most of the very limited time on the part of the administrator for direct supervision and coaching of teachers, one ESOL program administrator trained staff in peer coaching to facilitate adoption of new teaching strategies and ameliorate the typical difficulties experienced in learning and practicing new strategies.

The program administrator may also participate in the selection and interviews of new ESL teachers and regular classroom teachers who will be assigned to schools with large ESOL populations. Once again, it becomes the responsibility of the ESL program administrator to ensure that teachers who work with ESOL students have a positive attitude toward doing so, which is especially important when so many of these teachers lack knowledge about and skills in ESL programming. The program administrator in districts with larger ESOL populations may assume responsibility for supervising any testing personnel who evaluate initial classification of students' English-proficiency level and academic background. Especially in the early implementation of a new program or during the initial implementation of major changes to an existing program, the administrator's visibility is important at various school sites. During the earliest phases of implementation of a new model or refinements to a well-established program, the administrator becomes an instructional leader through coaching, supporting, reinforcing and clarifying roles, strategies, and material use.

Communication takes up a large segment of the program administrator's time—responding to calls from administrators, teachers, parents, and even secondary-level students who have questions or concerns about the program. A program newsletter for parents and, in larger programs, for staff are monthly publications that become the domain of this position. The administrator may also collaborate with the district spokesperson when media request information on the program. Considerable additional communication focuses on coordinating ESL variations of general programs in the district, such as Reading Recovery or Special Education/ESL programming needs. In addition, the administrator represents the district at state-level organizations.

Typically, the program administrator is responsible for, or is at the least a consultant in, program budget development for the ESL program, and compiles and reports data as required by state and federal agencies (OCR, Title VII funding). In the BASD, the English-Acquisition Program coordinator initiated development of a database when consultants suggested that such data would be extremely useful in longitudinal program evaluation and in gaining insights about the outcomes of the program. This database permits rapid retrieval of information on students and individual schools, and is extremely helpful to those who are interested in collecting valid and reliable research data.

The parameters of this position since vary considerably based on the demographics of the ESOL population, the perspective of the district leadership, and the management skills of the individual holding the position. In early phases of program development and implementation, the position parameters should remain flexible, so they can be redesigned to meet the needs of the staff and the emerging program.

Building Principals and the ESL Program

While a program administrator is important for ensuring the success of a district's program for ESOL students, school site leadership is critical to the support and ultimate success of the program. Teddlie and Stringfield (1993) found that three factors, administrative appropriateness, teacher preparedness, and student readiness, combine to determine the effectiveness of any particular setting, and no single factor alone can account for positive outcomes. Principals must work closely with the ESL program administrator and are responsible for implementing the program in their building, integrating the ESL programming into the general curriculum, and citing context variables that affect implementation of the selected model and may call for some variations. Principals are also the supervisors and, therefore, the evaluators of the teachers in the program (both ESL teachers and regular content-area teachers or grade-level teachers).

The principal must also serve as the liaison between teachers who work with ESOL students currently in the program and those who serve exited students. Therefore, principals need to develop an understanding of CLD instruction. In school districts that serve a moderate number of ESOL students (10% to 30%), the majority of principals have not developed a sensitivity to the needs of the students in their buildings, or to the issues and problems experienced by the teachers and parents of these students. In successful programs, principals are strong advocates for the program at the district level and, as such, need to collaborate with teachers and the program administrator in ensuring sufficient resources, and on important issues such as ESOL student assessment, program refinement or changes, or contextually necessary program changes. They may also provide support for the program in configuration of class size and as advocates in the greater community through activities such as making presentations to citizen groups and business leaders, notifying the media for coverage of positive activities, and developing a climate of acceptance of cultural and linguistic differences (Diaz-Rico & Weed, 1995). Diaz-Rico and Weed also cited four other techniques principals can use to establish the importance of ESOL program (Diaz-Rico & Weed, 1995, p. 266):

- monitoring grading policies to ensure that all students have equal opportunities for high grades;
- providing for time to allow staff members with expertise in ESL, second-language learning, or bilingual education to serve as mentors to other teachers;
- appointing a building-level coordinator for ESL programs who can represent the principal at districtwide meetings or serve on districtwide committees;
- encouraging leaders in the building to become models of respect and encouragement for students with culturally and linguistically diverse backgrounds; and
- providing staff development opportunities that meet the needs of the entire staff.

As long as clear and consistent communication between the principal and the building coordinator is achieved, the coordinator can help reduce direct responsibility for the program from frequently overburdened principals, and bring about empowerment of faculty members in regard to planning and assessing programs for ESOL students, and foster development of new leadership in the educational community. Principals may also foster parent involvement by encouraging parents of ESOL students to participate in committees to advise and consent on program practices, making school facilities available for meetings of parents and community groups, and investigating and providing resources for parent English-language learning, GED preparation, school library use, and other programs that can be held in the school (Diaz-Rico & Weed, 1995). Collaboration between the principal and ESL program administrator is critical to program success.

Teacher Knowledge and Attitudes
Regarding Working with ESOL Students

The increasing multicultural and multilingual diversity of students in American classrooms contrasts sharply with the demographics of the current population of American teachers. At the elementary level, the majority of classroom teachers are white, female, monolingual speakers of English who represent mainstream values, behaviors, and experiences. Concomitantly, fewer minority-group members are selecting a career in education as equal opportunities in other fields become more readily available (Olson, 1993). Farrell (1990) found that only 40% of the teachers working with

ESOL students shared the native language of their students, a proportion that is decreasing rapidly with the increasing numbers of ESOL students whose home language is not Spanish. Less than 20% of the teachers working with ESOL students hold certification in either bilingual education or ESL (Fleischman & Hipstock, 1993).

In 1985, Waggoner and O'Malley conducted a national survey that determined that one in four of their teacher subjects had LEP students in their classrooms that year, but only 6% of these teachers had taken one or more credit or noncredit courses that focused on how to teach students who were ESOL learners. While 90% of the students identified as LEP received some type of special services, the majority of ESOL students received most of their instruction from regular classroom teachers who have little or no training specific to working with this population of students (Enright & McCloskey, 1985). Many students who are culturally and linguistically different pass the screening tests administered when they enter a school district and do not receive special services related to their diversity. Students who have met the district's criteria for mainstream classroom instruction often have English-language proficiency at only an interpersonal communication skills level.

These students tend to appear fluent in English, but nevertheless are likely to lack the English-language skills necessary to deal with the abstract nature of much classroom academic instruction. At the same time, the vast majority of American classroom teachers continue to use lecture or recitation as the primary vehicle for instruction, and many ESOL students who have been assessed as fully English proficient and have exited the program lack the background knowledge or English proficiency to be able to learn successfully in context-reduced, abstract instructional settings. Even classroom teachers who work solely with FEP students should become aware of the need to adapt their instruction to students who are not native English speakers. Perhaps the most difficult challenge faced by administrators of districts and schools that have steadily or rapidly increasing ESOL populations is convincing teachers that the education of these students is the responsibility of every teacher, not just ESL teachers.

Teachers also must recognize the reality that they are language teachers, including secondary teachers who teach courses such as calculus and economics. Seeing themselves as language teachers appears to be threatening to current teachers, and while there have only been a few studies examining the attitudes and knowledge base of regular classroom teachers, the data currently available indicate that extensive staff development is needed, as are changes in the content of preservice teacher curriculum if districts are to be successful in providing equal educational opportunity for ESOL students.

Penfield (1987) conducted a research study to determine what regular classroom teachers know about teaching ESOL students. She discovered that the majority of elementary teachers know very little about the conditions and strategies that foster achievement of LEP students in regular classroom settings. Many of Penfield's teacher subjects actually expressed fear that LEP students would do poorly in their classes because they were not trained in how to address these students' cultural and language needs. Respondents to Penfield's survey also believed that efforts to meet these needs would negatively affect meeting the needs of the native-English-speaking students. A more recent survey conducted by Abramson, Pritchard, & Garcia (1993) identified teachers' dissatisfaction with their own lack of knowledge, both about teaching English-language skills and adapting academic-content instruction to meet the needs of ESOL students. These teachers asserted that while they were aware of the need to be sensitive to diverse cultures and ethnicity, and they recognized the value of integrating culturally and linguistically diverse students into the mainstream classroom, they did not know the methodologies nor did they have access to the resources to do so successfully.

Simons and Connelly (unpublished data, 1997) recently conducted a more extensive study of teacher attitudes toward and knowledge about instructing ESOL students. This grounded theory study not only replicated the results of studies conducted earlier that documented that teachers still concurred 10 years after the Penfield (1987) study that they are lacking in knowledge about second-language development and strategies for simultaneously teaching academic content and fostering English-language development, but also documented that many teachers have extremely negative attitudes about the need to provide special services to ESOL students whom they viewed all too frequently as the responsibility of ESL teachers, rather than part of their own professional responsibilities.

Simons and Connelly (unpublished data, 1997) employed methods based on qualitative field studies (Bogdan & Biklen, 1992; Glaser & Strauss, 1967; Goetz & LeCompte, 1981; Spradley, 1979) to collect and analyze data about teacher attitudes and knowledge

related to teaching ESOL students in regular mainstream classrooms. Ethnographic interview methodology was used that allowed
for eclectic data collection techniques and methods of data analysis
grounded in the data themselves, enabling the investigators understand individual informants' perspectives while permitting development of generalizations from these perspectives toward the purpose
of gathering information on the current knowledge base and attitudes of regular classroom teachers (K–12). Grounded theory
methodology involves a constant comparison method of data analysis simultaneous with data collection, thus producing a study that is
grounded in the perceptions of the teachers themselves and those of
the participant observers (researchers).

Data from 274 inservice teachers and 85 preservice teachers were
analyzed. Thirty-six ESL teachers also completed the questionnaire.
Thirty-one inservice teachers, 12 ESL teachers, and 6 inservice
teachers were interviewed to triangulate data and explore perspectives in more depth. The investigators also conducted classroom observations. Practicing teacher respondents represented teachers in
seven Pennsylvania school districts. Student teachers were currently
placed in schools in Philadelphia, six suburban counties in Pennsylvania, and two suburban districts in New Jersey. These districts
range in demographic makeup from Philadelphia's highly urban and
diverse system to smaller city districts with ESOL student populations to affluent suburban districts with ESOL populations that did
not exceed 5% of the total student population of a particular district.
Note that in the past 15 years almost all districts in Pennsylvania
have experienced a rapid increase in the number of ESOL students.
A series of open-ended questions on the questionnaire and ethnographic interviews that followed, and classroom observations, were
used to collect data on the subjects' attitudes and knowledge. A constant comparison methodology was employed to analyze the data.
The main findings of the study are discussed below.

Background Knowledge

Mainstream classroom teachers in grades K–12 lacked basic understanding of language development. Mainstream classroom teachers
were almost equally divided between viewing language development from a learning theory perspective or as the outcome of an interaction of genetic and environmental variables. In subsequently
conducted interviews, only 6% of the respondents were aware of a
difference between language learning and language acquisition.

Classroom teachers' understanding of the nature of second-language development was equally limited. Teachers simply did not have a holistic view of the process of second-language learning and had an even more narrow perspective on the challenges facing students who are learning English and academic content at the same time while trying to acculturate and integrate socially. When asked to describe the differences between first- and second-language development, mainstream teachers responded as follows: 23% said there was no difference between L1 and L2 development; 11% responded that learning the L2 was more difficult; 88% indicated that the most important difference between the L1 and L2 was age; 43% commented on the fact that L2 learners often confuse the L1 and L2; and 10% believed that inhibitions about speaking the L2 as the major difference. This gross oversimplification of second-language learning development and the misperceptions about the processes indicated that many teachers make instructional decisions about their ESOL students based on inaccurate knowledge of the cognitive and psychosocial factors related to L2 development.

ESL Techniques

Survey results indicated that only 10% of the population of mainstream classroom teachers and prospective teachers had ever taken a course related to second-language learning or instruction of ESOL students, in spite of the fact that just over 80% of the teachers had worked with ESOL students in their classrooms. Both practicing teachers and student teachers had extremely limited strategies for adapting instruction to meet the multiple needs of ESOL students. There were no significant differences in knowledge between the practicing teachers and student teachers, but ESL teachers had significantly more extensive strategies for facilitating academic-content learning and English-language development than the regular classroom teachers and student teachers. In addition, ESL teachers had very different views of who was responsible for educating ESOL students; they viewed the responsibility as shared between ESL and regular classroom teachers, while regular classroom teachers and student teachers both had a less collaborative viewpoint, with English-language learning activities viewed as the responsibility of the ESL teacher and content-area instruction the responsibility of the mainstream teacher, but only after ESOL students had gained advanced proficiency in English.

Only 23% of the regular classroom teachers felt their classroom strategies facilitated language development. While a majority of teachers who worked with kindergarten, first, and second graders (60%) said they included opportunities for fostering development of listening and oral language skills in their classrooms, only 30% of third- through sixth-grade teachers believed they consistently provided instruction in listening and oral language skills. At the middle- and high-school levels, only 24% and 10%, respectively, of teachers said they fostered language learning. It is important to note that of the secondary teachers who said that they fostered listening and oral skills in English, 85% were English teachers. If this self-assessment is accurate, very few ESOL students in mainstream classrooms receive the support and activities necessary to extend their English-language learning once they exit a program that provides support for them as English-language learners. Elementary teachers, especially those in the first three grades, appeared to be significantly more confident in their ability to teach English-language skills than middle- or high-school teachers. However, this difference was not the result of staff development or personal knowledge about strategies for meeting the needs of ESOL students, but rather the coincidence of these teachers' practice of "whole language" strategies.

Responsibility for ESL Students

Fifty-six percent of secondary teachers said it was not their job to teach language. Most of the secondary teacher respondents asserted that it was their job to teach a particular academic-content area, and that teaching English was incompatible with achieving the goals and objectives of their courses and curricula. Even more distressing is the fact that the majority of these teachers thought it was the ESL teachers' job to teach English, and they did not collaborate with the ESL teachers to integrate language learning and content. In fact, 50% were adamant that ESOL students should not be in classrooms with regular students because they were not ready for academic learning until they were proficient in English. This view contrasted with the view of elementary-level teachers who believed that students with limited proficiency might be able to benefit from their classroom activities.

Teachers who report they facilitated language development in their classrooms suggested a wide range of activities for doing so, including: (1) vocabulary development before teaching content (90%); (2) opportunities for oral language and listening-skill practice (96% of the elementary teachers); (3) writing activities (76%); (4) modeling proper English (94% of all teachers; 54% of secondary teachers); and (5) introduction of grammar conventions or writing mechanics (38%). A variety (56) other strategies were mentioned by respondents, but less than 20% identified any one of these strategies.

Teacher Preparation

Responses about teaching strategies indicate that teachers are entering classrooms with ESOL students without sufficient knowledge of what their students might not understand; why they might understand it; and what they could do to facilitate the students' task of learning abstract concepts in English. Teachers felt they were not prepared to meet the needs of ESOL students (98%). Respondents who were regular classroom teachers largely agreed (98%) that they had not succeeded in involving parents of LEP students into their programs, and the majority (78%) said they did not feel LEP parents were interested in their children's education. Analysis of the data clearly presents a dismal picture of the level of preparation of teachers for working with culturally and linguistically diverse students in grades K–12.

Every respondent reported the need for staff development with follow-up observations in the classroom. Seventy-nine percent acknowledged that inservice tended to have no follow-up or support for implementation of the ideas presented in the sessions. The results of this study document that preparation of teachers for working with ESOL students is largely unchanged from 10 years ago, and that many teachers do not have minimal proficiencies for teaching ESOL students in their classrooms. Exhibit 8.2 outlines the competencies required for teachers of language-minority students as outlined by the National Association of State Directors of Teacher Education (1984).

Staff Development: Content

Hamayan (1990) suggests four major knowledge areas for staff development of teachers working with ESOL students: (1) second-language learning, (2) bilingualism, (3) sheltering instruction, and (4) grouping practices. Education of regular classroom teachers and administrators in teaching CLD students is a developmental process. Learning the basic information is not difficult, but provid-

Exhibit 8.2
NASDTEC Standards for Certification:
*Competencies Required for Teachers of Language-Minority Students**

In Bilingual Multicultural Education Context	*Corresponding Higher Education Courses*
1. Proficiency in L1 and L2 for effective communication	Foreign language and English
2. Knowledge of history and cultures of L1 and L2 speakers	Cross-cultural studies, history and civilizations, multicultural education, ethnic studies, literature
3. Historical, philosophical, and legal bases for Bilingual Education (BE) and related research	Foundations of BE
4. Organizational models for programs and classrooms in BE	Foundations of BE
5. L2 methods teaching (including ESL methods)	Methods of teaching L2
6. Communication with students, parents, and others in culturally and linguistically different communities	Cross-cultural studies, school/community relations
7. Differences between L1 and L2 language and dialect differences across geographic regions, ethnic groups, social levels	Sociolinguistics, educational psychology

In ESOL	
1. Nature of language, language varieties, structure of the English language	General linguistics, English phonology, morphology, and syntax
2. Demonstrated proficiency in spoken and written English	English courses
3. Demonstrated proficiency in L2	Foreign language courses
4. L1 and L2 acquisition process	Language acquisition
5. Effects of sociocultural variables on language learning	Language acquisition, cross-cultural studies, sociolinguistics
6. Language assessment, program development, implementation, and evaluation	Language assessment, program development evaluation

*Supplemental to general standards required of all teachers.
Source: National Association of State Directors of Teacher Education and Certification, 1984.

ing the support to teachers to implement what they learn appears to be difficult to manage. Therefore, a multiformat approach to preparing teachers to effectively meet the needs of ESOL students is suggested. As in the case of most of the position papers that suggest the content of staff development related to quality instruction of ESOL students, Hamayan's view is a start, but likely will not produce teachers who have the attitudes, knowledge, and skills needed to provide equal educational opportunity to teachers unless these four points are integrated into teacher-education programs and ongoing staff development and support. If our goal is to produce elementary- and secondary-level teachers who are capable and confident, the scope and sequence of training must be more inclusive. Appendix I outlines a scope and sequence of a high-quality staff development model for preparing teachers working with ESOL students in a structured-immersion setting. Sessions should be spaced over at least a three-month period to foster processing and experimentation between sessions.

Administrators need to recognize that commitment of time and resources is critical for successful change (Fullan & Stiegelbauer, 1991). Teachers are skeptical of "one-shot" staff development ventures that generally lack opportunities for follow-up and support for implementation of innovations. One approach that may offer a practical remedy for this criticism is the *study support group model*, (see below), which empowers teachers to solve context-specific issues and concerns and at the same time provides support by developing site-based resource persons who may continue to support one another and the wider faculty.

Support Between Teacher and Supervisor

Martinez (1992) suggests using the process of teacher decision making as a framework to advance mainstream teachers' skills in teaching ESOL students. This approach allows teachers to analyze their own decisions during instruction according to the interactive decision-making models described by Peterson and Clark (1971) and Shavelson and Stern (1981), which help teachers trace the path of their thinking during a "particular decision-making point" (DMP). A DMP is a point when the teacher must try an alternative instructional strategy because a planned strategy is not working. Teachers focus on the variables that may indicate a change in approach: student learning, attitudes, and behavior; content, procedures, and materials; time issues and cultural variables that may include culturally-divergent teacher-student interaction, and language barriers which impede understanding. Teachers are encouraged to videotape their instruction, and review the tape with a supervisor, noting each DMP and considering the following questions:

- What were you thinking at this point?
- Were you thinking of any alternative actions or strategies that influenced your actions
at this point?
- Was there anything the student said or did not say at this point that influenced your actions?
- Did any specific student behavior or reaction cause you to act differently from how you planned? If so, what?
- Was there anything specific about a student's behavior to suggest that he or she didn't understand, or wasn't paying attention?
- Did you have any instructional objectives in mind at this point?

The supervisor uses a matrix developed by Marland (1977) to analyze teacher responses and specifies areas in which the teacher could benefit from training. This method allows for multiple approaches to assess teacher effectiveness beyond student achievement alone.

Teacher Supporting Teacher: The Study Support Group Model

While this staff development process provides access to knowledge and skills necessary to avoid the "watered-down curriculum" phenomenon, it does not provide for attitude change. Many teachers do not feel at all comfortable working with linguistically or culturally different students. They long for the status quo, and fear that change will cause them to be less effective. In most cases, teachers who have negative attitudes about working with ESOL students believe that these students should not be included in mainstream classes until they have acquired English-proficiency skills at the advanced level.

Other teachers may be prejudiced or may discriminate against CLD students. Administrators should take a strong stand with these teachers and not hesitate to use the prescribed disciplinary system if they do not respond after a prescribed sequence of staff development offerings. Whenever possible, teachers who are openly discriminatory or prejudiced should not be assigned these students. Unfortunately, there is no guarantee that staff development will effect attitude change. Since attitude change is difficult and is generally a long process, we encourage the use of a study support group model to supplement districtwide staff development. Study groups are useful to foster faculty and staff participation and input by all professional staff (Murphy, 1999).

One hope for fostering attitude change may come from the use of a study support group model to increase the ownership of school improvement by the entire staff and to expedite the improvement process (Francis, Hersh, & Rowland, 1994). There is no documented best makeup for a study support group. In some districts, it is the entire staff of a school, but because of the lack of context sensitivity of districtwide staff development, the study support group is an excellent parallel strategy that complements districtwide staff development offerings. Groups should meet one hour each week, either as whole faculty in a small elementary school or as smaller groups of eight participants each. The groups meet to study, reflect, and develop contextually sensitive strategies for providing equal educational opportunities for ESOL students. Study groups may identify curricular, assessment, and/or school climate issues and concerns that need to be addressed in positive, proactive ways to ensure full participation of CLD students and their parents. Throughout the country, success in making lasting change in student achievement, group and individual teacher development as leaders, and attitude change has been brought about by the study support team. Teachers participating in these groups try new ideas and, most important, manage to change their own classroom behaviors and those of their students. They develop a joint vision of how school and education should be and strive to realize their vision. The study groups offer the needed support and produce collegial pressure to implement change initiatives. Increased knowledge bases, improved professional dialogue, increased trust, improved classroom instruction, improved staff morale, institution of a professional code of conduct, and development of a shared vision are outcomes experienced by one elementary school in Dallas, Texas, as a result of implementing this study group process of staff development (Francis, Hersh, & Rowland, 1994).

Murphy (1999) recommends whole-faculty groups to integrate personal and organizational learning through a supportive yet challenging set of personal relationships because such groups bring individual and institutional needs together to support implementation of instructional innovation, integrate the school's many disconnected models and programs, collaboratively plan for the whole school's achievement, and study research on teaching and learning. Murphy (1999) further states that the success or failure of study groups is directly attributable to the support and technical assistance provided by district administration. While we know that only about 10% of teachers trained to use a new procedure actually implement it in their classrooms at a level that affects student growth, study support groups are able to provide teachers with the companionship and sharing necessary to boost the proportion of teachers who implement new strategies introduced in staff development. After initial training and implementation of study support groups to examine issues of interest, peer coaching may be used to provide ESL and regular classroom teachers the opportunity for feedback and learning.

Ongoing processing of feedback and teacher observation is a key factor in the eventual adoption and success of program development. However it is critical to any program's success, and preferable, to provide training for the staff *prior* to implementing a new model whenever possible. Unfortunately, this does not happen in most districts where, due to a variety of legal, social, and political factors, programs are implemented or altered first, and staff are trained later. This sequencing is risky because teachers may experience frustration or anger at the changes, and in some cases may transfer their negative attitudes to ESOL students, or ESL teachers, and even prove uncooperative in implementing the program as designed, thereby crippling or invalidating adequate program evaluation.

Program Evaluation

While no single model applies to every program evaluation, the following points are characteristic of any evaluation process. First, program evaluation is intended to support and direct *decision making*, so it is decision driven rather than hypothesis driven (as a research project is, for example). Second, *applicability of the results* of a program evaluation is a primary criterion for determining whether the evaluation has succeeded. Third, from the beginning of any evaluation, the form of the evalution and the results must be shown to *serve the needs* of an institution or district. Fourth, all shareholders must be *actively involved* in all phases of the evaluation, and, finally, *trust* in the evaluation process itself is essential for its success and acceptance by the broader community.

Both formative and summative evaluations are valuable in ongoing program development and refinement. Formative evaluation gathers information that will assist program improvement. Summative evaluation may also be used for program refinement, but it generally gathers and uses data to document the program's effectiveness and value.

Approaches to evaluation range on a continuum between evaluator-controlled on the one hand to client-controlled on the other. Many school districts require both internal and external evaluations, with the external or "expert judgment" (Eisner, 1985) being used most commonly. If an expert consultant is engaged to conduct an assessment or evaluation of a program, the evaluation design should be structured to be acceptable to both the internal parties (administration, teachers, staff) and the external ones (evaluators), with mutual agreement on what evidence will be useful, who collects the data, time required for the study, and what potential uses the results might serve. These and any other pertinent criteria should be stated clearly in advance, and if observational data are to be gathered, more than one evaluator is required to ensure reliability. Evaluations are of limited usefulness if the program itself is already hampered by vaguely formulated policy statements, faulty or limited curricula, and strategies, and evaluations will be of limited value when marked discrepancies exist between what a program claims to do and what it actually delivers.

Management-oriented evaluation helps administrators by providing a *management information system* for ongoing formative evaluation. As an example, Stufflebeam's (1995) model consists of four types of concurrent evaluation that may be of use:

- *Context evaluation* considers program variables and planning decisions at a site, such as identifying the population of students needing ESL services. Parents, teachers, and principals may have differing views on this point.
- *Input evaluation* involves identifying and assessing available resources, alternative strategies, and what plans or modifications will best accomplish the desired results identified by the context evaluation. These first two evaluations are part of an ongoing needs assessment process within the program.
- *Process evaluation* examines the extent to which the program is implemented as currently designed, what problems are

emerging, and the means by which the problems are addressed.

* *Product evaluation* examines the overall outcomes or results of a program in a given time period. These results might include results in exiting programs, what proficiency was achieved, and what academic performance was reached. As part of this evaluation, reflection on what may need improvement or correction is indicated.

Rossi and Freeman (1993) point out the need for administrators to consider the following points during any program evaluation: First, has the program achieved its stated goals (impact assessment)? Second, are program costs appropriate to benefits received, compared with other programs (cost-benefits assessment)? Third, what are the numbers and characteristics of the students served (coverage assessment)? Fourth, have all anticipated services been provided? By qualified providers? With expected quality (service delivery assessment)? Fifth, is there appropriate accountability for the budget (accountancy assessment), and, sixth, have provisions been made for real or possible legal concerns (legal assessment)?

ESOL programs may be subject to additional evaluation and assessment by the Office for Civil Rights (OCR). Such an assessment or audit is not uncommon, nor is there a presupposition of deficiency or dereliction in a program under audit. The questions presented in this book in chapters seven and eight regarding program design and evaluation are essentially the kinds of questions and answers that the OCR may want to review in a district. We suggest that the administrator consult the program checklist found in Lyons (1992) or similar checklists to help formulate responses to an OCR audit.

Political Contexts and Evaluations

All evaluations create some pressure on administration and staff, and while internal evaluations may appear less threatening on the surface, the evaluator may be under some pressure concerning how and when to convey negative findings within the program. External evaluators may create more tension, especially when their findings do not flatter the efforts of some of the shareholders in the overall evaluation. The perception of an evaluation as threatening will often make data collection difficult and slows down the evaluation process. Administrators or staff under such pressure have been known to delay or postpone interviews, raise last-minute objections or refinements to the data collection process, or be reluctant to elicit the full cooperation of staff, teachers, and parents in the overall procedure. A skilled external evaluator anticipates some measure of reluctance or lack of cooperation, but the program evaluation can only be damaged, and the program itself hindered, by such tactics. The evaluator needs to take steps to restore the fundamental trust in the process required for successful evaluation.

Further Considerations for Program Evaluation

One way to foster cooperation in the evaluation process is, as always, proper planning. The evaluation team should try to anticipate potential problems, identify sources of friction, and discuss these openly with the consultants or evaluation coordinator. Problems may be avoided if (1) the questions that need answers are articulated clearly; (2) a reasonable time schedule is established and followed; (3) shareholders' expectations and rights to the results are established; and (4) the responsibilities and scope of administrator's (or staff) editing of the results are made clear. These responsibilities, and any others that are required by the team, the administration, and the external consultant(s), should be put in writing and acknowledged or signed by all parties. Furthermore, when working with outside evaluators, the evaluation team or its leadership should obtain a written understanding of what findings may be published by the evaluators and where.

Regarding the instrument or process of evaluation to be used, several questions should be considered in advance. For example, the members of the evaluation team may wish to rank in importance the questions and issues covered in the evaluation. The consultant may use these or offer alternative viewpoints on pertinent questions and issues prior to any evaluation. The team and consultants may wish to specify a means for modifying the instruments of evaluation in case this becomes necessary. Additional, unforeseen questions may arise that may become part of the evaluation process, and a method for handling these should be clarified.

The team may want to identify (or designate a subgroup to do so) any possible ethical or controversial issues that may arise from the evaluation process, and have in place some person or group to speak to these issues. If the consultants have no obligations in this regard, the team may want to designate one or more of its members to research related questions and issues that may surface during the evaluation, so that data on what other districts are doing can be made available.

As the evaluation is set up and gets underway, it may become apparent that certain decisions or choices may have to be made sooner rather than later. The consultant or evaluation leadership should advise administrators of any trade-offs in study design, implementation, or analysis as these arise, and should offer advice if required. The evaluation leadership should be prepared to articulate any constraints or limitations on the evaluation process as they arise. For example, it may become readily apparent that not every teacher or site implements a program as designed. These patterns cannot always wait until the end of the evaluation; if such a situation arises, the evaluation team must be informed.

As the evaluation process moves along, the coordinator and team should be sure that the team members or consultant actually doing the composition of the report delineate their interpretation of the findings from other issues, such as recommendations or advocacy. Last, the final report should include a list of the qualifications or competencies of those who compiled it and those on the evaluation team as a whole (Hoaglin et al. 1984).

Chapter Nine

Resources

The administrator today is well positioned to take advantage of the many professional and educational resources available through the Internet and other professional and academic sources. This chapter provides an annotated overview of the key sites and works that an administrator may find helpful in gathering available information on program design, staffing, and evaluation. The sites presented here are organized under the following headings: (1) federal government sources, (2) state and local sources, (3) national organizations and databases for bilingual and ESL programs and related topics, (4) sources for program design and development, and (5) sources for bilingual and/or ESL teachers and teacher training. All sites are subject to change and updates, and are listed here only as starting points for more detailed searches. All sites listed here are or may be protected by applicable copyright laws, and are cited here for reference purposes only. At press time, the addresses and content are accurate, but changes do occur. The sites given are those of major organizations and their affiliates, and are likely to prove more stable and enduring than typical Internet flux allows.

Federal and Government-Affiliated Sources

U.S. Department of Education (http://www.ed.gov/) The sites listed here are a valuable starting point for researching policy updates and program resources, particularly research and evaluation.

Office of Bilingual Education and Minority Languages Affairs (OBEMLA) at (http://www.ncbe.gwu.edu/obemla/index.html) provides information on implementing equal opportunities for ESOL students (language minorities) within districts.

Office for Civil Rights (OCR) at (http://www.ed.gov/offices/OCR/index.html), housed within the Department of Education, consists of 12 regional enforcement offices responsible for defining, identifying, and correcting inequity in educational opportunities and programs. The OCR is the primary agency responsible for conducting compliance reviews of district programs according to the mandates set forth under Title VI of the Civil Rights Act. We recommend that administrators obtain from OCR the publication *The Provision of an Equal Education Opportunity to Limited English Proficient Students* from OCR, U.S. Department of Education, Office for Civil Rights, Customer Service Team, 330 C Street, S.W., Washington, D.C. 20202.

Office of Special Education Programs (OSEP) at (http://www.ed.gov/offices/OSERS/OSEP/) has a role analogous to that of the OCR in helping districts ensure that the requirements for equal educational opportunity are met for special-needs students, as these requirements are stated under the Individuals with Disbilities Education Act (IDEA).

FedWorld at (http://www.fedworld.gov/) is one of the easiest and most accessible ways to begin a search for any government Web site.

Several **federal branches of government** can be searched at (http://whitehouse.gov/), (http://www.senate.gov/) and (http://www.house.gov/). Data on LEP demographics may be searched through the **U.S. Census Bureau** at (http://www.census.gov/).

Legislative information can be searched through **Thomas: Legislative Information** at (http://thomas.loc.gov/) and through the *Federal Register.* Actual court findings and summaries may be searched via **FindLaw** at (http://www.findlaw.com/) and, of course, through the more specialized search engines such as **Lexis-Nexis**.

Ongoing federal and state legal developments are monitored carefully by J. W. Crawford, who maintains a site at (http://ourworld. compuserve.com/homepages/JWCRAWFORD). Crawford's own work on the issues surrounding bilingual education in the United States is available for order through this site.

To keep abreast of research topics, see the **Office of Educational Research and Improvement** Web site at (http://www.ed.gov/offices/OERI/) and the **National Library of Education** at (http://www.ed.gov/NLE/).

State and Local Sources

Sites of individual state departments of education are available through the **Department of Education** at (http://www.ed. gov/Programs/bastmp/SEA.html), and (http://www.ncbe.gwu.edu/ states/index.htm/). Of interest to the administrator is the online *Summary Report of the Survey of the States' Limited English Proficient Students and Available Educational Programs and Services 1994–1995*. This report was prepared by R. Macias and C. Kelly at the **University of California Linguistic Minority Research Institute** (http://lmrinet.gse.ucsb.edu/) and may be found through the National Clearinghouse for Bilingual Education (NCBE) at (http://www.ncbe.gwu.edu/ncbepubs/seareports/94-95/ summary.html). The report is an overview of the enrollments and educational conditions of LEP students throughout the country, and available programs at state and federal levels. For a survey of current state requirements for certification in ESL or bilingual education, we recommend Fleischman et al., 1995.

Both the **National Association of State Boards of Education** (http://www.nasbe.org) and the **National School Boards Association** (http://www.nsba.org) are useful starting points for determining the status of ESL/bilingual certification or endorsement policies for individual states. A brief overview of states with certification or endorsement status may be found at the **NCBE** site (http:// www.ncbe.gwu.edu). An excellent resource for data on bilingual education and programming, the NCBE is funded by the OBEMLA.

Several states have been addressing ESL and bilingual education issues for some time, and professional organizations in these states are rich sources of information. In particular, the reader may consult **California Association for Bilingual Education (CABE)** at (http://www.bilingualeducation.org/) and **California Teachers of English to Speakers of Other Languages (CATESOL)** at (http://www.catesol.org) See also the following state organizations for information: **New York State Association for Bilingual Education (NYSABE)** (search under acronym NYSABE), the **New Jersey Teachers of English to Speakers of Other Languages/ Bilingual Education (NJTESOL-NJBE)** at (http://www.union-city.k12.nj.us/njtesol/), the **Michigan Association for Bilingual Education (MABE)** at (http://pilot.msu.edu/user/solisjes/mabe. html), and **the Illinois Association for Multilingual/Multicultural Education** at (http://www.iamme.com/).

National Organizations and Databases

A number of national professional organizations serve the needs and interests of major constituencies in ESL/bilingual education. The following sites are indicative of those organizations serving administrators and teachers and their ongoing training and development, and organizations promoting quality program development. National databases are available as sources for research and information on ESL programs and funding and faculty enrichment and development.

The site **AskERIC** (http://ericir.syr.edu) and the **ERIC Database** are helpful starting points for Internet searches along many parameters: program development, grant resources, and teacher education, to name a few. **ERIC** (Educational Resources Information Center) offers a number of clearinghouses (http://www.ed.gov/EdRes/EdFed/ERIC.html) maintained by several different organizations, each dealing with a particular interest area. The **Center for Applied Linguistics (CAL)** at (http://www.cal.org) operates and maintains a clearinghouse on languages and linguistics (http://www.cal.org/ericcll). CAL contains many useful sites, including such database projects as *The Benchmarks Study of Title VII Programs*, *Directory of Two-Way Bilingual Immersion Programs in the U.S.*, and *Total and Partial Immersion Language Programs in U.S. Schools*. These can be valuable resources in identifying successful program qualities and organization.

Professional organizations to keep educators informed of issues and advances in program design and curriculum innovations, teacher development, and continuing education, and to link educators across the nation and the world can be reached via the Internet. Of particular interest to the ESL/bilingual education community are the **National Association of Bilingual Educators** (NABE) at (http://www.nabe.org) and **Teachers of English to Speakers of Other Languages, Inc**. (TESOL), at (http://www.tesol.org). At the TESOL and NABE sites, the addresses of regional or state affiliates are available, as are interest sections dedicated to program administration. Organizations such as the **National Education Association** at (http://www.nea.org) and the **American Federation of Teachers** (http://www.aft.org) may serve as a starting point for information on issues of nationwide concern, including the status of LEP populations in the United States. Organizations for administrators include the **National Association of Elementary School Principals** (http://www.naesp.org) and the

National Association of Secondary School Principals (http://www.nassp.org).

Program Design and Development Sources

Sites of organizations providing information on program development and resourcing include the **Association for Supervision and Curriculum Development** at (http://www.ascd.org). Of particular interest for bilingual/ESL educators and administrators are the **Bilingual Education Network** (BiEN), at (http://goldmine.cde.ca.gov/cilbranch/bien.htm), maintained by the California Department of Education, and the **Clearinghouse for Multicultural/Bilingual Education** at (http://www.weber.edu/MBE/). The **Department of Education** page at (http://www.ed.gov/EdRes/index.html) is a helpful starting point for investigating program resources online. Although not specifically designed to cover only ESL/bilingual education issues, the **National Foreign Language Resource Centers** (NFLRCs) at (http://search.ed.gov/csi/language/html) covers a variety of topics on second-language instruction and resourcing.

Teacher Training and Professional Development

The NABE and TESOL sites have valuable links to sites with additional information on teacher training, continuing education, and conferences. The NCBE site has a page offering specific information on bilingual education and teacher education programs available by individual states (http://www.ncbe.gwu.edu/links/biesl/teachered.html). Two sites of interest to teachers in bilingual education are the Bilingual Education Network, a site maintained by the California Department of Education (http://goldmine.cde.ca.gov/cilbranch/bien.htm), and the ESL/Bilingual Education Site at (http://cc.usu.edu/~graceh/esl.htm).

These selections are intended to help start the search for pertinent and up-to-date information, and are intended as representative, not exhaustive, listings. Many sites are available, and a wealth of information on ESL/bilingual education and related issues is easily available through the Internet.

Appendixes

Appendix A

Selected Studies and Position Papers Comparing Native-Language Instruction (Bilingual-Education) Programs to Structured-Immersion Programs

Baker, K. (1987). Comment on Willig's A meta-analysis of selected studies on the effectiveness of bilingual education. *Review of Educational Reseach, 57*, 276–282.

Baker, K., & DeKanter, A. (1981). *Effectiveness of bilingual education: A review of the literature.* Washington, DC: U.S. Dept. of Education, Office of Planning, Budget and Evaluation.

Danoff, M. N., Coles, G. J., McLaughline, D. H., & Reynolds D.J. (1977). Evaluation of the impact of ESEA Title VII Spanish/English Bilingual Education Programs (Vol. 1, Study Design and interim findings). Palo Alto, CA: American Institute.

Donovan, R. H. & Hodson J. K. (1995). Espanol aumentivo: A transitional bilingual education program for secondary Hispanic preliterates, Evaluation Report, Year IV (ED3888045).

Genesee, F. (1985). Second language learning through immersion: A review of U.S. programs. *Review of Educational Research, 55,* 541–561.

O'Malley, J. M. (1978). Review of the evaluation of impact of ESEA Title VII Spanish/English Bilingual Education Programs. *Bilingual Resources, 1,* 6–10.

Rossell, C. (1998). Mystery on the bilingual express: A critique of the Thomas and Collier study. *READ Perspectives, 2,* 65–78.

Russell, G., & Woodward, J. (1995). A longitudinal study of transitional and immersion bilingual programs in one district. *Elementary School Journal, 95.*

Secada, W. (1987). This is 1987, not 1980: A comment on a comment. *Review of Educational Research, 57,* 377–384.

Tobias, R. (1994). Education progress of students in bilingual and ESL programs: A longitudinal study, 1990-1994, OER Report (ED 378817).

Willig, A. (1985). A meta-analysis of selected studies on the effectiveness of bilingual education. *Review of Educational Research, 55,* 269–317.

Willig, A. (1987). Examining bilingual education research through meta-analysis and narrative Review: A response to Baker. *Review of Educational Research 57,* 362–376.

Yates, J. R., & Ortiz, A. A. (1983). Baker and de Kanter review: Inappropriate conclusions of the efficacy of bilingual education. *NABE Journal, 7,* 377–384.

Appendix B

State-by-State Contact Person and Program Mandates for ESOL Students

Contact Person	Program Mandates
Alabama Diane Courtney (334) 242-9700	No Mandate
Alaska Anne Kessler (907) 465-8716	Bilingual/bicultural education. Mandate for districts with 8 or more LEP students, students who are English proficient but speak another language. Districts may apply for waiver.
Arizona Nancy Mendoza (602) 542-3204	All schools must provide either bilingual or ESL programs for all LEP students.
Arkansas Andre Guerro (501) 682-4213	No mandate. State requires all courses be taught in English, but school districts may establish ESL programs.
California Leroy Hamm (916) 657-3699	Schools having at least 10 LEP students who speak one language must provide a program.
Colorado Dr. Roger Martinez (303) 866-6771	All instruction must be conducted in English, except LEP transitional programs, which may be ESL or bilingual.

Connecticut
George DeGeorge   Any school or school district with
(860) 566-2169   20 or more LEP students who speak a
                         single language must provide a bilingual
                         program. Three-year limit on TBE
                         programs.

Delaware
Sister Margie Loveland   No statute or regulations. By law,
(302) 739-2770   English is the only language of
                         instruction.

Florida
Bernardo A. Garcia   Either an ESL or bilingual program
(904) 487-4495   must be provided if 15 students speak the
                         same language in a school.

Georgia
Beth Arnow   Schools must provide programs for LEP
(404) 656-4495   students designed to develop English
                         skills and American culture concepts for
                         participation in regular classroom
                         instruction.

Hawaii
Dr. Alan Ramos   Both ESL and bilingual education
(808) 733-4495   programs are allowed.

Idaho
Irene Chavolla   English required as language of
(208) 332-6907   instruction, but transitional programs
                         may be provided for children who do
                         not speak English at home. A consent
                         decree requires a uniform, comprehen-
                         sive, and appropriate program statewide.

Illinois
Rene Valenciano
(314) 814-3986

All students must be served by either a transitional bilingual education program or a transitional program. Any school that has 20 or more students who speak one language must have a TBE program. Any school with fewer than 20 students speaking a single language must have a transitional program.

Indiana
Darlene Slaby
(317) 232-0555

School districts must provide bilingual/bicultural programs for students whose L1 is not English, who speak another language more often than English, or who live in a home where the language spoken most often is not English. Program goal is to assist students in reaching their full academic achievement and to preserve awareness of cultural and linguistic heritage.

Iowa
Dan Chavez
(515) 281-3805

No mandate. Code allows for TBE and/or ESL programs.

Kansas
Kimberley Kreiker
(913) 296-7929

Schools required to establish program for LEP students that integrates them into regular educational programs. Schools may enter into a small multi-district arrangement to share program costs.

Kentucky
Nancy LaCount
(502) 564-2672

No statutes or regulations.

Louisiana
Sally M. Tyler
(504) 342-3454

No statutes or regulations.

Maine
Dr. Barney Berube
(207) 287-5984

State law requires English as the
language of instruction, but permits
bilingual or ESL programs for LEP
students.

Maryland
Jill Bayse
(410) 767-0344

State law establishes guidelines for
creating both bilingual and ESL
programs. Each school must establish
one of the two for LEP students.

Massachusetts
Tony Delorenzo
(617) 388-3300

Any school district with 20 or more
LEP students at any grade level of a
particular language group must offer a
TBE program. BE programs may
include English-proficient students.
Multigrade classrooms with up to a
4-year age spread are permitted.
Districts may petition to waive this
requirement due to hardship.

Michigan
Jesus Solis
(517) 373-4580

Schools required to provide ESL or
bilingual programs, but only bilingual
programs receive funding.

Minnesota
Joyce Biagini
(612) 296-6104

State does not require bilingual or ESL
programs, but any district with either
program is required to prevent LEP
student isolation for any substantial part
of school day, and to facilitate integration into "nonverbal" subjects such as
art, music, and PE.

Mississippi
Dr. Ada Belton
(601) 359-3513

No statutes or regulations.

Missouri
Dr. Joel Judd
(573) 751-8281

State statutes provide for special programs for students who are in danger of dropping out of school. Bilingual and ESL programs are included under this provision to address needs of LEP students.

Montana
Lynn Hinch
(406) 444-3095

No statutes or regulations.

Nebraska
Mary L. Peterson
(702) 687-9200

State board adopted regulations endorsing both bilingual and ESL instruction programs.

New Hampshire
Christine Noon
(603) 271-3494

Various policies in each district's compliance plan that require individual approval by the Bureau of Equality at the New Hampshire Department of Education, but largely uses ESL programs and permits bilingual programs.

New Jersey
Linda Carmona-Bell
(609) 292-1211

Any school district with 20 or more LEP students in any language is required to establish a bilingual education program. This requirement can be waived if the district can demonstrate it is impractical; then district is required to implement a special alternative instructional program for these students. Districts with fewer than 10 LEP students must provide services to improve students' English proficiency. When there are more than 10 LEP students in a school, ESL must be provided.

New Mexico
Lupe M. Castillo
(505) 827-6566

Bilingual education programs are a local option and are not mandated. All programs must be reviewed by the School Board, State Department of Education, and a required parent advisory board at regular intervals.

New York
Carmen Perez Hogan
(518) 474-8775

Each district receiving state funds for English learners that has 20 or more LEP students in the same grade in same building must have a bilingual education program. May not keep children in program for more than 3 years without extension by state Commissioner of Education. All LEP students' English proficiency must be assessed annually to determine if student should remain in program.

North Carolina
Jame S. Cowan
(919) 715-1796

The Department of Public Instruction requires each district to adopt a ESL, bilingual, or other program for LEP students.

North Dakota
Mari B. Rasmussen
(701) 328-2958

No statutes or regulations.

Ohio
Dan Fleck, Ph.D.
(614) 466-3641

No mandate for a particular program, but schools with a bilingual education program have one certified bilingual education teacher for every 25 students. ESL, structured-immersion, and tutoring programs are also implemented.

Oklahoma
Dr. Van Anderson
(405) 321-3301

Schools must provide bilingual classes or other options as necessary to meet needs of students who enter school unable to speak and understand English. English is still considered the language of instruction, but other languages may be used.

Oregon
Merced Flores
(503) 378-3569, ext. 675

No specific program required, but bilingual programs are permitted. Special courses offered until students can benefit from classes taught solely in English.

Pennsylvania
Myrna Delgado
(717) 787-1890

No statutes or mandates. One curriculum regulation exists that says every district must provide a program for students whose predominant language is not English. Program must be either bilingual/bicultural or ESL.

Rhode Island
Maria Lindia
(401) 277-4600

Each district is required to design a program to assist its LEP students; most use ESL programs.

South Carolina
Jaqui Asbury
(803) 734-8500

No statutes or regulations.

South Dakota
Margo Heinert
(605) 773-3282

No statutes or regulations.

Tennessee
Julie P. McCargar   State civil rights act requires each
(615) 532-6245   district to design its own LEP program
                           that is evaluated regularly. ESL pro-
                           grams are endorsed and taught by
                           certified ESL teachers. District must
                           provide transportation to ESL program
                           if not provided by school.

Texas
Maria Seidner   State statutes require districts with 20 or
(512) 463-9551   more LEP students in same grade level
                           in "any language classification" to
                           provide bilingual program in grades 1
                           through 6 only. Students in higher
                           grades must be receive ESL or bilingual
                           program.

Utah
Kathy Akin   Statutes require all districts to provide
(801) 538-7830   programming for LEP students; may be
                           bilingual, ESL, or other established
                           alternative.

Vermont
Jim McCobb   No statutes or regulations.
(802) 658-6342

Virginia
David E. Cox   State laws mandate instruction in
(804) 225-2593   English; programs must include means
                           for identification, assessment, and place-
                           ment in appropriate program.

Washington
Roger Barron   School district board of directors must
(360) 753-2573   make available a TBE or alternative
                           instructional program if TBE is not
                           feasible. Programs are to last no longer
                           than 3 years.

West Virginia
Amelia Davis   No statutes or regulations.
(304) 558-2691

Wisconsin
Tim Boals   State law requires bilingual/bicultural
(608) 266-5469   programs if there are 10 or more LEP
                            students in grades K–3 and 20 or more
                            in grades 4–12. Students are to be
                            taught by bilingual teachers with
                            bilingual counselors available to high-
                            school students. Certified ESL teachers
                            may be used when bilingual teachers
                            are not available with approval of state
                            superintendent.

Wyoming
Paul Soumokil   No statutes or regulations.
(307) 777-7673

Collaborative Planning Worksheet*

Content Area _____ Grade ____ Teacher _____

Concept(s) _____

Content-Area Teacher	*ESL Teacher*

1. Identify the objectives

The student will identify the planets in the solar system.	The student will name the planets and will be able to discuss each one.

2. Select the instructional strategies

Use a film of the solar system. Use a model of the solar system. (Plan a trip to planetarium.)	Use visuals to create conversations and activities. Use mnemonic devices to reinforce names of planets.

3. Check for understanding

Use Jeopardy game questions	Use a graphic organizer.

4. Re-teach the concept

Use visuals to discuss each planet in small groups.	Have ESOL students build a model of the solar system and hang it from the ceiling of the mainstream classroom.

Other:

*Adapted from BASD with permission.

Appendix D

Stages of English Acquisition for Oral/Aural, Reading, and Writing Development: Bethlehem Area School District

Stages are not exact points but describe a continuum from the beginning of a stage to its upper limit. Stages overlap at all levels. An occasional non-English word is acceptable at even the higher stages. An accent is acceptable at all stages.

Beginner Level for Elementary Schools

Oral/Aural Language Stages in English

Stage 1:
    Understands little or no English
    Uses no English except for a word or two
    Names objects

Stage 2:
    Understands only slow, simple speech; requires repetitions
    Speech is slow except for short patterns
    Is able to use functional words and phrases
    Is unable to use English for significant communication
    Vocabulary is limited to basic personal and survival areas

Stage 3:
    Understands simplified speech with repetitions and rephrasing
    Speech is hesitant and uneven; some sentences left incomplete
    Uses simple speech and gestures with predominantly present tense verbs
    Demonstrates errors of omission; leaves words out; leaves off endings
    Vocabulary is limited preventing continuous conversation

Reading Stages in English
Stage 1:
   Attends to pictures and objects, but not print
Stage 2:
   Beginning to understand conventions of print such as reading
   from left to right and the concepts of letters and words
Stage 3:
   Participates in choral reading activities and/or can identify
   some sound/symbol relationships along with some high-
   frequency words
Stage 4:
   Decodes simple sentences without assistance but may not
   associate meaning

Writing Stages in English
Stage 1:
   Draws a picture
   Has no knowledge of the written word
   Writes name only
   Writes isolated letters or words only
Stage 2:
   Writes in phrases and simple patterned sentences only
   Uses limited vocabulary, and mostly present tense verbs
   May use temporary spellings

Intermediate Level for Elementary Schools

Oral/Aural Language Stages in English
Stage 1:
   Understands simplified speech with repetitions and rephrasing
   Speech is hesitant and uneven; some sentences left incomplete
   Uses simple speech and gestures with predominantly present
   tense verbs
   Demonstrates errors of omission; leaves words out; leaves off
   endings
   Vocabulary is limited preventing continuous conversation
Stage 2:
   Understands adult speech but requires repetition and
   rephrasing
   Speech may be hesitant because of rephrasing and groping for
   words
   Uses some complex structures

Overgeneralizes rules of grammar
Has difficulty with choice of verb tense, verb tense consistency,
some word use
Difficulties

Reading Stages in English
Stage 1:
Decodes simple sentences without assistance, but may not
associate meaning
Stage 2:
Reads some words and simple sentences without assistance and
is able to retell the meaning of a simple passage

Writing Stages in English—Intermediate
Stage 1:
Writes in phrases and simple patterned sentences only
Uses limited vocabulary, and mostly present tense verbs
May use temporary spellings
Stage 2:
Writes concrete description of a picture/idea commensurate
with the student's oral ability
Writes sentences centered on one idea, not necessarily in
sequential order
Has some knowledge of rules of punctuation and capitalization,
but may not use them consistently
Uses readable, invented spellings

Advanced Level for Elementary Schools

Oral/Aural Stages in English
Stage 1:
Understands adult speech, but requires repetition and
rephrasing
Speech may be hesitant because of rephrasing and groping for
words
Uses some complex structures
Overgeneralizes rules of grammar
Has difficulty with choice of verb tense, verb tense consistency,
and subject/verb agreement
Vocabulary is adequate to carry on basic conversation; some
word use difficulties.

Stage 2:
  Understands most adult speech except some advanced
  structures
  Responds in detail, often with hesitations or digressions that do
  not impede narrative
  Errors made are not uncommon among proficient speakers of
  standard American English and do not detract from story line
  Uses most basic grammatical structures with occasional error in
  syntax; some errors in a young learner may be developmental
  Vocabulary is sufficiently varied to express ideas clearly

Reading Stages in English
Stage 1:
  Reads some words and simple sentences without assistance and
  is able to retell the meaning of a simple passage
Stage 2:
  Uses reading strategies to understand the main ideas
  appropriate to the student's grade level, but may need ESL
  support to understand more advanced concepts

Writing Stages in English
Stage 1:
  Writes concrete descriptions of a picture/idea commensurate
  with the student's oral ability
  Writes sentences centered on one idea, but not necessarily in
  sequential order, with errors consistent with with student's
  oral ability
  Has some knowledge of rules of punctuation and capitalization,
  but may not use them consistently
  Uses readable, invented spellings

Competent—Ready for the Regular Elementary Program

Oral/Aural Stages in English
Stage 1:
  Understands most adult speech except some advanced
  structures
  Responds in detail, often with hesitations or digressions that do
  not impede narrative
  Errors made are not uncommon among proficient speakers of
  standard American English and do not detract from story line

Uses most basic grammatical structures with occasional error in syntax; some errors in a young learner may be developmental
Vocabulary is sufficiently varied to express ideas clearly
Stage 2:
Able to express self adequately to succeed in a regular education program with no
ESL support

Reading Stage in English
Stage 1:
Demonstrates reading ability appropriate to succeed in a regular education program with decreasing ESL support
Stage 2:
Demonstrates reading ability appropriate to succeed in a regular education program with
ESL support only as needed

Writing Stages in English
Stage 1:
Has story line and/or central idea present
Able to write a summary of a story in correct sentences
Shows sequential relationship between sentences
Uses some compound and complex sentences
Demonstrates general control of most basic grammatical structures (e.g., subject/verb agreement, standard word order, consistent verb tense), but still contains errors
Uses punctuation and capitalization correctly most of the time. Some conventional and invented spellings
Stage 2:
Demonstrates writing ability appropriate to succeed in a regular classroom education program with ESL support only as needed

Appendix E

BASD English Acquisition at the High School Level

Program of Studies

No. Periods	EAP I: Grades 9–10
	Courses
2	Composition/reading development
2	Oral language development
1	Keyboarding (2nd semester)
1	Math 1
1	English-Acquisition Resource Room
1	Physical education/elective (one semester each)

	EAP II—Grades 10–11
	Courses
1	English-language development
1	Life science
1	World geography
1	English-Acquisition Resource Room
2	Vo-tech/business classes
1	Physical education/elective/keyboarding

	EAP III—Grades 10–12
	Courses
1	English-language development
1	Science
1	World geography
1	EAP Resource Room
1	Vo-tech/business classes
	All other classes in regular program

No. Periods	TEP I—*Grades 9–10*
	Courses
1	Composition/reading development
2	Oral language development
1	English-Acquisition Resource Room
1	Keyboarding (first semester)
1	Mathematics
1	Physical education/elective

	TEP II—*Grades 9–11*
	Courses
2	English-language development
1	Science concepts
1	Social studies concepts
1	English-Acquisition Resource Room
	All other classes are in regular program

	TEP III—*Grades 9–12*
	Courses
1	Transitional English
1	English 9B
1	Content-area reading
1	Government/economics
1	Physical science
1	English-Acquisition Resource Room
	All other classes are in regular program

Change of English-Acquisition Program Form

Bethlehem Area School District

Please submit a copy of this completed form, along with copies of the required documentation, to CLA, Marvine School. The original copy of this form must be filed in the student's guidance folder. The principal/administrative designee will set up a building review team and assign teachers to provide documentation. Team members should include the ESL teacher, classroom teacher, principal, and/ or other staff such as the reading specialist.

Student _____ Student # _____

Social Security #_____ DOB _____

Current School _____ Current level _____ GR _____

School student will attend after program change:_____

Recommended program level: _____

Complete the following with the student's stage levels:

Oral English Proficiency Stage:_____

Reading Stage: (photocopy one-page passage read and story retelling) _____

Writing Stage: (photocopy writing sample, classroom teacher's signature, and date) _____

Comments:

Staff member assigned to notify parent of change: _____

_____   _____
Principal   ESL Teacher

_____   _____
Classroom Teacher   Date

White copy: Student's folder   Canary copy: CLA folder   Pink copy: School

Appendix G

Home Language Survey

Bethlehem Area School District

Home Language Survey
Under Bethlehem Area School District policy, survey is
required to identify children by dominant language.

Student: _____
          Last   First   Middle   Date of Birth

Address: _____
Phone: _____

School: _____ Grade: _____ Date: _____

1. What was the FIRST language this student spoke? _____

2. At home, what language is MOST often spoken? _____

3. At home, does this student FREQUENTLY speak a language besides
   English? _____ YES _____ NO

4. Is the student being cared for by a non-English-speaking person?
   _____ YES _____ NO

5. Has this student ever received bilingual or ESOL services?
   _____ YES _____ NO

If the answers to questions 1 and 2 indicate a language other than English, and if
any questions 3–5 are YES, this student MUST be referred to the CLA-Marvine
Office.

Principal or Designee must call CLA (865-XXXX) for an appointment if child is
referred for English-language assessment.

Child referred for English-language assessment _____ YES _____ NO

If yes, date and time for testing: _____

_____
Signature of person giving information   Relationship

    CLA-white copy   School-canary copy   Parent-pink copy

Appendix H

Request for Language Assessment*

Center for Language Assessment
Bethlehem Area School District

Complete **ALL** information below:
*CLA will test students only if a school has a concern about student placement or student's progress that cannot be addressed by school-based personnel. Re-evaluation for exit or movement within levels is to be determined as described in the memo "Program changes for ESOL Students."

Referral Date _____ Referred by _____

Student Data

Student Name _____ D.O.B. _____

Home Address _____ Phone # _____

School _____ Grade _____ Current Program _____

Home School _____ Home Language (s) _____

Student Schooling

Initial CLA Evaluation Date _____

Initial CLA Recommendation:

Program _____ School _____ Grade _____

Special Education Status: (if any) _____

Support Services _____

Specific Reasons for Referral

_____

CLA Evaluation Results

Evaluation Date _____ Evaluator _____

Recommendation: Program _____ School_____ Grade _____

All Kindergarten students who are now at the beginner, intermediate, or advanced levels will be retested by CLA during the month of May to determine program needs for the new year. This testing will be done in each school building.

Appendix I

Scope and Sequence
of Staff Development

Session 1: (Full day or two half-days recommended)
1. What does it mean to learn a language?
2. Language acquisition vs. language development
3. Intercultural Communication
4. Multicultural Education
5. Helping all students to benefit from the language and cultural diversity in their classrooms

Session 2: (Full day or two half-days recommended)
1. School language vs. social language
2. Adapting teacher discourse
3. Strategies for content-area instruction
4. ESL strategies to integrate into content instruction

Session 3: Collaboration (Full day)
1. Team-building/trust-building/goal-setting activities for ESL teachers and their regular classroom instructional teams
2. Strategies for collaborating for academic success of ESOL students
3. Language and culture difficulties vs. learning difficulties: Assessment and documentation.

Session 4: (Four two-hour sessions)
Elementary Teachers
1. Developmental reading and the ESOL student; reading difficulties and the ESOL student
2. Using graphic organizers
3. Acculturation and social integration
4. Assessment and the ESOL Student

Secondary Teacher
1. Content-area reading, study skills, and the ESOL student
2. Using graphic organizers
3. Acculturation and social integration
4. Assessment and the ESOL student

Session 5: (one 2-hour session with both elementary and secondary, and one 2-hour session divided according to elementary and secondary grade levels)
1. Assessing English-language development
2. Assessing academic content and learning
3. Assessing exiting the ESL program
4. Assessing competency by benchmarks

Appendix J

Program Design Checklist

Does the program

_____ view programming for ESOL students as developmental rather than remedial?

_____ provide for equal access to core curriculum at all levels?

_____ meet the contextual needs of the community?

_____ provide services/experiences to foster social integration into the class, the school, and the community?

_____ affirm all students' linguistic and cultural heritage?

_____ integrate English-language learning and academic-content learning?

_____ incorporate students' home languages and cultural experiences into both curriculum and instruction?

_____ strive for frequent interactive communication from the students' homes

_____ prepare all staff to be culturally sensitive?

_____ use methods and material that promote self-esteem and self-confidence?

_____ provide for peer interaction by emphasizing experiences across language groups and proficiency levels and with native English speakers?

_____ regard grammar and other components of language learning as means to enhance communication rather than ends?

_____ emphasize the development of critical thinking skills?

_____ include curricular and extracurricular activities that provide opportunities for students to interact in a positive manner with native-English speakers?

_____ plan and implement staff development programs that support a commitment to meeting the needs of ESOL students?

_____ have a library containing a variety of materials for beginner, intermediate, and advanced students in English and in the home languages of ESOL students?

_____ provide regularly scheduled opportunities for collaboration between ESL teachers and academic-content teachers?

_____ use a variety of approaches that are sensitive to students' age, language levels, and communication needs?

_____ frequently provide activities for ESOL students that are student-centered and activity-based?

_____ have a designated program administrator?

_____ have a means of validly assessing ESOL students' level of English proficiency?

_____ have a means of validly assessing ESOL students' academic-content area knowledge?

_____ provide integrated social services on site?

_____ include multicultural materials as an integral part of mainstream curriculum?

_____ have a realistic budget for reaching program goals?

_____ have a database appropriate for longitudinal data collection?

_____ focus attention on ESOL students' content and fluency rather than form?

_____ encourage parents and community members to volunteer in the classroom?

_____ gather information on student learning styles that are culturally and individually appropriate?

Appendix K

Checklist for the
Orientation of LEP Students

Name _____ Date of registration _____

Country of origin _____ Home language _____

Age _____ Length of residence in U.S. _____ Years in school _____

To what extent has this student's education been interrupted _____
_____

Language(s) used in previous schooling _____

Grade level in last school attended _____

Name of lst school _____

Orientation tasks:

_____ Student is taught the names of key people, especially teacher.

_____ Student is assigned buddy who speaks student's home language.

_____ Student is introduced to daily schedule for courses.

_____ Student is informed of time of arrival and dismissal.

_____ Student is aware of lunch breaks, other breaks.

_____ Student is informed of eligibility for scholarship competition.

_____ Student is informed of bus schedule.

_____ Student is familiar with academic calendar, including holidays.

_____ Student is informed of meaning of bells.

_____ Student is taught location of classroom, cafeteria, lockers, restrooms.

_____ Student is informed of designated areas (bus stops, area where classes line up).

_____ Student is aware of off-limits places.

_____ Student is familiar with procedures for entering/leaving classroom/school.

_____ Student understands class participation and how to be recognized in class.

_____ Student understands how to ask to use the lavatory.

_____ Student understands procedure for lining up.

_____ Student understands when talking is permitted and when it is considered cheating.

_____ Student understands traffic patterns in hallways.

_____ Student understands how do deal with absences, permissions, excuses.

_____ Student understands attendance and lateness policies.

_____ Student understands how to ask for tutorial help.

_____ Student understands how student work is evaluated.

_____ Student is aware of options for extracurricular activities.

_____ Student understands graduation requirements for ESOL students.

_____ Student understands rules and consequences for infractions.

_____ Student understands how to make a phone call home.

_____ Student understands emergency signals and procedures (e.g., fire alarm).

_____ Student understands how to get home when bus is missed.

_____ Student understands transportation system and how to access it.

_____ Student understands homework policy and procedures.

_____ Student is provided with a bilingual dictionary.

_____ Student is introduced to available technology.

Glossary

academic language   Language used in learning academic subject matter in formal educational settings; these are the aspects of language associated with literacy and academic achievement that include terms specific to a particular discipline, technical language, and jargon related to fields of study.

acculturation   The process of adapting to a new culture.

additive bilingualism   Process by which individuals develop proficiency in an L2 subsequent to or simultaneous with the development of proficiency in the primary language; the addition of the second language and culture are unlikely to replace the first language and culture.

affective filter   Students acquire a new language more readily when affectively engaged in classroom learning that fosters motivation, self-confidence, and low anxiety. The affective filter is high under conditions of stress and defensiveness, and low under the conditions mentioned.

basic interpersonal communication skills (BICS)   One of two related language skills proposed by Cummins (1984, 1989), BICS involves those skills that allow individuals to communicate in everyday contexts. It is language that involves participants providing feedback to one another, and where the situation itself provides clues to meaning as opposed to cognitive-academic learning proficiency (CALP) which includes language needed to perform school tasks successfully. Most second language learners acquire BICS in 6 months to 2 years, whereas proficiency in CALP may require 5 to 7 years.

biculturalism   Native or near nativelike understanding of two cultures; including the ability to respond effectively to the demands of both cultures.

bilingual education   A generic term referring to a variety of programs designed to help students whose home language is not English succeed in school; the term is used to refer to programs that promote academic and linguistic development in two languages, or to denote programs that support the learning of ESOL students but do not support bilingualism.

body language   The gestures and mannerisms by which a person can communicate with others with or without sound.

CALP   Cognitive-academic learning proficiency. *See BICS.*

communicative competence   Refers to the set of competences that define appropriate language growth and ability. These competences include not only grammatical accuracy, but also practical, situational, and discursive appropriateness.

comprehensible input   A construct that describes understandable and meaningful language directed at second-language learners under optimal conditions; characterized as the language the learner already knows plus a range of new language made comprehensible by the use of certain planned strategies.

content-based ESL   A model of language education that features the integrated use of academic-content materials/instruction and language instruction as context for ESL instruction.

dual immersion   Programs that provide academic and language instruction in two languages over a period of years to foster bilingualism and biculturalism. This model is also referred to as two-way immersion and enrichment immersion.

ESL   The field of English as a second language; courses, classes, and programs designed for students learning English as a second language.

ESL standards   ESL Standards for Pre-K–12 Students published by TESOL, Inc., outlines goals, standards, explications of the standards, descriptors of the standards, progress indicators, vignettes, and discussions organized by grade level clusters to address the needs of ESOL students with different English-proficiency levels (beginning, intermediate, advanced, and limited formal schooling).

ESOL student   Learners who are identified as still in the process of acquiring English as an additional language; students who may not speak English at all or who at least do not speak, understand, read, or write English with the fluency of their classmates, generally because they speak another language at home.

FEP   Fully English proficient, a speaker of English as another language whose English-language skills are sufficiently proficient so as not to need support services as assessed by a standardized measure.

home language   Language(s) spoken in the home of a student by significant others such as family members or caregiver; sometimes this term is used as a synonym for first language, primary language, or native language.

immersion A model or program of language instruction that at times refers to a "sink or swim" approach to instruction where unmediated accommodation to the new language is demanded, or to a variety of programs where the language of instruction is the target language, but is carefully structured to support student participation. Such immersion programs are found in the Canadian school system and in enrichment immersion and two-way immersion programs in the United States. See Lessow-Hurley, 1996, for an excellent introduction to the variety of immersion programs.

L1, L2 First (native or home) language and second language, respectively.

language acquisition/language learning The sum cognitive and linguistic processes and practices whereby command of one or more languages is possible. Some researchers see first-language acquisition and second-language learning as mediated by the same cognitive and linguistic mechanisms, whereas others see the processes as quite different (see chapter two).

language minority Anyone who comes from a home in which a language other than English is primarily spoken, and who has acquired a first language other than English.

language proficiency Level of competence at which an individual is able to use language for both basic interpersonal communication and academic purposes.

late-exit TBE Late-exit transitional bilingual education describes those programs where the bilingual component of the educational program transitions to English instruction, typically in the (late) middle-school years, in contrast to elementary or early/middle years.

LEP Limited English proficiency.

linguistic competence The cognitive framework that encompasses and defines phonological, morphological, syntactic, semantic, and strategic capabilities required to use language.

mainstream or regular classroom Class with or without ESOL students that does not systematically accommodate the language-learning needs of ESOL students; may be a regular elementary- or secondary-level class in which all instruction is provided in English.

maintenance bilingual education A program that supports not only education and communication in the student's primary language, but also in the student's heritage and culture; this model is also known as developmental bilingual education.

multilingualism   The ability to speak two or more languages; proficiency in several languages.

native language   First spoken language or primary language of an individual.

NEP   Non-English proficient.

PEP   Potentially English-proficient.

pull-out ESL   Associated with immersion models, this term refers to a continuum of service models, from ones that separate ESOL students from the mainstream students to provide remedial instruction in English with no collaboration between the ESL teacher and the regular classroom teacher and no continuity between the ESL class content and classroom content to programs in which there is careful, ongoing collaboration between ESL teachers and regular classroom teachers to ensure continuity between students instruction in ESL classes and academic-content instruction in the mainstream classroom.

sheltered instruction   An approach in which students develop knowledge in specific subject matter through the medium of English with their teachers adjusting the language demands of the lesson in terms in speech rate, tone, use of context clues and models, graphic organizers, and adapting language of texts to make academic instruction more readily accessible to students with different levels of English proficiency.

specially designed academic instruction in English (SDAIE)   A program for ESOL students that is designed to simultaneously foster English-language development, teach academic content, practice higher-level thinking skills, and advance literacy skills (Law & Eckes, 1990).

structured immersion   Programs of instruction that provide language-minority students with instruction in an ESL setting. Similar to transitional-bilingual and ESL-only instruction. Structured-immersion programs may vary in quality.

submersion   Programs in which students receive instruction in English with English monolingualism as the goal; also referred to as the "sink or swim" model, ESOL students receive no support as they simultaneously learn English and content. This model is illegal in U.S. public schools.

subtractive bilingualism   The learning of a majority language at the expense of the first language; refers to programs in which primary language and home culture have low status and, because of this, learners are encouraged to divest themselves of the first language and replace it with the new language.

transitional bilingual education (TBE)   Programs for ESOL students whose goal is to mainstream students into English-only classrooms. Two variations of this model exist: early-exit and late-exit. In early-exit models there is initial instruction in the child's L1 with all other instruction in English, while in late-exit models students are given approximately 40% of their instructional time in the primary language in content areas, remaining in this program through the sixth grade, even if they are reclassified as fully English proficient.

References

Abramson, S., Pritchard, R., & Garcia, J. (1993). Teacher education and limited English proficient students: Are we meeting the challenge? *Teacher Education Quarterly, 20*, 53–65.

Ada, A. F. (1989). *Los libros magicos: A small miracle among parents in the Pajaro valley*. San Francisco: California Tomorrow.

Anderson, T., & Boyer, M. (1970). *Bilingual schooling in the United States*. Austin, TX: Southwest Educational Laboratories.

Arreaga-Mayer, C., Carta, J. J., & Tapia, Y. (1994). Ecobehavioral assessment: A new methodology for evaluating instruction for exceptional culturally and linguistically diverse students. In S. B. Garcia (Ed.), *Addressing cultural and linguistic diversity in special education: Issues and trends* (pp. 10–29). Reston, VA: Division for Culturally and Linguistically Diverse Exceptional Learners, Council for Exceptional Children.

Arreaga-Mayer, C., & Greenwood, C. (1986). Environmental variables affecting the school achievement of culturally and linguistically different learners: An instructional perspective. *Journal of the National Association of Bilingual Education, 10*, 113–135.

Au, K. H., & Jordan, C. (1981). Teaching reading to Hawaiian children: Finding a culturally appropriate solution. In H. T. Trueba, G. P. Guthrie & K. H. Au (Eds.), *Culture and the bilingual classroom*. Rowley, MA: Newbury House.

August, D., & Garcia, E. E. (1988). *Language minority education in the United States: Research, policy and practice*. Springfield, IL: Charles C. Thomas.

Baca, L., & Cervantes, H. (1989) *The bilingual special education interface* (2nd ed.). Columbus, OH: Merrill.

Bain, B. (1974). Bilingualism and cognition: Towards a general theory. In S. T. Carey (Ed.), *Bilingualism, biculturalism and education: Proceedings from the conference at College of Saint Jean* (pp. 119–128). Edmonton: University of Alberta.

Bain, B., & Yu, A. (1980). Cognitive consequences of raising children bilingually: One parent one language. *Canadian Journal of Psychology, 34*, 304–313.

Baker, K. (1987). Comment on Willig's "A meta-analysis of selected studies in the effectiveness of bilingual education." *Review of Educational Research, 57*, 351–362.

Baker, K., & DeKanter, A. (1981). Effectiveness of bilingual education: A review of the literature. Washington, DC: Technical Analysis Report Series, U.S. Department of Education.

Benavides, A. (1989). High risk predictors and pre-referral screening for language minority students. In A. A. Ortiz & B. A. Ramirez (Eds.), *Schools and the culturally diverse exceptional student* (pp. 19–31). Reston, VA: Council for Exceptional Children.

Bennett, C. (1990). *Comprehensive multicultural education: Theory and practice* (2nd ed.). Old Tappan, NJ: Allyn & Bacon.

Ben-Zeev, S. (1977). The influence of bilingualism on cognitive strategy and cognitive development. *Child Development, 48,* 1009–1018.

Bermudez, A. B., & Padron, Y. N. (1987). Integrating parental education into teacher training programs: A workable model for minority parents. *Journal of Educational Equity and Leadership, 7,* 235–244.

Bethlehem Area School District. (1993). *English Acquistion Program Handbook.*

Bilingual Education Act of 1992 (Title VII of Improving America's Schools Act, P. L. 103-382, 108 Stat. 3716.

Bloomfield, L. (1933). *Language.* New York: Holt, Rinehart and Winston, Inc.

Bloomfield, L. (1942). *Outline guide for the practical study of foreign languages.* Baltimore: Publisher?

Bogdan, R., & Biklen, S. K. (1992). *Qualitative research for education: An introduction to theory and methods.* San Francisco: Freeman.

Bronfenbrenner, U. (1979). *The ecology of human development: Experiment by nature and design.* Cambridge, MA: Harvard University Press.

Brooks, N. (1964). *Language and language learning* (2nd ed.). New York: Harcourt Brace and World.

Buck, K., Byrnes, H., & Thompson, I. (Eds.). (1989). *The ACTFL oral proficiency interview tester training manual.* Yonkers, NY: American Council of Teachers of Foreign Languages.

Campos, J., & Keatinge, R. (1988). The Carpinteria language minority student experience: From theory to practice to success. In T. Skutnabb-Kangas & J. Cummins (Eds.), *Minority education: From shame to struggle* (pp. 299–307). Clevedon, England: Multilingual Matters.

Canale, M., & Swain, M. (1980). Theoretical bases of communicative approaches to second language teaching and testing. *Applied Linguistics, 1,* 1–47.

Carey, S. (1997). Language management, official bilingualism, and multiculturalism in Canada. *Annual Review of Applied Linguistics, 17,* 204–23.

Cartagena, J. (1991). English only in the 1980s: A product of myths,phobias, and bias. In S. Benesch (Ed.), *ESL in America: Myths and possibilities.* Portsmouth, NH: Heinemann.

Carter, T. P., & Chatfield, M. L. (1986). Effective bilingual schools: Implications for policy and practice. *American Journal of Education, 95,* 200–232.

Castaneda v. Pickard, 648 F.2d 989 (5th Cir. 1981).

Chamot, A. U., & O'Malley, J. M. (1994). *The CALLA handbook: Implementing the cognitive academic language learning approach.* Menlo Park, CA: Addison Wesley.

Charles, L., & Clark, P. (1995). Study groups in practice. *Journal of Staff Development, 16* (3), 49–53.

Chastain, K. (1971). *The development of modern-language skills: Theory to practice.* Philadelphia, PA: The Center for Curriculum Development, Inc.

Chomsky, N. (1957). *Syntactic structures.* The Hague: Mouton.

Chomsky, N. (1975). *Reflections on language.* New York: Pantheon Books.

Chomsky, N. (1976). *Aspects of the theory of syntax.* Cambridge, MA: MIT Press.

Cintron v. Brentwood Union Free School District Board of Education, 455 F. Supp. 57 (E. D. N. Y. 1978).

Clair, N. (1993). Mainstream classroom teachers and ESL students. *TESOL Quarterly*, 189–195.

Cloud, N. (1993). Language, culture and disability: Implications for instruction and teacher education. *Teacher Education and Special Education*, *16* (1), 60–73.

Cochran, C. (1989). *Strategies for involving LEP students in the all-English medium classroom: A cooperative learning approach*. Program Information Guide Series, Number 12, National Clearinghouse for Bilingual Education.

Constantino, R. (1994). A study concerning instruction of ESL students comparing all-English classroom teacher knowledge and English as a second language teacher knowledge. *The Journal of Educational Issues of Language Minority Students*, *15*, 123–145).

Cornell, C. (1993a). Factors contributing to Hispanic students' tendency to drop out of school. MIDTESOL Regional Conference, Lincoln, NE, October, 1993.

Cornell, C. (1993b). Language and culture monsters that lurk in our traditional rhymes and folktales. *Young Children*, *48*, 45–51.

Cornell, C. (1995). Reducing failure of LEP students in mainstream classrooms and why it is important. *Journal of Educational Issues of Language Minority Students*, *15*, 123–145.

Crawford, J. (1991). *Bilingual education: History, politics, theory, and practice* (2nd ed.). Los Angeles, CA: Bilingual Education Services.

Crawford, J. (1992a). *Hold your tongue: Bilingualism and the politics of English only*. Reading, MA: Addison Wesley.

Crawford, J. (Ed.), (1992b). *Language loyalties: A source book on the official English controversy*. Chicago, IL: University of Chicago Press.

Cummins, J. (1976). The influence of bilingualism on cognitive growth: A synthesis of research findings and explanatory hypothesis. *Working Papers on Bilingualism*, *9*, 1-43. Toronto: Institute for Studies in Education.

Cummins, J. (1984). *Bilingualism and special education: Issues in assessment and pedagogy*. Clevedon, England: Multilingual Matters.

Cummins, J. (1989). *Empowering minority students*. Sacramento: California Association for Bilingual Education.

Cummins, J. (1994). Primary language instruction and the education of language minority students. In California State Department of Education, *Schooling and language minority students: A theoretical framework* (2nd ed.,pp. 3–46). Los Angeles: California State University, Evaluation, Dissemination and Assessment Center.

Darcy, N. T. (1953) A review of the literature on the effects of bilingualism upon the measurement of intelligence. *Journal of Genetic Psychology*, *82*, 21–57.

DeAvila, E. (1987). Bilingualism, cognitive function, and language minority group membership. In P. Honel, M. Pallij, & D. Aaronson (Eds.), *Childhood bilingualism: Aspects of linguistic, cognitive, and social development*. Hillsdale, NJ: L. Lawrence Erlbaum and Associates.

DeAvila, E. A., and Duncan, S. E. (1977). Pre-Language Assessment Scales (Pre-LAS). Corte Madera, CA: Linguametrics Group.

DeAvila, E. A., and Duncan, S. E. (1977). Language Assessment Scales, I, II. (LAS, 2nd ed.). Corte Madera, CA: Linguametrics Group.

Delgado-Gaitan, C. (1994). Sociocultural change through literacy: Toward the empowerment of families. In B. M. Ferdman, F. M. Weber, & G. Ramirez (Eds.), *Literacy across languages and cultures*. Albany: State University of New York Press.

Diaz, R. (1983). Thought and two languages: The impact of bilingualism on cognitive development. *Review of Research in Education, 10*, 23–34.

Diaz, S., Moll, L. C., & Mehan, H. (1986). Sociocultural resources in instruction: A context-specific approach. In *Beyond language: Social and cultural factors in schooling language minority students*. Los Angeles: California State University, Evaluation, Dissemination and Assessment Center.

Diaz-Rico, L. T., & Reed, K. Z. (1995) *The crosscultural, language and academic development handbook: A complete K–12 reference guide*. Boston, MA: Allyn & Bacon.

Doyle, W. (1983). Academic work. *Review of Educational Research, 53*, 287–312.

Ehrman, M.E. (1996). *Understanding second language learning difficulties*. Thousand Oaks, CA: Sage Publications, Inc.

Eisner, E. (1985). *The educational imagination*, 2nd ed. New York: Macmillan.

Enright, D. S.(1986). "Use everything you have to teach English": Providing useful input to young language learners. In P. Rigg & D. S. Enright (Eds.), *Children and ESL: Integrating perspectives* (pp. 115–162). Washington, DC: Teachers of English to Speakers of Other Languages.

Enright, D. S. & McCloskey, M. L. (1985). Yes talking!: Organizing the classroom to promote second language acquisition. *TESOL Quarterly, 19*, 431–453.

Enright, D. S. & McCloskey, M. L. (1988). *Integrating English: Developing English language and literacy in the multilingual classroom*. Reading, MA: Addison-Wesley.

Epstein, J. (1990). Paths to partnerships: What we can learn from federal, state, district, and school initiatives. *Phi Delta Kappan, 72* (5), 344–349.

Epstein, J. (1992). *School and family partnerships Report No. 6*. Center on families, communities, schools, and children's learning. Baltimore, MD: The Johns Hopkins University Press.

Esterlin, R. A., Ward, D., Bernard, W. S., & Rueda, R. (1982). *Immigration*. Cambridge, MA: Harvard University Press.

Faltis, C. J. (1993). *Jointfostering: Adapting teaching strategies for the multilingual classroom*. Upper Saddle River, NJ: Merrill/Prentice Hall.

Farrell, E. J., (1990). On the growing shortage of Black and Hispanic teachers. *English Journal, 79*, 39–46.

Fine, M., & Weis, L. (Eds.), (1993). Beyond silenced voices: *Class, race,and gender in United States schools*. Albany, NY: State University of New York Press.

Fleischman, H. L., & Hipstock, P. J. (1993). *Descriptive study of services to limited English proficiency students.* Arlington, VA: Development Associates.

Fradd, S. H., & Correa, V. I. (1989). Hispanic students at risk: Do we abdicate or advocate? *Exceptional Children, 56,* 105–110.

Fradd, S. H., & Weismantel, M. J. (1989). *Meeting the needs of culturally and linguistically diverse students: A handbook for educators.* Boston: College-Hill Press.

Francis, S., Hersh, S. & Rowland, E. (1994). Improving school culture through study groups. *Journal of Staff Development, 15* (2), 12–15.

Fries, C. C. (1945). *Teaching and learning English as a foreign language.* Ann Arbor: University of Michigan Press.

Fuchs, V. R., & Reklish, D.M. (1992). America's children: Economic perspectives and policy options. *Science, 225,* 41–46.

Fullan, M. G., & Stiegelbauer, S. (1991). *The new meaning of educational change* (2nd ed.). New York: Teacher College Press.

Garcia, A. & Morgan, C. (1998). A Fifty-state survey of requirements for the education of language minority children. *READ Perspectives, 5*(1), 56–73.

Garcia, E. E. (1994). *Understanding and meeting the challenge of student cultural diversity.* Princeton, NJ: Houghton Mifflin.

Gay, G. (1993). Ethnic minorities and educational equity. In J. A. Banks & C. A. McGee Banks (Eds.), *Multicultural education: Issues and perspectives* (pp. 171–192). Boston, MA: Allyn & Bacon.

Gersten, R., & Woodward, J. (1994). The language of minority students and special education: Issues and paradoxes. *Exceptional Children, 60,* 310–322.

Gibson, M. (1987). Punjabi immigrants in an American high school. In G. Spindler & L. Spindler (Eds.), *Interpretive ethnography of education: At home and abroad.* Hillsdale, NJ: Lawrence Erlbaum and Associates.

Glaser, B., & Strauss, L. (1967). *The discovery of grounded theory: Strategies for qualitative research.* Chicago: Aldine.

Glenn, X. L. (1988). *The Myth of the common school.* Cambridge, MA: Harvard University Press.

Glick, P. C. (1988). Fifty years of family demography: A record of social change. *Journal of Marriage and the Family, 50* (4), 861–73.

Goetz, J., & LeCompte, M. (1981). Ethnographic research and the problem of data reduction. *Anthropology and Education Quarterly, 12,* 51–70.

Goldberg, A. (1997) Follow-up study on the Bethlehem, PA school district's English acquisition program. *Read Perspectives, 4,* (1), 59–93.

Goldenberg, C. (1996). The education of language minority students: Where are we, and where do we need to go? *The Elementary School Journal, 96* (3), 353–361.

Gollnick, D. (1992). Multicultural education: Policies and practices in teacher education. In C.A. Grant (Ed.), *Research and multicultural education* (pp. 211–239). Washington, DC: Falmer Press.

Gonzalez, M. L., Huerta-Macias, A., & Tinajero, J. V. (Eds.). (1998). *Educating Latino students: A guide to successful practice.* Lancaster, PA: Technomic Publishing Co., Inc.

Gonzalez, R. (1990). When minority becomes majority: The changing face of English classrooms. *English Journal, 79*(1), 16–23.

Gonzalez, V. (1991). *A model of cognitive, cultural, and linguistic variables affecting bilingual Spanish/English children's development of concepts and language.* (Doctoral dissertation,The University of Texas at Austin (ERIC Document Reproduction Service No. ED 345–562).

Gonzalez, V, Brusca-Vega, R., & Yawkey, T. (1997). *Assessment and instruction of culturally and linguistically diverse students with or at-risk of learning problems.* Needham Heights, MA: Allyn & Bacon.

Goodenough, F. L. (1926). Racial differences in the intelligence of children. *Journal of Experimental Psychology, 140,* 3–10.

Gottlieb, J., Alter, M., & Gottlieb, B.W. (1991). Mainstreaming academically handicapped children in urban schools. In J. W. Lloyd, N. N. Singh, & A. C. Repp (Eds.), *The regular education initiative: Alternative perspectives on concepts, issues and models* (pp. 95–112), Sycamore, IL: Sycamore.

Grossman, H. (1991). Special education in a diverse society: Improving services for minority and working class students. *Preventing School Failure, 36,* 19–27.

Guadalupe Organization v. Tempe Elementary School District No. 3, 587 F.2d 1022 (9th Cir. 1978).

Hakuta, K. (1986). *Mirror of language.* New York: Basic Books.

Hakuta, K., & Diaz, R.M. (1984). The relationship between bilingualism and cognitive ability: A critical discussion and some new longitudinal data. In K.E. Nelson (Ed.), *Children's Language* (pp. 310–344). Hillsdale, NJ: Lawrence Erlbaum and Associates.

Hamayan, E. V., & Perlman, R. (1990). *Helping language minority students after they exit from bilingual/ESL programs. A handbook for teachers.* Washington DC: National Clearinghouse for Bilingual Education.

Handscombe, J. (1989). A quality program for learners of English as a second language. In P. Rigg and V. G. Allen (Eds.), *When they don't all speak English* (pp. 1–14). Urbana, IL: National Council of Teachers of English.

Heath, S. B. (1983). *Ways with words: Language, life, and work in communities and classrooms.* Cambridge: Cambridge University Press.

Hernandez, M. (1997). *A profile of Hispanic Americans: Executive summary.* Princeton, NJ: Population Resource Center.

Hernandez, H. (1989). *Multicultural education: A teacher's guide to content and process.* Riverside, NJ: Macmillan.

Highsmith, J. (1990). Educating the new immigrants. *CSU Academic Senator, 19* (3), 3.

Hoaglin, D. D., Light, R. J., McPeek, B., Mosteller, V. & Soto, M. A. (1984). *Data for decisions: Information strategies for policy makers.* Cambridge, MA: Abt Books.

Hodgkinson, H. L. (1989). *The same client: The demographics of education and service delivery systems.* Washington, DC: Institute for Educational Leadership.

Hodgkinson, H. L. (1992). *A demographic look at tomorrow.* Washington, DC: Institute for Educational Leadership.

Ianco-Worrall, A. D. (1972). Bilingualism and cognitive development. *Child Development, 43*, 1390–1400.

Individuals with Disabilities Education Act of 1990 20 U.S.C., Sections 1400–1485, Education of the Handicapped Amendments of 1990.

Jensen, J.V. (1962). Effects of childhood bilingualism. *Elementary English, 39*, 132–143.

Joyce, B., & Showers, B. (1988). *Student achievement through staff development.* White Plains, NY: Longman.

Krashen, S. (1981). *Second language acquisition and second language learning.* Oxford: Oxford Pergamon.

Krashen, S. (1982). *Principles and practices of second language acquisition.* Oxford: Oxford Pergamon.

Krashen, S. (1987). *Principles and practices in second language acquisition.* Englewood Cliffs, NJ: Prentice Hall.

Krashen, S. and Biber, D. (1988). *On course: Bilingual education's success in California.* Sacramento, CA: California Association for Bilingual Education.

Krashen, S. (1991). *Bilingual education: A focus on current research.* Washington, DC: National Clearinghouse for Bilingual Education.

Lado, R. (1957). *Linguistics Across Cultures.* Ann Arbor: University of Michigan Press.

Lado, R. (1964). *Language Teaching: A scientific approach.* New York: McGraw Hill.

Lambert, W. E. (1984). An overview of issues in immersion education. In California State Department of Education, *Studies on immersion education: A collection for U.S. educators.* Sacramento, CA: Author.

Laosa, L. M. (1984). *Social policies toward children of diverse ethnic, racial and language groups in the U.S.* In H. W. Stevenson & A. E. Siegel (Eds.), *Child development research and social policy.* Chicago: University of Chicago Press.

Larsen-Freeman, D., & Long, M. (1993). *An introduction to second language acquisition research.* New York: Longman, Inc.

Lau v. Nichols, 414 U.S. 563 (1974).

LaVelle, M. (1997). The importance of learning English: A national survey of Hispanic parents. *READ Perspectives, 4* (1), 7–16.

Lee v. Johnson 404 U.S. 1215 (1968).

Leitch, M., & Tangri, S. (1988). Barriers to home-school cooperation. *Educational Horizons, 66* (2), 70–74.

Leopold, W. (1939). *Speech development of a bilingual child: A linguist's record: Vol. 1. Vocabulary growth in the first two years.* Evanston, IL: Northwestern University Press.

Levine, D., & Adelman, M. (1982). *Beyond language: Intercultural communication for English as a second language.* Englewood Cliffs, NJ: Prentice Hall.

Liedtke, W. W., & Nelson, L. D. (1968). Concept formation and bilingualism. *Alberta Journal of Educational Research, 14*, 225–232.

Lucas, T, Henze, R., & Donato, R. (1990). Promoting the success of Latino language minority students: An exploratory study of six high schools. *Harvard Educational Review, 60,* 315–340.

Lyons, J. (1992). *Legal Responsibilities of Education Agencies Serving National Origin Language Minority Students.* Washington, DC: Mid-Atlantic Equity Center.

Malave, L. (1991). Conceputual framework to design a programme intervention for culturally and linguistically different handicapped students. In L. Malave & G. Duquette (Eds.), *Language, culture and cognition.* Clevedon, England: Multilingual Matters.

Marland, P. E. (1977). A study of teachers' interactive thoughts. Unpublished doctoral dissertation, The University of Alberta, Edmonton, Canada.

Martinez, R. (1992). Staff development for improving teaching skills of mainstream teachers of limited English proficient students. *The Journal of Educational Issues of LanguageMinority Students, 11,* 163–174.

Mattes, L. J., & Omark, D. R. (1984). *Speech and language assessment for bilingual handicapped.* San Diego, CA: College Hill.

Matute-Bianchi, M. (1991). Situational ethnicity and patterns of school performance among immigrant and nonimmigrant Mexican-descent students. In M. Gibson & J. Ogbu (Eds.), *Minority status and schooling.* New York: Garland.

McLaughlin, B. (1987). *Theories of second-language learning.* London: Edward Arnold.

Memorandum from J. Stanley Pottinger, Director OCR/DHEW to school districts with more than five percent national origin minority group children regarding identification of discrimination and denial of services on the basis of national origin, May 25, 1970.

Meyer v. Nebraska, 262 U.S. 390 (1923).

Minicucci, C., & Olsen, L. (1993). Caught unawares: California secondary schools confront the immigrant student challenge. *Multicultural Education, 1* (2), 16–19, 38.

Miramontes, O. B. (1993). ESL policies and school restructuring: Risks and opportunities for language minority students. *Journal of Education Issues of Language Minority Students, 12,* 77–96.

Moll, L. C., Amanti, C., Neff, D., & Gonzalez, N. (1992). Funds of knowledge for teaching: Using a qualitative approach to connect homes and classrooms. *Theory into Practice* 31, 2, 132–41.

Moll, L. C., & Diaz, S. (1987). Some key issues in teaching latino students. *Language Arts, 65,* 465–472.

Moll, L. C., Velez-Ibanez, C. G., & Greenberg, J. (1988). *Project implementation plan. Community knowledge and classroom practice: Combining resources for literacy instruction.* (Technical Report No. L-10). Tucson: University of Arizona, College of Education anf Bureau of Applied Research in Anthropology.

Murphy, C. U. (1999). Use time for faculty study. *Journal of staff development* 20, 2, 20–25.

Nash, R. (1976). *Teacher expectations and pupil learning.* Boston: Routledge.

National Association of State Directors of Teacher Education (NASDTEC, 1984). http://www.nasdtec.org/.

National Council for Accreditation of Teacher Education (NCATE, 1987) http://www.ncate.org/.

National Council of La Raza (1986). *The Education of Hispanics: Status and implications.* Washington, DC: Office of Research, Advocacy and Legislation.

Northwest Arctic School District v. Califano, No. A-77-216 (D. Alaska Sept. 29, 1978).

Oakes, J. (1985). *Keeping track: How schools structure inequality.* New Haven. CT: Yale University Press.

Olsen, L. (1988). *Crossing the schoolhouse border: Immigrant students and the California public schools.* San Francisco: California Tomorrow.

Olsen, L., & Mullen, N. (1990). *Embracing diversity: Teacher's voices from California classrooms.* San Francisco: California Tomorrow.

Olson, R. (1993). A survey of LEP and adult ESL enrollments in U.S. public schools. In *Language minority student enrollment data.* Symposium conducted at the 27th Annual TESOL Convention, Atlanta, GA.

Ortiz, A. (1997). Learning disabilities occurring concomitantly with linguistic differences. *Journal of Learning Disabilities,* 321–332.

Ortiz, A. A., Yates, J. R., & Garcia, S. B. (1990). Competencies associated with serving exceptional language minority students. *Bilingual Special Education Perspective, 9,* 9.

Ortiz, A.A., & Ramirez, B. A. (1989). *Schools and the culturally diverse exceptional student: Promising practices and future directions.* Reston, VA: Council for Exceptional Children.

Padilla, A. M., Fairchild, H. H., & Valdez, C. M. (1990). *Bilingual education: Issues and strategies.* Newbury Park, CA: Sage Publications, Inc.

Padilla, A. (1982). Bilingual schools: Gateways to integration or roads to separation. In J. Fishman and G. Keller (Eds.), *Bilingual education for Hispanic students in the U.S.* (pp. 48–70). New York: Teachers College Press.

Page, R. N. (1991). Lower-track classrooms: A curricular and cultural perspective. New York: Teachers College Press.

Pallas, A. M., Natriello, G., & McDill, E. L. (1990). The changing nature of the disadvantaged population: Current dimensions and future trends. *Educational Researcher, 18,* 16–22.

Payan, R. (1984). Language assessment for bilingual exceptional children. In L. Baca & H. Cervantes (Eds.). *The Bilingual special education interface.* St. Louis, MO: Times Mirror Mosby.

Penfield, J. (1987). ESL: The regular classroom teacher's perspective. *TESOL Quarterly, 21,* 21–39.

Peregoy, S. F., & Boyle, O. F. (1993). *Reading, writing, and learning in ESL: A resource book for K–8 teachers.* New York: Longman.

Peterson, P. L., & Clark, C. (1971). Teachers' reports of their cognitive processes during teaching. *American Educational Research Journal, 15* (1), 555–565.

Pinker, S. (1995). *The language instinct*. New York: Harper Perennial.

Pinker, S. (1996). *Language learnability and language development*. Cambridge, MA: Harvard University Press.

Plyler v. Doe, 457 U. S. 202 (1982).

Policy Analysis Center of the Council of the Raza (1990). *Hispanic education: A statistical portrait, 1990*. Washington, DC: National Council of La Raza.

Porter, R. (1990). *Forked tongue: The politics of bilingual education*. New York: Basic Books.

Porter, R. (1996). On the state of bilingual education 1990–1995: *Forked Tongue* continued. *READ Perspectives, 3* (1), 5–61.

Ramirez, D., Yuen, S., Ramey, D. and Pasta, D. (1991). *Final report: Longitudinal study of structured English immersion strategy, early exit, late exit transitional bilingual education programs for language minority children, Vol. 1*. San Mateo, CA: Aguirre International.

Rasinski, T., & Fredericks, A. (1989). Dimensions of parent involvement. *The Reading Teacher*, 180–182.

Reyhner, J. (1992). American Indian bilingual education: The White House conference on Indian education and the tribal college movement. *NABE News, 15* (7), 7, 18.

Rios v. Reed, 73 F. R. D. 589 (E. D. N. Y. 1977), 480 F. Supp 14 (E. D. N. Y. 1978).

Rodriguez, R. (1982) *Hunger of memory: The education of Richard Rodriguez*. Boston.

Rodriguez, R., Prieto, A., & Rueda, R. (1984). Issues in bilingual/multicultural special education. *Journal of the National Association for Bilingual Education 8* (3), 55–65.

Rosenthal, R., & Jacobson, L. (1968). *Pygmalion in the classroom*. New York: Holt, Rinehart and Winston.

Rossi, P. H., & Freeman, H. E. (1993). *Evaluation: A Systematic Approach*. Newbury Park, CA: Sage Publications, Inc.

Rumberger, R. (1983). Dropping out of high school: The influence of race, sex and family background. *American Educational Research Journal, 20* (2), 199–220.

Ruiz, R. (1984). Orientation to language planning. *NABE Journal, 8* (2), 15–34.

Seifeddine, S. (1994). *Changing mosaic: A needs assessment of immigrant youth in Edmonton Mennonite Centre for newcomers*. Edmonton, Alberta.

Serna v. Portales Municipal Schools, 351 F. Supp. 1279 (D. N. M. 1972), *aff'd*, 499 F.2d 1147 (10th Cir. 1974).

Shavelson, J., & Stern, P. (1981). Research on teachers' pedagogical thoughts, judgments, decisions, and behavior. *Review of Education Research 54*, 455–498.

Simons, J. (1992) Unpublished longitudinal data on BASD English Acquisition Program.

Simons, J., Connelly, M., & Goldberg, A. (1995). The Bethlehem, PA, school district's English acquisition program: A blueprint for change. *READ Perspectives, 2* (2) 53–116.

Simons, J. & Connelly, M. (1997) Unpublished data on qualitative survey of teacher knowledge of ESL instructional issues.

Slobin, D. (1993). *Adult language acquisition: a view from child language study.* In C. Perdue (Ed.), *Adult language acquisition: cross-linguistic perspectives.* Cambridge: Cambridge University Press.

Snow, M. A., & Brinton, D. M. (Eds.). (1997). *The content-based classroom.* White Plains, NY: Longman.

Sosa, A. S. (1994). *20 years after Lau: In pursuit of equity not just a language response program.* San Antonio, TX: Intercultural Development Research Association.

Spradley, J. (1979). *The ethnographic interview.* Fort Worth, TX: Holt, Rinehart and Winston, Inc.

Stevens, F. I., & Grimes, J. (1993). *Opportunity to learn: Issues of equity for poor and minority students.* Washington, DC: National Center for Educational Studies.

Stufflebeam, D. (1995). *A portfolio for evaluation of school superintendents.* Kalamazoo, MI: Center for Research in Educational Accountability and Teacher Evaluation.

Suarez-Orozco, M. (1987). Towards a psychosocial understanding of Hispanic adaptation to American schooling. In H. Trueba (Ed.), *Success or failure? Learning and the language minority student.* Boston: Heinle & Heinle.

Sugai, G. (1989). Educational assessment of the culturally diverse and behaviorally disordered student: An examination of critical effect. In A. A. Oritiz & B. A. Ramirez (Eds.), *Schools and the culturally diverse exceptional student* (pp. 63–75). Reston, VA: Council for Exceptional Children.

Suzuki, B. (1989). Asian Americans as the "model minority." *Change, 21,*12–19.

Swedo, J. (1987). Effective teaching strategies for handicapped limited English proficiency students. *Bilingual Special Education Newsletter, 6,* 1–5.

Teachers of English to Speakers of Other Languages. (1997). *ESL standards for pre-K–12 students.* TESOL, Inc.

Teddlie, C., & Stringfield, S. (1993). *Schools make a difference: Lessons learned from a 10-year study of school effects.* New York: Teachers College Press.

Tikunoff, W., Ward, B., Romero, M., Lucas, T., Katz, A.,Van Broekhuizen, L., & Castaneda, L. (1992). *Addressing the instructional needs of the limited English proficient student: Results of the exemplary SAIP descriptive study.* Symposium conducted at the American Educational research Association, Chicago.

Torrance, E. P., Wu, J. J., Gowan, J. C., & Alliotti, N. C. (1970). Creative functioning of monolingual and bilingual children in Singapore. *Journal of Educational Psychology,61,* 72–75.

Trueba, H., Cheng, L., & Ima, K. (1993). *Myth or reality: Adaptive strategies of Asian Americans in California.* Washington, DC: Falmer Press.

U.S. Department of Education, (1990). *Staffing the multilingually impacted school of the 1990's.* Washington, DC: Office of Bilingual and Minority Language Affairs.

U.S. Department of Education, Office of Policy and Planning (1993). *New land, new knowledge: An evaluation of two education programs serving refugee and immigrant students. Final Report.* Washington, DC.

U.S. Department of Education. (1994). Improving America's schools act. Conference report on H. R. 6. Title VII: *Bilingual education, language enhancement, and language acquisition programs.* Washington, DC: National Clearinghouse for Bilingual Education.

U.S. General Accounting Office (1987). *Bilingual education: A new look at research evidence.* Washington, DC: U.S. General Accounting Office.

U.S. General Accounting Office (1994). *Limited English proficiency: A growing and costly challenge facing many school districts.* Washington, DC: U.S. General Accounting Office.

Valentin, T. (1993). Getting ready for the ESL onslaught: Steps the principal should take. *NASSP Bulletin,* 30–38.

Valverde, S. (1987). A comparative study of Hispanic high-school dropouts and graduates: Why do some leave school early and some finish? *Education and Urban Society, 19* (3), 320–329.

Waggoner, D. (1993). The growth of multilingualism and the need for bilingual education: What do we know so far? *Bilingual Research Education.*

Waggoner, D., & O'Malley, J. M. (1985). Teachers of limited English proficient children in the United States. *The Journal for the National Association for Bilingual Education,* 9 (3), 25–42.

Watt, D., Roessingh, H., & Bosetti, L. (1994a). *ESL drop-out: The myth of educational equity. Alberta Journal of Educational Research, 40* (3), 283–296.

Watt, D., Roessingh, H., & Bosetti, L. (1994b). Some you win, most you lose: Tracking ESL student dropout in high school (1988–1993). *English Quarterly, 26* (3), 5–7.

Watt, D., Roessingh, H., & Bosetti, L. (1996). Success and failure stories of ESL students' educational and cultural adjustment to high school. *Urban Education, 31* (2), 199–221.

Waxler-Morrison, N., Anderson, J., & Richardson, E. (1990). *Cross-cultural caring: A Handbook for health professionals in Western Canada.* Vancouver: University of British Columbia Press.

Wedel, E., & Cornell, C. (1991). Hispanic parents' non-participation in their children's schooling: Causes and cures. Southern regional TESOL Conference, Atlanta, GA.

Weinreich, U. (1953). *Languages in contact.* The Hague: Mouton.

Willig, A. C. (1985). A meta-analysis of selected studies on the effectiveness of bilingual education. *Review of Educational Research, 55 (3),* 269–371.

Willig, A. C. (1987). Examining bilingual education research through meta-analysis and narrative review: A response to Baker. *Review of Educational Research,57* (3), 363–376.

Willig, A. C., Swedo, J. J., & Ortiz, A. A. (1987). *Characteristics of teaching strategies which Result in high task engagement for exceptional limited English proficiency Hispanic students.* Austin: University of Texas, Handicapped Minority Research Institute of Language Proficiency.

Wong-Fillmore, L. (1980). Learning a second language: Chinese children in the American classroom. In J. Alatis (Ed.), *Georgetown University round table on languages and linguistics 1980: Current issues in bilingual education.* Washington, DC: Georgetown University Press.

Wong-Fillmore, L. (1982). Language minority students and school participation: What kind of English is needed? *Journal of Education, 164,* 143–156.

Wong-Fillmore, L., & Valadez, C. (1985). Teaching bilingual learners. In M. C. Wittrock (Ed.), Handbook of research on teaching (3rd ed.). New York: Macmillan.

Wong-Fillmore, L. (1986) Research currents: Equity or excellence? *Language Arts, 63,* 474–481.

Wong-Fillmore, L. (1991). When learning a second language means losing the first. *Early Childhood Research Quarterly,* 6 (3), 323–346.

Wong-Fillmore, L., & Meyer, L. (1990). The classroom as a social setting for language learning. Oakland, CA: Celebrating Diversity Conference.

Yates, J. R., & Ortiz, A. A. (1995). Linguistically and culturally diverse students. In R. S. Podemski, G. E. Marsh II, T. E. C. Smith, & B. J. Price (Eds.), *Comprehensive Administration of Special Education* (2nd ed., pp. 129–155), Englewood Cliffs, NJ: Prentice Hall.

Zuniga-Hill, C. & Yopp, R. H. (1996). Elementary school teachers of second language learners. *Teacher Education Quarterly, 23,* 83–96.

Index

Penfield, J., 7, 26–27, 167
Peregoy, S. F., v
Peterson, P. L., 173
Pinker, S., 40, 46
Plyler v. Doe, 54
Porter, R., 8, 13, 74
Posner, M. I., 46
Pottinger, J. S., 54, 56–57
primary language instruc-
    tion. *See* bilingual pro-
    grams
program administrators.
    See ESL program ad-
    ministrators
program design: integra-
    tion of curriculum
    with, 146–47, 151,
    160–61; questions prior
    to, 63, 142–43, 146,
    151; process of, 147;
    TESOL standards and,
    111–13
program design team,
    144–49
program development:
    curriculum develop-
    ment in, 160–61;
    checklists for, 86,
    142–43, 150–51; goals
    of, 146
program effectiveness:
    checklist for, 86, 146;
    research on, 65, 84–86
program evaluation, 176–80
programs. *See* ESL pro-
    grams; *see also* bilingual
    programs
pull-out ESL, 96–97
push-in ESL, 96–97

Rasinski, T., 130
Reyhner, J., 90
Riley, R. W., 60
Rios v. Reed, 59
Rodriguez, R., 58
Rodriguez, R., 24
Rossell, C., 190
Rossi, P. H., 178
Ruiz, R., 9
Russell, G., 190

Secada, W., 190
Seifeddine, S., 82

*Serna v. Portales Municipal
    Schools*, 59
Shavelson, J., 173
sheltered English, 94, 220;
    See also ESL programs,
    structured-immersion
Simons, J., 7, 18, 26–28,
    74, 167–71
Slobin, D., 45
Snow, M. E., v
Spradley, J., 167
staff development, 171–73
Stevens, F. I., 23
structured immersion. *See*
    ESL programs
Stufflebeam, D., 177–78
Suarez-Orozco, M., 12, 25
submersion, 7, 220
subtractive programs,
    68–69, 221
Sugai, G., 23–24
Suzuki, B., 25
Swedo, J., 23

*Task Force Findings Specify-
    ing Remedies Available
    for Eliminating Past
    Educational Practices
    Ruled Unlawful under
    Lau v. Nichols*. See Lau
    remedies
TBE (transitional bilingual
    education). *See* bilin-
    gual programs
teachers: administrative
    support of, 32, 51,
    110–11; attitudes of,
    26, 165–68; back-
    ground knowledge of,
    81–82, 168–69; collab-
    oration of, 101–103;
    ESL techniques and,
    28, 169–70; families
    and, 123–31; prepara-
    tion of, 26–28, 70–72,
    171–73; responsibilities
    of, 29–30, 38, 44,
    170–71; shortage of,
    70–71; support of, 157,
    173–76; successful
    characteristics of,
    26–28
Teachers of English to

Speakers of Other Lan-
    guages (TESOL):
    standards, Pre-K–12, x,
    50–51, 111–13, 142,
    150, 160, 184
Teddlie, C., 164
TESOL. *See* Teachers of
    English to Speakers of
    Other Languages
Tikunoff, W., 31, 149
Title VII, 7, 16–17
Tobias, R., 190
Torrance, E. P., 6
transitional bilingual edu-
    cation (TBE). *See* bilin-
    gual programs
Trueba, H., 26, 30

University of California
    Linguistic Minority
    Research Institute, 183
Unz initiative. *See* Califor-
    nia Proposition 227
U.S. Department of Edu-
    cation, 181, 185
U.S. General Accounting
    Office (GAO), 17,
    22–23

Valverde, S., 82

Waggoner, D., 14–15, 25,
    166
Watt, D., 82
Waxler-Morrison, N., 82
Weinreich, U., 6
Willig, A. C., 190
Wong-Fillmore, L., 26, 48,
    83, 124

Yates, J. R., 154, 190

Zuniga-Hill, C., 28

About the Authors

Mark Connelly, S.J., Ph.D., is an assistant professor in the Graduate School of Education and Allied Professions at Fairfield University, Fairfield, Connecticut, and teaches in the department of ESL and Bilingual Education. He holds a doctorate in linguistics from Harvard University, and his professional interests include first- and second-language phonology acquisition and reading acquisition.

Judith Simons, Ed.D., is an associate professor and chair of the Education Department at Cedar Crest College, Allentown, Pennsylvania. A former primary grade and preschool teacher, Dr. Simons earned a doctorate in elementary education from Lehigh University and an M.Ed. in early childhood education from Georgia State University. She currently teaches courses in emergent, developmental literacy, mathematics, and instructional strategies for the ESOL student in the general education classroom.